His California Story

Teacher's Supplement

His California Story
Teacher's Supplement

By Lesha Myers M.Ed.

Published by Cameron Academy
P.O. Box 21383
Concord, CA 94521
www.Cameron-Publishing.com

Cameron Academy
www.Cameron-Publishing.com

Originally 1995, revised 1996.

Picture Credits:
Line drawings by Melody Chapman and Lesha Myers
Photographs by Reneé Werner and Lesha Myers

Table of Contents

Introduction 6

California Indians 17

The Explorers 29

Spanish Units 51

Mexican Units 81

Gold Rush Units 111

American Units 135

Appendices

A—Character Sketches 156
B—Class Project 165
C—California Date Song 180
D—Geography 183
E—Co-ops 189
F—More Articles 191

Teaching Aids

Teacher's Overview

CALIFORNIA IS ONE OF THE RICHEST lands in the world. If it were an independent nation, it would be one of the wealthiest and most productive. The story of how this came to be and the many ways God directed the development of the state are presented in the book *His California Story*. This *Teacher's Supplement* has been written to help you to effectively use *His California Story* as you teach your student about California's exciting past. This introduction is intended to present an overview of the *Teacher's Supplement* and offer suggestions on how to use it.

Worldview

Understanding the concept of a worldview is one of the most important components of this California history course. A student reading *His California Story* will hear many statements from modern writers or field trip docents that contradict what he or she has been taught. He will need to understand why and be able to evaluate what he is hearing in terms of God's truth. The introduction to *His California Story* discusses the concept of a worldview and why students will hear contradictory statements. Use this opportunity to begin to teach your students discernment.

Course Contents

Teaching materials for each unit are divided into two sub-sections. The activities presented in "How to Teach the Unit" are what I feel should constitute a basic course of study. Those offered in "Supplemental Activities," while not required, will offer further understanding and enrichment.

Class Organization

California history classes can be organized in many ways such as a conventional classroom, a homeschool, or a cooperative class. This manual has been designed to support all three options. I have taught California history to my own children. Our year was filled with discovery and family field trips, as we knew almost nothing about California's past. I also taught California history classes for several years. The advantage to this method is that craft projects and field trips are easier since the workload is shared, and the discipline imposed by a class schedule helps keep the study on course.

Lesson Planning

As you prepare your lesson plans, read through the following sections and select the activities you will use. Suggestions for the basic course and a few supplements appear at the beginning of each section. Additionally, ample space has been provided for you to write notes as you consider what you feel should be emphasized in a study of California's history. (See Appendix E for issues concerning a cooperative class.) Your California history class can be taught over an entire school year by completing approximately one unit a month or in three quarters, leaving the fourth quarter to study local or American history.

Materials Needed

Each student will need a copy of *His California Story*, a notebook in which to file completed assignments, and normal school supplies. You will also need other supplies, depending on what activities you select to accompany your study.

Materials needed for each activity are listed in the directions for the project. The remainder of this introduction to the *Teacher's Supplement* discusses the elements of each section.

Teaching Older Students

His California Story and this *Teacher's Supplement* have both been written for upper elementary students; however, the course is easily adaptable for older students. Use the units as a framework, and flesh them out with books, projects, and articles. With that idea in mind, I've included book suggestions in each unit for strong readers and adults. Older students, those in middle school and high school, will benefit from most of these books.

Additionally, at the beginning of some units in this *Teacher's Supplement* and in Appendix F, I've reprinted articles that I wrote for the *CHEA Parent Educator* magazine. They have been revised where needed and will add additional information and perspective. The first two articles follow.

Finally, older students will benefit from the article excerpts in the Source Documents section of this supplement.

Why Bother?

IT'S THE START OF THE SCHOOL YEAR, AND MANY OF US are beginning our study of history—local, California, United States, or world. If your children are like mine, they may protest. "Why do we have to do this?" they may mutter. "All of these people are dead. What do we care about these meaningless dates and details?" A good question. Why should we even bother?

Increase Our Faith

We study history to draw closer to our Lord. As we learn more about God, our character grows and our faith increases.

It is not always easy to see the providence of God when we are in the midst of a situation, but with historical eyes we can clearly see how God has ordained events to bring about His purposes. In California's history, we see that although God allowed the Spaniards to colonize California and protected the fledgling province, He never allowed it to become strong. This prevented California from becoming an independent nation when the Spanish colonies around the world revolted in the early 1800s. A strong, independent nation would not have petitioned for statehood. Numerous instances of God's care and overriding provision are found throughout California's history, including the delayed gold discovery.

Stand Alone

History encourages us to stand alone when we see how the faith of one man can be used to change a situation. God sent His servants to minister during the wild and tumultuous early days in San Francisco. One man, named Rev. Wheeler, held services in a friend's home. After a few Sundays, in which the house was empty, Wheeler was encouraged to quit. San Francisco was just too hard his friend told him; it would be best to move on. Rev. Wheeler however would not be deterred. He stayed his course and after four weeks, the house was filled to overflowing. God used the efforts of men like Wheeler to tame San Francisco.

Build Character

Studying history builds character. There is a story of a missionary named William Taylor who was sailing around the horn to his field in California. One Sunday during the monotonous journey, Taylor was quietly reading his Bible on deck. Suddenly there arose a clamor and men rushed to the side to see a shark streaming through the clear water. Excitement and merriment followed as the shark was finally captured for the evening meal.

After the commotion had died away, the men found that Taylor had not even looked up from his prayers. When questioned Taylor replied, "Colonel, if I was talking to a king on important business, and if in the middle of the conversation I ran off over some small excitement, like a shark killing, wouldn't I be showing great disrespect? I have just been reading a message from and talking to the Great King. If I were to run away to see a fish killed on this His holy day, I would not be treating the Lord with courtesy." When we see dedication of this magnitude, we realize that our faithfulness needs to improve.

Manage Our Time

History can help us to manage our time. So often we are willing to put off until tomorrow whatever we may. But history will show us that this attitude can result in many missed opportunities, even to the extent of jeopardizing our lives. The Donner Party is an excellent example. They missed surmounting the summit of the Sierra Nevada by just one day. If they had pushed harder at the beginning of their journey, moved a bit quicker through the untried "shortcut" they elected to take, or cut their rest in the Truckee Valley, they would have made it safely to Sacramento. One day's delay cost the lives of almost half of the party.

Root Out Sin

God can use our study of history to root out sin in our lives. Many of our forefathers saw the blessings and curses of God in the weather. A prolonged drought would be reason to call for a day of personal examination, humiliation, prayer, and fasting. We've experienced at least three droughts since I've moved to California and I've rarely heard a minister suggest that the hand of God was upon us, let alone encourage us to pray or fast. One of the most railed-against sins of the previous century was Sabbath-breaking. Today very few of us even know how to keep the Sabbath holy. Our conscience has been seared as we daily face situations that our forefathers never imagined.

With the exception of the Bible itself, the Lord has used my study of history more than any other circumstance to bring me closer to Him. In fact, when viewed properly, history is the study of Him. This is why it is such a great loss to have Christianity censored from our children's textbooks. The study of history blesses us and is one of the ways God equips us to live faithfully in the presence.

You Can't Revise the Truth

HERE'S A $64 WORD FOR YOU: SESQUICENTENNIAL. IT means 150th anniversary and it describes several commemorations that took take place a few years ago in California. Books and articles have been written about these events so that people of today will know what they are celebrating. What is interesting about these writings is that they differ from those composed in times past. California's history, it seems, is being revised.

How is History Written?

How is history written? How does a person living today determine the truth concerning events covered with 150 years of historical dust? Let's look at how today's college students, who are tomorrow's historians, are instructed to do historical research.

All historians are instructed to look for and use what are called primary or source documents. Source documents are those written by people who actually witnessed the events being described. Newspapers, magazine articles, diaries, letters, census and military records, and in some cases books, are all examples of primary sources.

The book that results when primary sources are utilized is called a secondary document. If a book was written using diaries and letters, and then a subsequent textbook was authored using that book as its source, we would say the subsequent textbook was written using secondary sources. Any further book which used the subsequent book as its source would also be considered a secondary document, so it would be possible to get far away from the actual facts if only secondary documents were used. If we examine the bibliographies of modern history books, we find a preponderance of secondary sources, but this is only part of the problem.

External and Internal Criticism

After sources are selected, they are evaluated. Students are asked to apply external and internal criticism. External criticism is used to determine whether or not the document is authentic. For example, if a letter used the modern-day name of a town instead of the common name of the time, it could be a forgery.

Internal criticism is a way to evaluate the accuracy and worth of the document selected by examining the viewpoint of the writer. Students are offered this advice from a college textbook:

> Even a competent observer, if sufficiently biased in the direction of a given point of view, may record an untruthful record of the occurrences in question. If the author of a document or maker of a statement has some interest to be promoted by the acceptance of a particular point of view, one may expect that this viewpoint will be put forth, whether truthful or not. Historians must often delve to a considerable degree into the race, political party, religious group, and social status of the observer in an effort to appraise the likelihood of prejudices or biases.

In other words, the perspective and value system of the writer must be evaluated to see if what he has to say is acceptable. What is remarkable about this process is that we would agree with it completely and consider it a fine preliminary plan when appraising research materials. Why then do we have such a problem with what is being written today?

The answer is that our evaluation criteria differs. Modern writers often reject outright the writings of a person exhibiting a Christian bias, while a Christian would very carefully read the writings of an author exhibiting an anti-Christian inclination. Neutrality is impossible with respect to Christianity, for as Jesus Christ said, "He that is not with me is against me" (Matthew 12:30).

It also is not possible to be completely without bias. Every person evaluates life through a set of presuppositions based upon his beliefs, life experiences, and value system. Today, the saying "without bias" often becomes a euphemism for "without Christianity."

Of course an open mind is absolutely necessary for historical research. When I began to study the Spanish period of California's history, I formed a preliminary conclusion that the Spanish missions were destroyed in judgment because the missionaries had so mistreated the Indians. With further research I discovered that the missions were destroyed by the sin of man, and the missionaries had showed abundant love and kindness towards the Indians. It would have been prejudicial to hold to my original conclusion.

The rewriting of California's history is not an historical problem, it is a religious one. Only when men evaluate all of life from God's perspective, using the Bible as their standard, will we have the possibility of truth in the historical record. Perhaps in the bicentennial!

Teaching the Basic Course

Lesson Plans

The basic California history course consists of the following topics, each of which will be discussed in turn: Objectives, God's Providence, Character Sketches, Date Memorization, Geography, Notebook, and Roundup Questions. Although literature suggestions and the projects section are included under supplemental activities, the completion of a book report and a class project (see Appendix B) should be considered part of the basic course.

Objectives

The objectives listed at the beginning of each unit provide a framework from which to teach the unit. Out of all of the information presented in each chapter, the main points to emphasize are listed in the objectives. They may be used as the basis of a class lecture or for discussion and review of assigned reading.

God's Providence

Definition of "Providence" from Noah Webster's *First Edition of the American Dictionary of the English Language*, 1828:

1. The act of providing or preparing for future use or application. Providence for war is the best prevention of it. [Now little used.] Bacon.
2. Foresight; timely care; particularly active foresight, or foresight accompanied with the procurement of what is necessary for future use, or with suitable preparation. How many of the troubles and perplexities of life proceed from want of providence!
3. In theology, the care and superintendence which God exercises over His creatures. He that acknowledges a creation and denies a providence, involves himself in a palpable* contradiction; for the same power which caused a thing to exist is necessary to continue its existence. Some persons admit a general providence, but deny a particular providence, not considering that a general providence consists of particulars. A belief in divine providence, is a source of great consolation to good men. By divine providence is often understood God Himself. [*Plain; obvious; easily perceptible.]
4. Prudence in the management of one's concerns or in private economy.

Definition of "Providence" from Webster's *New International Dictionary*, second ed. 1951

1. One who exercises providential power. Specif: a God, conceived of as guiding men as a race and as individuals to ends He has in view for them or as preserving individuals from danger through His prescience, loving care, or intervention.

Definition of "Providence" from The Heidelberg Catechism, Lord's Day 10, Questions 27-28:

Question 27. What dost thou mean by the providence of God?

Answer: The almighty and everywhere present power of God; (a) whereby, as it were by his hand, he upholds and governs (b) heaven, earth, and all creatures; so that herbs and grass, rain and drought, (c) fruitful and barren years, meat and drink, health and sickness, (d) riches and poverty, (e) yea, and all things come, not by chance, but be his fatherly hand. (f)

(a) Acts 17:25 Neither is worshipped with men's hands, as though he needed any thing, seeing he giveth to all life, and breath, and all things; Acts 17:26 And hath made of one blood all nations of men for to dwell on all the face of the earth, and hath determined the times before appointed, and the bounds of their habitation; Acts 17:27 That they should seek the Lord, if haply they might feel after him, and find him, though he be not far from every one of us: Acts 17:28 For in him we live, and move, and have our being; as certain also of your own poets have said, For we are also his offspring. Jer.23:23 Am I a God at hand, saith the LORD, and not a God afar off? Jer.23:24 Can any hide himself in secret places that I shall not see him? saith the LORD. Do not I fill heaven and earth? saith the LORD. Isa.29:15 Woe unto them that seek deep to hide their counsel from the LORD, and their works are in the dark, and they say, Who seeth us? and who knoweth us? Isa.29:16 Surely your turning of things upside down shall be esteemed as the potter's clay: for shall the work say of him that made it, He made me not? or shall the thing framed say of him that framed it, He had no understanding? Ezek.8:12 Then said he unto me, Son of man, hast thou seen what the ancients of the house of Israel do in the dark, every man in the chambers of his imagery? for they say, The LORD seeth us not; the LORD hath forsaken the earth. (b) Heb.1:3 Who being the brightness of his glory, and the express image of his person, and upholding all things by the word of his power, when he had by himself purged our sins, sat down on the right hand of the Majesty on high; (c) Jer.5:24 Neither say they in their heart, Let us now fear the LORD our God, that giveth rain, both the former and the latter, in his season: he reserveth unto us the appointed weeks of the harvest. Acts 14:17 Nevertheless he left not himself without witness, in that he did good, and gave us rain from heaven, and fruitful seasons, filling our hearts with food and gladness. (d) John 9:3 Jesus answered, Neither hath this man sinned, nor his parents: but that the works of God should be made manifest in him. (e) Prov.22:2 The rich and poor meet together: the LORD is the maker of them all. (f) Matt.10:20 For it is not ye that speak, but the Spirit of your Father which speaketh in you. Prov.16:33 The lot is cast into the lap; but the whole disposing thereof is of the LORD.

Question 28. What advantage is it to us to know that God has created, and by his providence does still uphold all things?

Answer: That we may be patient in adversity; (a) thankful in prosperity; (b) and that in all things, which may hereafter befall us, we place our firm trust in our faithful God and Father, (c) that nothing shall separate us from his love; (d) since all creatures are so in his hand, that without his will they cannot so much as move. (e)

(a) Rom.5:3 And not only so, but we glory in tribulations also: knowing that tribulation worketh patience; James 1:3 Knowing this, that the trying of your faith worketh patience. Ps.39:9 I was dumb, I opened not my mouth; because thou didst it. Job 1:21 And said, Naked came I out of my mother's womb, and naked shall I return thither: the LORD gave, and the LORD hath taken away; blessed be the name of the LORD. Job 1:22 In all this Job sinned not, nor charged God foolishly. (b) Deut.8:10 When thou hast eaten and art full, then thou shalt bless the LORD thy God for the good land which he hath given thee. 1 Thess.5:18 In every thing give thanks: for this is the will of God in Christ Jesus concerning you. (c) Ps.55:22 Cast thy burden upon the LORD, and he shall sustain thee: he shall never suffer the righteous to be moved. Rom.5:4 And patience, experience; and experience, hope: (d) Rom.8:38 For I am persuaded, that neither death, nor life, nor angels, nor principalities, nor powers, nor things present, nor things to come, Rom.8:39 Nor height, nor depth, nor any other creature, shall be able to separate us from the love of God, which is in Christ Jesus our Lord. (e) Job 1:12 And the LORD said unto Satan, Behold, all that he hath is in thy power; only upon himself put not forth thine hand. So Satan went forth from the presence of the LORD. Job 2:6 And the LORD said unto Satan, Behold, he is in thine hand; but save his life. Acts 17:28 For in him we live, and move, and have our being; as certain also of your own poets have said, For we are also his offspring. Acts 17:25 Neither is worshipped with men's hands, as though he needed any thing, seeing he giveth to all life, and breath, and all things; Prov.21:1 The king's heart is in the hand of the LORD, as the rivers of water: he turneth it whithersoever he will.

His California Story presents the story of how God formed the thirty-first state in the nation. So often this perspective is omitted from modern history books. However, if God is the Creator and Sustainer of all life (and He is), if He has a plan

for each individual, community, state, and nation (and He does), then omitting any mention of God, Christian workers, or providential events is a grievous error. When we read older books, those written by people who lived in California before about 1930, we frequently hear about the Lord's work in the state. *His California Story* is a humble attempt to redeem some of that lost knowledge.

The God's Providence section repeats the observations of California's early settlers and pioneers. Often providential acts were a major turning point in the history of the state, but they came about by the small, faithful deeds of individuals. Use these instances to increase the faith of your students and exhort them to be faithful in whatever ways the Lord calls them.

Character Sketches

Almost all of the modern California history textbooks approach history in a similar way: they talk about California's past in generalities, omitting the contribution of individuals. When individuals are discussed, little is said about their character—what they believed—and their value system. By studying the character of the men and women who lived in California before us, we see both admirable and dishonorable qualities. Students' own character can be strengthened by learning how godly people responded to difficult circumstances.

For example, we learn of duty and loyalty when we read how Lewis Manly risked his life to return to Death Valley and rescue the remainder of his party (see p. 135). We learn how the Lord honors those who abide by His word when we read of the blessing received by Elihu Anthony during the Gold Rush (see p. 140). Our own desire to share the gospel with the lost is fueled when we learn of the hardships faced by the Owen family as they traveled to California (see pp. 142-143). Our esteem for God almighty increases when we learn that William Taylor would not interrupt his ship-board devotions to see a shark (see p. 155-156).

See Appendix A for a description of a character sketch and examples prepared by my students. The following is a list of my favorite California history characters. I hope you will enjoy "meeting" these people as much as I have.

Juan Bautista de Anza
Father Lasuén
Jedediah Smith
John Bidwell
William Taylor
William Coleman
Theodore Judah

California Date Song

For many years I felt that dates were not important. What mattered was learning about how God worked in history, not memorizing a list of dates. Plus, date memorization is hard work. However, the more I studied history, the more I realized that we have to know some dates in order to be able to see the big picture. For example, if we know that Francis Drake came to California in 1579 and held the first Protestant service at that time, when we study the Pilgrims we learn that they followed Drake by only forty years, in 1620. A few dates, introduced slowly, provide a framework for future historical studies. Learning what God has done is just as important as learning when He did it.

If your students have trouble memorizing dates, you might consider omitting some of those I've chosen. Important dates include the beginning of each time period, the Gold Rush, statehood, and the completion of the transcontinental railroad. Use your own judgment as to whether or not you will include others.

Since I insisted that my students memorize a framework of dates so that they could grasp the connections in history across geographical boundaries, and since students struggled with the effort, one of my students solved the problem. Karen Schachterle, who is now a college graduate, wrote a song to help her memorize the dates. She shared the song (see Appendix C) and made the task easier for all of the California history students that followed her. The song is a delightful way to learn California's chronology.

Geography

Geography is a sorely neglected part of many history classes. We need to know what God has done, when He did it, and why He did it (His providence), but we also need to know *where* He did it. This is geography. I have tried to include maps or descriptions of all the places mentioned in *His California Story*. The geography section of this *Teacher's Supplement* continues by introducing the students to the physical features of California's landscape.

Introduce these features slowly, a few at a time, while frequently reviewing. I began with an outline of California on the white board, and I invited students to draw in all of the mountains, valleys, and other features we have been studying.

See Appendix D for a further discussion of geography. After all geographical features have been learned, you might have your students create a salt, water, and flour map of California. This project is described in the Class-Time Activities section of the American Units of this supplement.

Journal

The journal portion of each section lists questions that require research or reasoning skills. These assignments could be used as an alternative to the Roundup Questions listed below.

Unit Roundup Answers

The roundup questions listed in the text *His California Story* are meant to provoke thought and discussion. They also have been designed to help students absorb and remember what they have read. Sometimes it is easier to retain information by reading and then writing about it. Answers to the questions are provided in each section of this manual.

Supplemental Activities

The second part of each section of this manual contains supplemental activities. Two potential dangers present themselves at this point. The first is that teachers might become discouraged, thinking that they have to include all of these activities. Remember, they are *supplemental*. You know your students' abilities and your own goals. If these activities fit in with your overall objectives for California history, by all means use them. Otherwise, don't feel guilty about passing them by.

The second danger is that a teacher will want to do everything in this section. Keep in mind that the study of California history at the upper elementary level is meant to be a survey. If you do all of the activities in the California Indians Unit, you might find that the year has gone by and you are still studying the California Indians. Choose your supplemental activities carefully so that your study can move ahead.

Literature Suggestions

Supplemental reading and literature should be chosen with care. There are four basic types of books available: those that are anti-Christian, those that do not mention Christianity at all or only in passing, those that are Christian, and those that take the modern child and all of his modern viewpoints and place him in a historical setting.

The anti-Christian materials should, of course, be avoided unless you are trying to teach your child discernment. Even then, they should be used with care. Books in the other three categories can be used by a student reading *His California Story* since he will already understand the providential viewpoint. Sometimes "neutral" books can add detail and depth to your study. Christian books are preferred, and many more are being written each year as Christians redeem California history. Finally, there are many books that although set in a historical context reflect modern values and perceptions rather than those of the time being studied. Many of Scott O'Dell's books, as well as the *American Girl* series, fall into this category. The books recommended in each of the Literature and Supplemental Reading sections are all "neutral" or Christian.

Field Trips

Field trips are a great way to experience California's history and we are fortunate that so many of our historical sites have been preserved. Field trips can also be wearing, so use your time wisely. I took my class on three field trips each year, visiting two sites each day for a total of six sites. Individual families sometimes take weekend field trips, especially when living history days are offered. You might consider a family vacation to some historical sites or an overnight or weekend camping trip to an area (for example Sacramento).

In the pages that follow, many general suggestions for field trips are offered. To find the historical sites that are close to your area, consult the following resources:

Books

- *Fun and Educational Places to Go With Kids and Adults in Southern California* by Susan Peterson
- *Fun Places to Go With Children in Northern California* by Elizabeth Pomada.
- *AAA TourBook* for California and Nevada, available to members from the American Automobile Association.
- *Sunset Guides* published by Lane Publishing Co.
- *Historic Spots in California* (Stanford University Press). This book lists many historical sites by county. It's substantial and expensive—you might look for it in your local library.

Encourage your students to take pictures, write reports, and collect brochures from the places you visit. These should be saved in your students' notebooks or in a specially-created field trip memory book.

California State Park System

- For sites that have been designated historical landmarks by county, go to http://ohp.parks.ca.gov (Type "landmarks" in the search bar.)
- For information on California's parks and California's historical parks, go to http://www.parks.ca.gov. In addition to information about the parks' facilities, many are accompanied by informative videos that preview the parks' history. The site also contains information about how to organize reduced-cost and free school field trips.

Virtual Field Trips

With the advent of the Internet, you and your students can visit almost anywhere in California from the comfort of your classroom.

- The SCORE (Schools of California Online Resources for Education) project was begun in 1995 and is an attempt to provide ideas, support, and materials to public school teachers. To find virtual tours of historical sights created by teachers, go to http://score.rims.k12.ca.us/virtual/scorewebmuseums/
- To locate other virtual field trips, search on "California virtual field trips" or "California virtual tours."

Class-Time Activities

The class-time activities have been designed to accommodate those students who learn best by doing. Most require inexpensive, easily-obtained materials. If you do not wish to include the activity described, you might substitute another listed in the Project Section. Remember, however, that these activities are supplemental.

Oral Review Questions

Another way that many students learn is by hearing. The oral review questions are designed to help these students. They may be used to quiz an individual student or to play a game. In addition to the ones below, you will find a wide variety of review games on the Internet, from Bingo, to Who Wants to Marry a Millionaire, to puzzles, to games that require movement. To find them, just search for review games.

Review Games

A simple game requires two teams. The first person in each line tries to answer the question. If he or she can, he earns two points. If he needs help from his teammates, he earns one point. If the team cannot answer or answers incorrectly, the opposing team gets to try for one point. I like this game because the student can always ask his

team for help and does not feel awkward if he cannot answer the question.

Around the World

In this game the classroom is the world and the student tries to travel around it. One student stands next to the student he is challenging while the teacher asks the questions. The student who answers correctly moves on to challenge the next student, while the other sits in the newly vacated seat. The object of the game is to travel "around the world." If no one travels the whole way, the one who travels the farthest wins.

PowerPoint Jeopardy

You can make jeopardy posters by hand and create question cards, or if you have a PowerPoint projector, you can make a PowerPoint version. Download one or both of the templates located at http://www.educationworld.com/a_lesson/lesson/lesson306.shtml (or search for PowerPoint Jeopardy). This site also contains some other fun and creative review games.

Project Suggestions

The California history project is one of the most challenging, rewarding, and interesting elements of a study of California's history. It allows students to pursue an in-depth study of some aspect of California's history and introduces them to several important skills: researching, report-writing, public speaking, and project presentation. See Appendix B of this manual for a description of the class project. A list of suggested projects is presented in each section of this *Teacher's Supplement*.

Source Documents

The final part of each section of this manual is a selection of quotations from the many books I read to write *His California Story*, my sources. This section is for the adult or teen who would like to study more of California's history. Many of us have learned California history from a different perspective than that presented in *His California Story*. The source documents are meant as a starting place for further research.

Teacher's Supplement

California Indians

Unit 1

Teaching Aids—Unit 1

The California Indians

Teacher's Overview

THE STUDY OF THE INDIANS OF California is a favorite with most of my California history students. Students enjoy lots of fun projects as they try to understand life in California long ago. On the other hand, the study of the California Indians also offers challenges to the Christian student for two reasons.

Challenges

First, many modern books present the Indians as "noble savages," living happily and innocently in California before the land was "spoiled" by the Europeans. They follow the teachings of the French philosopher Rousseau who said that people were born naturally good and that civilization corrupted their innocence. Historical evidence does not substantiate these claims. However, even if there was no historical proof, we would know these assertions could not be true because they contradict the Bible. The Bible tells us that all men are born with a sin nature. No one can be good without the gift of redemption and grace through Jesus Christ. No culture can honor Him unless its members are redeemed by the blood of Christ.

The second challenge is to present the culture realistically, yet sensitively. Christians would consider many aspects of the California Indians' culture offensive including infanticide, homosexuality, licentiousness, and worship of nature. Many modern authors have glossed over these aspects and painted an edited picture of the California Indians. I have tried to paint a realistic picture, yet I've tried to be careful since this book will be read by elementary students.

Population

Before we get into teaching ideas and aids, I'd like to discuss a few problem areas that California Indian historians wrestle with. The first is population.

It is very difficult to determine the number of Indians who lived in California before the arrival of the Spaniards. Estimates range from 100,000 to 700,000. Estimates for the number of Indians living in California just prior to the Gold Rush range from 20,000 to 150,000. The actual number is important since the people who came to California during the Gold Rush are accused of decimating the Indians. Although there is no question that Indians were killed by disease, evil men, and in self-defense, no one is sure how many. If there were 20,000 Indians living at the beginning of the Gold Rush and 20,000 at the 1860 census, the problem was slight. However, if there were 150,000 Indians living in California in 1848 and only 20,000 in 1860, the problem was great indeed.

A person who relies strictly on anthropological evidence will have many challenges determining population since the Indians moved their homes three to five times per year. If an archaeologist examines an Indian village site and locates the remains of 100 huts which he estimates contained 50 people each, does he assume that 5,000 people lived in the village? Or, would he assume that five families rebuilt their huts on the site once a year for 20 years for a total of 250 people? There is a substantial difference between the two estimates.

"Native Americans"

I have chosen not to use the modern term *Native Americans* to describe the Indians of California. Although it is true that Columbus misnamed the people he found on his travels to North America *Indians*, thinking that he had arrived at the Orient, it is equally true that the term *native* pertains to a person born in a particular country, in this case America. I was born in this country and probably many of the parents, teachers, and students reading this book would also qualify for the term *Native American.* To be technically correct, the California Indians should be referred to as *aborigines*, that is the primitive inhabitants of a country, or those who lived there at the earliest time.

"Tribes"

Another term that presents problems with respect to the California Indians is the term *tribes*, because people immediately associate this term with the American Indians living further east, such as the Sioux or Cheyenne. The California Indians lived in small family groups or villages. There are two ways to categorize them: by language group and by culture. About twenty main language groups existed in California but with so many dialects that groups living next to each other could not communicate in the same tongue. There were six cultural groups but still a wide variety of beliefs, customs, and practices within each. Because of these difficulties, I have tried to avoid using the term *tribe* altogether.

A Caution

A word of warning is in order here. Many textbooks suggest that you teach your students Indian dances. Don't do this. Most of the dances were designed to worship the Indians' false "gods," the spirits they believed lived in nature. Many other aspects of the Indians' culture contain aspects of witchcraft (*poison*) and spiritism. Learn the origin of the dance to see if it is appropriate to include in your teaching plans.

Accusations

Finally, since this unit looks at the California Indian culture before contact with Europeans, it does not address accusations that the Europeans destroyed them through violence and disease. We will return to this topic; however, since these issues will arise, let me offer the very briefest of particulars.

First, it is very true that many Indians died from diseases that were introduced by Europeans because the California Indians had no natural immunity. The Spaniards had little knowledge of germ theory and grieved over the loss of life. Additionally, the Indians resisted many Spanish treatments and instead relied on their sweathouses and shamans. Besides this, we need to remember that the same European culture that introduced these deadly diseases has also made medical advances possible and has saved millions of lives. Indian taboos would have prevented these advances.

Second, Europeans did kill many Indians, both in self-defense and through evil designs; however, it is grossly unfair to lump all Europeans into one category and condemn them in the same way that it would be grossly unfair to stereotype the California Indians. Some Europeans and Americans introduced Indians to the One True God and eternal salvation. Some argued for their rights in civil courts, helped pass laws to protect them, and worked towards their material comfort and education. The same culture that produced people who perpetrated evil also produced critics of these evils and people who worked to stop them.

The most balanced perspective I have found on this topic is the excellent book *Converting California* by James Sandos, Yale University Press, 2004.

Teaching the California Indians' Unit

Lesson Plans

1. Read and discuss the preface to *His California Story* and Psalm 78:1-8. Make sure students understand what a worldview is and why people believe different ideas.
2. Introduction ideas
   - Students are fascinated with the Indians and many select some aspect of the Indians' culture for their class project. (See Appendix B.) By all means, encourage your students to have fun with this unit, but make sure that your presentation is balanced. Many students, especially those who like to spend time outdoors, might think of the Indians' way of life as one big camping trip. Instead, it was filled with hardship and fear.
   - Where appropriate ask your students questions such as, "What does the Bible say about this?" or "Does this aspect of the Indians' culture contradict any of God's commandments?" Ask your students how they would feel being a part of the culture. Ask the girls, "How would you feel if you had to pound acorns for every meal?" Ask the boys, "How would you feel if you had to sleep on the ground every night, even in the rain?" Try to let the students get a feel for what the culture was really like.
   - Many teachers find it valuable to give an overview of California's history to students along with a preview of what is ahead. This works especially well for students who think globally.
3. Teach the origin and beliefs of the California Indians (Ch. 1) and do Roundup questions. Look up the Bible verses and read them in context.
4. Introduce "The California Date Song" and teach the first verse.
5. Teach about life in the Pomo village (Ch. 2) and do Roundup questions.
6. Do acorn-pounding activity from the Class-Time Activities section.
7. Teach about medicine and illness (Ch. 3) and do Roundup questions.
8. Teach the bays and mountain ranges.
9. Do Things to Ponder questions from the Roundup.
10. Compare and contrast the Miwok flood legend to the Genesis flood and the Maidu creation legend to the Genesis account.
11. Make sure students understand how to receive the free gift of grace offered by Jesus Christ.

Objectives

At the completion of this unit students should be able to do the following:

1. Understand that the California Indians, like all men, descended from Noah. Their ancestors had knowledge of the One True God.
2. Describe what life was like in the Pomo culture including:
   a. Village life
   b. Dwellings
   c. The sweathouse
   d. Medicine and sickness
3. Refute the following half-truths about the California Indians:
   a. They were peaceful people.
   b. They lived in harmony with their environment or surroundings.
   c. Their beliefs allowed them to live

happy and prosperous lives.
   d. They respected all life.
4. Describe the Indians' religion correctly using the terms *spirits*, *power*, *poison*, and *shaman*.
5. Understand that the Indians like all people including the students themselves, were lost, without hope, and in need of the salvation that can only be brought by Jesus Christ.

God's Providence

I present no instances of God's providence in this section for two reasons. First, there is no recorded history for the California Indian period since the Indians' religion forbade the mention of the deceased. Second, this unit describes the culture rather than a chronological history. We will look at instances of God's providence beginning with the Explorers Unit.

Character Sketches

(For more information see Appendix A.)

The historical contribution of individual Indians who lived in California prior to the arrival of the Europeans is unknown due to the constraints of their religion. Character Sketches will begin with the Explorers Unit.

California Date Song

(See Appendix C for entire song.)

Some unknown years after the flood,
When all the land was dried from mud,
Maybe after our Savior shed His blood,
Came the California Indians.

Geography

(See Appendix D for geography expectations.)

Students should be able to locate and place the following on a map of California:

Bays

Humboldt	Santa Barbara
San Francisco	San Pedro
Monterey	San Diego

Mountain Ranges

Sierra Nevada	Klamath
Tehachapi	Santa Ana
Coast Range	San Gabriel

Journal

1. Answer "Thought Questions" for each chapter.
2. Answer the "Things to Ponder" questions on the Unit Roundup.
3. Think about and answer this question: Would you like to have lived as a California Indian? Give reasons for your opinion.
4. Record your thoughts about at least one aspect of the California Indians' culture.

Unit Roundup Answers

Chapter 1

1. Describe the two Biblical events that caused the people we call the California Indians to travel to California. *Two events were the flood of Noah's time which destroyed all of life on Earth and the Tower of Babel which confused all of the languages.*
2. What impressions or ideas about American Indians did you have that were not true for the California Indians? *Answers will vary and might include tribes, teepees, totem poles, birch bark canoes, fierce battles between tribes and settlers, or any customs belonging to the more organized Indian tribes to the east of California.*
3. Define these words:
   - Power: *A spiritual force or energy from certain objects like rocks, trees, streams, or mountains.*
   - Poison: *Sorcery or spiritual harm; witchcraft*
   - Taboos: *Rules or things that were forbidden. If the taboos were broken, the Indians believed harm would follow.*
4. Write a paragraph describing the Pomo beliefs. Make sure you use the words *spirits, power, poison,* and *taboos. Make sure the words are used correctly. Use the section entitled "The Pomo Beliefs" to check students' answers. Make sure the words students choose are their own, although ideas should align with the text.*
5. **Thought Questions:** If the California Indians descended from righteous Noah, why didn't they know about the One True God? Why did they believe in spirits, power, poison, and taboos? *Answers will vary but might include a discussion of a person's sin nature, the idea that parents who do not believe in the One True God will not pass this knowledge on to their children, or that people cannot learn about God unless they hear the gospel. If people reject the truth, they need to replace it with something that will keep order, otherwise people's sin natures will rule. The Indians' beliefs kept order in the village. Everyone had a specific place in the society.*

Chapter 2

1. The Pomo village contained the following buildings and structures. Describe each one and tell what it was used for.
   - Family Hut: *Living quarters for extended family—all relatives on the mother's side.*
   - Roundhouse: *Place where dances and religious ceremonies were performed.*
   - Sweathouse: *Men's gathering place. Place where men would be "fixed" as they sought power and obeyed the taboos to prepare for deer hunting or gambling.*
   - Acorn Granary: *Place to store acorns for winter use.*
2. What is a *professional*? Describe some of the Pomo professions. *A particular occupation for which men prepared. Examples include arrowhead and spear-making, fishing, money -making, hunting, gambling, and preparing to be shamans, poison men, and chiefs.*
3. How were acorns prepared for eating? Describe each step. *Gathered in the fall and stored in granaries. Shell cracked, meat extracted, pounded into fine flour, taken to water and washed or leached to remove bitter tannic acid.*
4. What is an *awihinawa*? *A best friend for life, the only person a Pomo could trust outside of his family.*
5. What activities might take place in the Pomo village? *Any of the professions listed in #2 above, prepare rabbit skins to make clothes, chop wood, make baskets, pound acorns.*

6. **Thought Question:** Why did the Pomo have to move their homes three times each year? *Answers will vary and might include the need to follow the food supply since the Pomo did not farm or the need to start a fresh since dwellings became vermin- and flea-infested.*

Chapter 3

1. Describe these words:
    - Shaman: *A combination doctor, religious leader, "witchdoctor." Provided a link between the material and spiritual world.*
    - Feud: *A fight between families or individuals that might begin over a small slight or insult and continue for many years with one side provoking and the other retaliating.*
2. How did the Pomo think sickness was created? *By Coyote, who wanted to receive money for curing sickness.*
3. What are three ways shaman treated sickness? *1) using medicinal plants, 2) trickery—sucking or singing cure, 3) calling on the spirits or demons.*
4. Why were the Pomo so careful and protective when one of their family became ill? (Hint: Think about what their enemies might try to do.) *The Pomo believed an enemy might add poison to the illness to make it worse and make the whole family ill.*
5. **Thought Question:** Why do we have sickness in our world? *Answers will vary but should include the concept that sin produced sickness. Before Adam and Eve's fall, there was no sickness. Everything was very good.*

Things to Ponder

This unit discusses several thoughts about the Pomo that are half-truths, something that is partly true, but mostly false. For each of the following half-truths, write a complete paragraph describing the full truth. Turn the half-truth into a topic statement, for example:

- "The Pomo were not peaceful people"
- "Compared to some of the eastern Indian tribes, the Pomo could be considered peaceful, but they still had wars"
- "In a way the Pomo were peaceful, but in many ways they were not."

Once you decide on a topic sentence, be sure to back it up with facts and examples.

Be sure that the paragraphs are written in proper form. They should have a good topic sentence that defines the student's position and then evidence to back their claims.

1. The Pomo were peaceful people. *Paragraphs might include idea that wars were small but frequent. Feuds were especially prevalent.*
2. They lived in harmony with their environment or surroundings. *Paragraphs might include the ideas that the Indians worshiped their environment and were not allowed to make any changes. Therefore, the environment constrained how they lived.*
3. The Pomo beliefs allowed them to live happy and prosperous lives. *Paragraphs might include a discussion of how the taboos and religious beliefs restricted the Indians and held them in bondage. They could not progress or change anything about their way of life. They lived in constant fear because they believed the spirits were capable of any action.*
4. The California Indians respected all life. *Paragraphs might include a discussion of the treatment of the newly born and the elderly. Babies were not real people until they were three days old, one twin could be left to die, if a woman's husband divorced her she could kill all her children, old men could be cruelly treated by the women, and those sick or elderly could be left in the woods to die.*

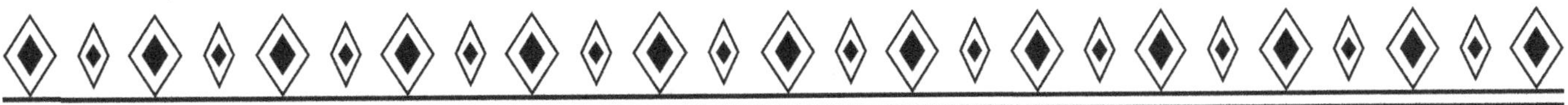

Supplemental Activities

Literature Suggestions

There is very little in the way of good literature to supplement a unit on the California Indians. The people themselves never developed an alphabet and therefore never produced any literature of their own. Some legends passed on orally for generations and subsequently written down are good, but others are often obscene. Choose your reading carefully.

Island of the Blue Dolphins by Scott O'Dell. This book is based on a true story about a woman who was accidentally left behind when her people were rescued from an island in the Santa Barbara Channel. The woman lived alone on the island for eighteen years before she was finally taken to live at Santa Barbara Mission. This book is a fictional account of those eighteen years.

Lone Woman of Ghalas-Hat by Rice Oliver (published by California Weekly Explorer
A shorter version of the above incident that adheres closer to the historical facts. Great illustrations.

Adopted by Indians by Thomas Jefferson Mayfield
In 1850, Mayfield's mother died and his father sent him to live with Yokut Indians in the Central Valley. This book is Mayfield's account of those years. It concentrates on the material aspects of the culture, how the people lived, while completely neglecting the reasons or beliefs that informed their actions. While we learn much about what the Chinoumne village ate, drank, wore, and did, we learn nothing about ceremonies, beliefs, initiations, taboos, and other aspects of the Yokuts' lives. Written for children and recommended with noted reservations.

California Indian Days, by Helen Bauer. Helen Bauer has written a series of books on the Indian, Mission, Rancho, and Gold Rush periods of California's history. These books offer detail on what life was like at the time while offering little in the way of interpretation.

Field Trips

Field trips are most students' favorite way to experience history. However, field trips to California Indian museums and sites could present a number of problems. Most docents in such places adhere to a non-Christian worldview. They probably will give you information contrary to that presented in this unit and in the historical record. They may say things like, "The Indians lived peacefully and happily in California until the white man came and killed them with the sword and disease," or "The Indians lived in harmony with their environment and used everything that they took from the earth. We need to learn from them." If you decide to take a field trip to an Indian museum or site, you will need to be prepared to address these issues.

Look for museums that offer hands-on activities you can do on your own, without the necessity of a docent. Some offer informative videos (and some that are not). Some also offer teaching trunks or kits that you can check out or rent for a short time and peruse on your own. Teaching trunks might contain replicas of Indian artifacts such as arrowheads, tule-filled balls for playing games, or baskets.

Special care should be used if you wish to view an ceremony. Bear in mind that the ceremony may have been used to worship the California Indians' "gods." Research the ceremony before proceeding.

Crafts & Activities

Acorn Pounding

1. Materials needed
   Acorns, which must be gathered in the autumn. When I cannot find acorns I use hazelnuts (filberts). Small Ziploc bags if you wish the students to take their nut flour home; bowls and garbage bags. Rocks and/or bricks for pounding. Plastic tarp to spread over the ground to contain mess. Broom and dustpan for cleanup.

2. Objective
   To gain an appreciation for the progress our Christian society has made possible. When the students return to class, talk about the taboos and prayers that were required to prepare acorns and how the Indian women were not allowed to change them. The students should gain an appreciation for supermarkets as well as the free market and the Christian society that encourages and permits them. I joke and tell my students that the purpose of this activity is to make them appreciate Safeway, but you may insert the name of your favorite grocery store.

3. Procedure
   Instruct the students on safety precautions to safeguard fingers. When one student is pounding, the others should keep their hands away—in their laps or under their legs perhaps. Crack the acorn shells and gather a small quantity of inner meat. Clean up the shells so they don't get mixed in with the flour then pound the inner nut meat into a fine flour.

   Sometimes the California Indians used rocks that looked like a huge mortar and pestle. If you do not have one of these, use rocks or bricks. Let each student take some of the acorn flour home in a small plastic bag, but warn them not to eat it. It contains tannic acid which could make them sick. If you think they might not be able to resist, you might consider keeping the flour.

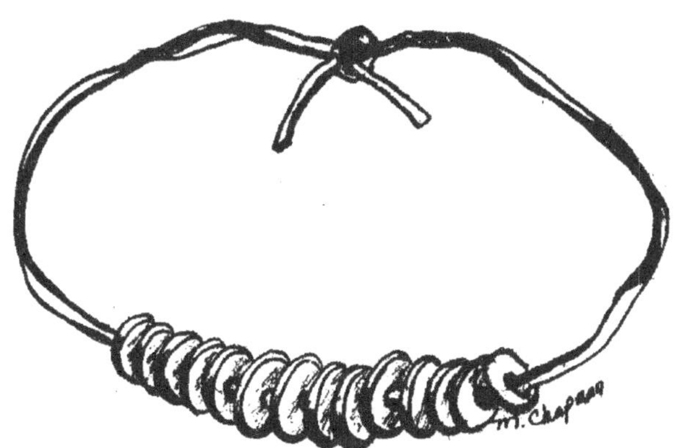

Indian Shell Necklaces

1. Materials Needed
   Shells (any flat shell such as oyster or clam). Leather or leather-like cord long enough to fit

over students' heads. Medium grade sand paper (1/2 sheet for each student). Plastic covers and newspapers to protect tables

2. Advance preparation
   Collect and wash shells. Break shells into pieces about the size of a quarter and drill a small hole in the center of each one. The hole should be big enough to thread a leather or plastic leather-like cord.

3. Objective
   To show the students one of the Indian professions: that of money-making. The shells had value because the Indians said they did (economists call this *fiat money*) and because of the amount of work that went into creating them. The amount of shell money in circulation was limited because only the money-maker was allowed to make it. The older the necklace, the more valuable it was. The Indians did not use shell money solely; they also had a barter system.

4. Procedure
   Use sand paper to smooth off the edges of the shell pieces. They should be as round and as uniform as possible. If a student finishes early, encourage him or her to go back and spend more time shaping the shell disks. When several are complete (5 to 10 shells), string them on the leather cord.

Making Baskets

Directions for making baskets is beyond the scope of this *Teacher's Supplement*, but should be available from library books, some Indian museums and historical sites. You may also check out the Internet.

Indian women made baskets using two different methods: coiling and twining. Twining is the easier of the two and might be more suitable for students to attempt. Each basket requires a quantity of rushes that must be soaked in water to become pliable.

Indian Games

The California Indians also played a variety of games that may be reproduced in the classroom. Unfortunately, most of these games were used for gambling. I found that problematic and have consequently have omitted them.

More Ideas

If you would like more craft and activity suggestions, I would recommend *The Chumash People, Materials for Teachers and Students* from the Santa Barbara Museum of Natural History. Although it deals with the Chumash only, it is excellent and many activities will apply to other California Indian groups as well. For more information, contact the museum by looking them up on the Internet (use your favorite search engine).

Oral Review Questions

You might use these questions for oral review games and/or team competitions.

1. What Biblical figure are the California Indians descended from? (Noah)
2. True or false: Some California Indian legends are similar to Bible stories. (true)
3. Why didn't the California Indians know about God? (knowledge suppressed)
4. True or false: The Pomo lived in the same place or village all year round. (false)
5. What is a tule? (rushes—grow in wet areas)
6. What did Chikokawe wear to keep warm? (tule coat, rabbit-skin blanket, mud)
7. What was a sweathouse? (gathering place for men)
8. How did the Pomo take baths? (sweat then plunge into an icy stream)
9. What was the Pomos' main food? (acorns)
10. What did the Pomo eat besides acorns? (buckeyes, berries, deer, grasshoppers, dried

seeds)

11. How did the California Indians cook food? (hot rocks in a basket)
12. How were acorns prepared for food? (cracked, pounded and tannic acid washed out along with chants, songs, and prayers)
13. What did the Pomo believe caused illness? (evil spirits)
14. Who supposedly cured an Indian of illness? (the shaman)
15. What kinds of tools did the shaman use to cure illness? (coyote paw, obsidian knife, rabbit bladder, feather headdress, human bone, herbs)
16. What is a taboo? (rule or prohibition)
17. Give some examples of taboos. (Men could not talk to mothers-in-law, shaman could not eat meat or grease for eight days when curing an illness, Indian women chanted and prayed while making acorns, no fresh meat in a family dwelling if someone were ill)
18. What did the Indians mean by poison? (witchcraft, casting a spell)
19. What was the purpose of the Indian dances? (visual forms of prayers to the spirits)
20. Did the Indians live in harmony with nature? (no, nature determined how they could live.)
21. Were the Indians peaceful? (no, some had small wars and feuds)
22. How were most women treated by the male Indians? (like slaves)
23. What is a feud? (a dispute or grudge between families or individuals)
24. What is a profession? (an occupation or vocation, a job)
25. Name some professions found in the Pomo village. (arrowhead and spear-making, fishing, money-making, hunting, gambling, shamans, poison man, and chief)
26. What is an *awihinawa*? (best friend)
27. Name some of the buildings found in an Indian village. (sweathouse, roundhouse, family hut)
28. What was a shaman? (combination doctor and priest—a link between the physical world and the spiritual world)
29. True or false: The California Indians lived in teepees, made birch bark canoes, and built totem poles. (false)
30. Describe a Pomo family dwelling. (Long tule-covered hut that looked like an overgrown haystack. An extended family of up to 50 people lived in one. Long aisle and each family had own fire pit.)
31. What are some activities men performed in the sweathouse? (prepare for baths, "fixing" for hunting or gambling, pass religious history on to grandsons)
32. When did babies become real people? (after three days)
33. Explain what the Pomo believed about how sickness was created. (Coyote)
34. In what ways did the shaman try to cure illness? (plants, trickery, calling on evil spirits)

Project Suggestions

1. Make a model of a California Indian village. Include the sweathouse, dwellings, roundhouse and perhaps some utensils (baskets, acorn-pounding rocks). You could use plaster of Paris to make the setting, aluminum foil for water, weeds for marshlands, and grass and twigs for structures.
2. Learn how to weave an Indian basket, make a soaproot brush, or other Indian tool. Some Indian museums offer instruction.
3. Research the different ways California Indians made their homes. Build or draw models of plank houses, tule huts, desert shelters, and earth mounds. (For help see *California Indian Days*, by Helen Bauer.) Discuss how the climate influenced the kind of houses the Indians made.

Source Documents

Reading Recommendations

If you would like to learn more about the Pomo, I'd like to recommend the book I used as the basis for my stories:

Aginsky, Burt W. & Ethel G., *Deep Valley*, Stein and Day, New York, 1967.

This book was written by a husband and wife who lead a team of researchers in Northern California in 1934-36, 1939-42, and 1946-48. Interviewing a number of Pomo who still remembered life before the Spaniards, the Aginsky's waited until 1967 to publish their book to protect the privacy of the people they consulted.

The reason I like *Deep Valley* is that it is a work of historical fiction, an accompaniment to the Aginsky's other scholarly works. It's hard to form a picture of everyday life from a list of facts and this book helps bring the culture to life. However, since it does portray the culture realistically, it will be offensive to some Christians, especially young people. I would rate it PG-13. Some high school students might benefit from it, but I would want to take a black marker to some sections first. You will probably have to look at some used book websites to find *Deep Valley*.

Teacher's Supplement

The Explorers

Unit 2

Teaching Aids—Unit 2

The Explorers

Teacher's Overview

THE EXPLORER PERIOD OF CALIFORNIA'S history overlaps about 250 years of the Indian period, including the first contact between the European, Asian, and Indian cultures. During this time, Cabrillo became the first Spaniard to discover California. Subsequently, the Manila Galleons sailed down the coast of California for 250 years without ever landing. These rich Spanish treasure ships attracted the attention of England and brought Sir Francis Drake to California's shores, while Cermenho and Vizcaíno tried to find suitable harbors for the Manila Galleons to re-supply in California. Additionally, there probably were other explorers who came to California from Asia and other parts of the world.

At first, the study of the explorers can seem dull and not germane to the subject of California history. Several of my students seem to endure this chapter so that they can get to the "real thing." The more I studied this era, the more I became fascinated with the explorers themselves.

Modern history books don't normally tell us why the explorers undertook many risks to sail into the great unknown. We learn their motivation when we read their logs and journals. Very often, the voyages were undertaken for the glory of God, to bring His Word to a lost people. Columbus believed that Christ could return in his own lifetime, but first the gospel had to be carried to the ends of the earth. He believed that he was chosen by God to help with this task, which is one reason he undertook his journey to the Indies. He also believed he would receive financial and status rewards from the monarchs of Spain.

The Spanish Church and State

It would be helpful to understand a little about the relationship between the church and state in Spain during the 1400-1600s, the time of the explorers. The established church was Catholicism, and no other options were allowed. The Jews were expelled from Spain in 1492, the same year that Columbus discovered America. Later, after the Reformation, Protestants were not tolerated. Anyone suspected of not adhering to the teachings of the Catholic church could be brought before the Spanish Inquisition, an institution that thankfully did not reach the North American frontier.

The church was under the direct control of the state and its head, King Charles V. The Catholic Pope gave King Charles V authority to administer the church in all of the Spanish colonies under an agreement known as the *Patronato Real* (Royal Patronage). The king decided where the missionaries were to go, where to build missions, and who would be appointed as priests or bishops. All of the expenses and salaries of the missions were paid from the royal treasury.

Since the church and state were so entwined in Spain's history, the Crown took on many responsibilities that today we leave in the realm of the church. It felt that it had the obligation to try to convert its subjects to Christianity. Beginning with the second voyage of Columbus, missionaries accompanied the explorers. They had three tasks: First, they attended to the spiritual needs of the sailors.

Second, they attempted to bring Christianity to the natives. Third, they made recommendations on the best places to build future missions or colonies.

Faith of the Explorers

In general, the explorers had a deep faith in God. They relied on Him for protection during their long, dangerous journeys. All men are sinners and there were plenty of scoundrels in the group we label "explorers," but as a whole, they were men of faith.

It is easy for those of us living in this age to look back on the explorers with scorn, and point to areas where they fell short of the Word of God. However, it would be helpful to remember that the common man did not have access to the Bible. He walked in the light that he had, which was much dimmer than that which we enjoy today. Samuel Eliot Morison, a Harvard historian, did a great deal of research on the lives and times of the explorers. He reports that every part of the sailors' day was replete with reminders of God and the sailors' duty towards Him. From morning prayers, to songs, to afternoon reminders, to evening prayers, sailors' lives were organized around reminders of God's daily presence. (See the Source Documents section for more information.)

Just as today where true belief is mixed with superstition or no belief, the sailors beliefs were also mixed. Some prayed to the true and living god, some to idols, and some to nothing. Morison's works contain stirring examples of the first and would be uplifting to read. The following are especially helpful:

Morison, Samuel Eliot, *The European Discovery of America - The Southern Voyages A.D. 1492 - 1616*, Oxford University Press, New York, 1974

Morison, Samuel Eliot, *Admiral of the Ocean Sea*, Little, Brown and Company, Boston, 1942

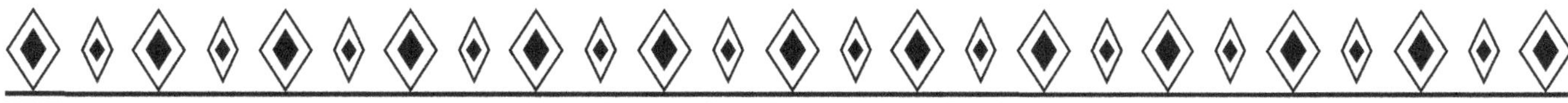

Teaching the Explorers' Unit

Lesson Plans

1. Introduction ideas:
   - Choose a hands-on activity such as the sea chest centers, explained in the activities section.
   - Explain the Mariners' Psalm (Psalm 107).
   - Act out the voyage to California, as explained in the activities section, so students understand why it was so difficult to reach and why it was colonized so late.
2. Begin teaching about the chain of explorers with Columbus and Cortés (Ch. 4) and do Roundup questions. If students have studied these explorers previously, make connections.
3. You might create a paper chain with very large links, each link containing the name of an explorer. Begin with Columbus near a map (outline) of Spain and end with Viscaíno in California. Make every chain link a different color. This physical object will help students understand the purpose of the unit and the contributions of each explorer.
4. Teach Cabrillo and Ferrelo, Drake, Cermenho, and Vizcaíno (Ch. 5). Introduce Cabrillo, Drake, and Vizcaíno by teaching their stanzas of the "California Date Song."
5. Accompany your discussion of the explorers with a discussion of geography. (See Geography section.) As the explorer is discussed, trace his route on the map found in the Class-Time Activities section. Color code the routes.
6. Explain the importance of the Strait of Anián. You might demonstrate its importance with physical objects in your room.
7. If you have not already done so, act out the journey to California, explained in the Class-Time Activities section. Additionally, explain the difficulties of scurvy. You might be able to find some pictures by searching the Internet for images of scurvy.
8. Teach about Spanish exploration after the visit of Viscaíno and the hidden San Francisco Bay (Ch. 5). Do the Roundup questions.
9. Choose one or two of the activities from the Class-Time Activities section, as many as you have time for.
10. Choose a writing activity. You might consider some character sketches, journal activities, or the Things to Ponder question from the Unit 2 Roundup.
11. Finish the unit with a review game based on the Oral Review questions.

Objectives

At the completion of this unit, students should be able to:

1. Explain why it was so difficult to reach California. Students should have an appreciation of not only the distances involved, but also the effects of geography.
2. Know the four main explorers to reach California: Cabrillo, Drake, Cermenho, and Vizcaíno. Students should be able to state the contribution of each.
3. State the three possible reasons why the entrance to San Francisco Bay was missed.
4. Understand what was happening in New Spain after the last sea voyage of Vizcaíno.
5. Define the word *providential*. (See

Introduction.)

6. List several providential events from this unit (see below).

God's Providence

7. Cortés, by conquering the Aztecs with only 500 men, paved the way for Christianity to reach Mexico, p. 25-26.
8. Drake was not able to return to California to build an English colony, p. 32.
9. God provided for Cermenho and his crew after his galleon was wrecked, p. 34.
10. Spain did not colonize California at the height of her power, after the voyage of Vizcaíno, p. 35.
11. The entrance to San Francisco Bay was hidden from the Spaniards, pp. 37-38.

Character Sketches

(See Appendix A for further detail on character sketches)

Beginning with this unit, students will be asked to do character sketches on certain historical figures. The purpose of this exercise is to teach the students to analyze the motivation of the various historical personalities that they study and to learn what the people did, but also, if known, why they did it. Students should record whether or not the person was a Christian (if this is known), and what character qualities he exhibited that are worthy of admiration. The character sketch form in Appendix A will be useful for this exercise.

Choose from the following:

Columbus	Drake
Cortés	Cermenho
Cabrillo	Vizcaíno

California Date Song

(See Appendix C for entire song)

1542 - Cabrillo (Discovery of California)
1579 - Drake (English visit to California)
1602 - Vizcaíno (Last major Spanish sea exploration)

In fifteen hundred and forty-two,
Cabrillo sailed the ocean blue.
Searching for a short cut through,
He discovered California.

In fifteen hundred and seventy-nine
Sir Francis sailed the *Golden Hind*,
The Strait of Anían to find,
But he only found Drake's Bay.

In sixteen hundred and only two,
Vizcaíno sailed the ocean blue,
Of Monterey Bay he wrote and drew,
The last of the explorers.

Geography

(See Appendix D for further discussion of geography.)

Students should learn the following locations:

Points and Capes

Cape Mendocino
Point Conception

Islands

Santa Catalina
San Clemente
Santa Rosa
Santa Cruz
San Miguel

One way to become familiar with the coastline of California, is to trace the routes of the explorers. This exercise is discussed in more detail under the Class-Time Activities section of this manual.

Journal

1. Write a paragraph explaining the effect geography had on the discovery and settlement of California.
2. Do character sketches on: Cabrillo, Drake, Cermenho, and Vizcaíno.
3. Trace the routes of the above explorers using colored pencils and the map provided (see following).
4. Write a short essay discussing the three reasons San Francisco Bay was missed by all the explorers, and which one you think is correct.
5. Read the Mariners' Psalm (Ps. 107:23-31) from the introduction to The Explorers Unit and tell why this portion of Scripture would be of comfort to the explorers.

Unit Roundup Answers

Chapter 4

1. Why did Columbus believe he had arrived in the Indies? *His maps, which did not include the North or South American continent, showed he had reached the East. San Salvador was located in about the same place he believed Cipangu (Japan) would be.*
2. What problems did Cortés' settlement in Baja California face? *Little water, little food, land could not be farmed, to difficult to get supplies, and many men died.*
3. **Thought Question:** What do you think might have happened if Columbus and Cortés had never lived? *Since the purpose of this question is to give students the opportunity to think and interact with the ideas of history, it could have many different answers. Possibilities range from North America would not have been discovered to someone else would have had the honor.*

Chapter 5

1. Identify each of the following explorers and tell what he did:
   Cabrillo—*First Spaniard to California*
   Drake—*The English privateer*
   Cermenho—*The man who wrecked his galleon*
   Vizcaíno—*The last Spanish explorer*
2. Explain why it was so hard to reach California. Use the words *wind*, *currents*, and *scurvy*. *Winds and currents made it very difficult to sail up the coast from Mexico. Sailors did not have enough fresh food to eat and got very sick with scurvy.*
3. Why was the valley around Los Angeles called the Bay of Smokes? *It filled with smoke from Indian campfires so that the mountains could not be seen.*
4. What is the Strait of Anían, also called the Northwest Passage? *A mythical passage (shortcut) across North America that united the Pacific and Atlantic Oceans.*
5. What is a *letter of marque*? What is the difference between a *pirate* and a *privateer*? *Special permission from the crown to attack enemy ships. A pirate steals. A privateer commits acts of war.*
6. What was a Manila Galleon? *A Spanish treasure ship.*
7. Why did the people of San Francisco build

Prayer Book Cross? *To remember the first Protestant service in California and the visit of Sir Francis Drake.*

8. Who are the Jesuits and what did they do? *Spanish missionaries. Built missions in Baja California.*
9. **Thought Question:** Think about how your life might be different if the Spanish or English had built a prosperous colony in California in the 1600s. Write a paragraph describing your thoughts. *Students should think about what life might be like if they spoke Spanish, ate Spanish food, and lived under a Spanish government. Perhaps some have been to Mexico and can draw on that knowledge. Or perhaps they have watched movies or read books about Spain or Mexico. Alternatively, they could think about living in the midst of British culture.*

Supplemental Activities

Literature Suggestions

Below are two very fine books about the explorer period of California's history.

What Cabrillo Found by Maude Hart Lovelace. This book is absolutely delightful. The author has consulted source documents to recount what is known of Cabrillo's journeys, beginning with his adventures with Cortés in New Spain. The author records the sailors' faith in an accurate and favorable manner.

Drake, the Man They Call a Pirate by Jean Lee Latham. The award-winning author of *Carry On Mr. Bowditch* brings life and color to the person of Sir Francis Drake, including his several voyages to the New World and California.

Field Trips

There are many possibilities for field trips to enhance your study of the explorers. Usually maritime museums have displays that feature early exploration methods. Sometimes military museums have these exhibits as well. In some of the larger harbor cities in California, you might see replicas of the incredibly small ships that the early explorers used.

If you don't have access to a maritime or military museum, you might try contacting a boating or yacht club to find someone willing to give your family or group a private tour of a boat, or even better, a ride. If you explain that you are teaching a group of well-behaved students about California's past, many people will be more than willing to accommodate you.

If you live near San Diego or your travels take you near this lovely city, you might make a stop at Cabrillo National Monument which commemorates Cabrillo's visit to California. It contains a huge statue of Cabrillo, some excellent tide pools, and a quaint lighthouse. The national park service website also contains a downloadable teacher's packet and field trip guide.

Point Reyes

Further north, you might visit Point Reyes National Seashore, one of the possible places where Cermenho lost his galleon and Drake repaired his ship. The Kenneth C. Patrick Visitors' Center explores this possibility. You may eat at the café or picnic on the beach under cliffs that look very similar to the white cliffs of Dover in England. (You can also see the cliffs online by searching "Drake's Beach Panorama.")

Additional attractions include miles of trails including one that shows evidence of the 1906 earthquake on the San Andreas Fault. The Point Reyes Lighthouse with its first order fesnel lens is one of my favorites—lots of steps, though. During certain times of the year, you might even see whales from the lighthouse platform. Be sure to visit Kule Loklo, a recreated Miwok Indian village.

There's enough to do here to warrant an overnight stay, and the Point Reyes Hostel might be an option. We reserved the Bunkhouse (twenty people maximum) and had our own bathrooms and private living room. We made our meals and ate in the very close Ranch House.

Class-Time Activities

The Discovery of Monterey Bay

This play recounts Vizcaíno's discovery of Monterey Bay. It can be performed by as few as two students and a parent, or by as many as ten students. The parts of Mates 1-8 can be played by the same person if desired. Costumes and/or props can be used in this play for more color.

Special thanks to Donna Miller for originally writing this play.

Scene One

Narrator: The activity of English sea dogs in the "Spanish Lake," as the Spaniards called the Pacific Ocean, have worried the king of Spain. Valuable Manila Galleons returning from the Philippines contain many riches. They must have a safe harbor where they can obtain fresh food and water, and an escort of Spanish warships as they make their way back to New Spain. Count Monterrey in New Spain has commanded Sebastian Vizcaíno to search for a good harbor in the territory called California. If his search is successful, the count will order that a colony be built to assist the Manila Galleons.

(Captain Vizcaíno and four of his men are standing by the side of the ship discussing the voyage. The men are grumbling and complaining.)

Mate 1: Captain Vizcaíno, how much longer until we get to the safe harbor Captain Cabrillo found? Our ship must be repaired and our food is almost gone!

Mate 2: It's been a rough trip! Every time we sail north, these blasted storms push us back! We've been trying for seven months to reach the harbor! Will we ever reach it?

Mate 3: Cabrillo's report is more than 150 years old. Maybe the harbor doesn't exist anymore. Maybe we'll just keep sailing up and down this coast. I've seen these same cliffs on the shore five times this month. Are we ever going to get far enough north to please Count Monterrey?

Mate 4: Well, if we don't reach it soon, we won't need to worry about a safe harbor for the Manila Galleon because we'll all be dead.

Captain Vizcaíno: Have faith men! Let's have no talk of death here. By the grace of God we will find that harbor.

Mate 5: *(Looking through a telescope towards land.)* Captain Vizcaíno! Look ahead! There's a harbor. It must be the one that Cabrillo found. What did he call it? San Miguel, I think.

Captain Vizcaíno: (Moving towards Mate 5 and taking the telescope.) Good work, mate! We'll walk on shore tonight! As to the harbor, we will name it San Diego since today is the day of St. Diego.

Mate 6: I hope we can find fresh food. I have not felt good for weeks. My gums are soft and spongy, my teeth are loose, and my mouth is bleeding and sore.

Mate 7: Me too! My joints are so swollen with this scurvy that I can hardly move.

Captain Vizcaíno: Head for shore! We will rest here for ten days to give the sick time to recover. Call for Father Ascension. He must say a Mass to thank God for a safe trip.

Mate 8: Look captain! I see natives! I wonder if they are friendly?

Captain Vizcaíno: Remember our orders. We

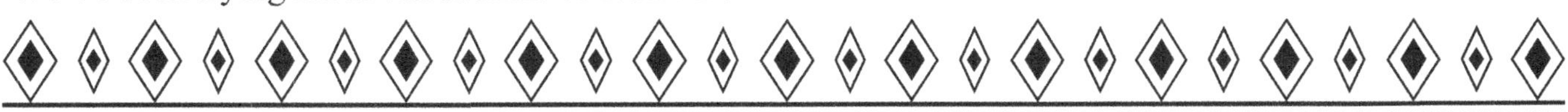

are to treat all of the natives well so that the missionaries can tell them about our Lord and Savior Jesus Christ. Now, bring the ship around and sail for shore!

Narrator: The natives were friendly. They gave the Spaniards food and water which allowed the men to recover from their scurvy. The ten days passed quickly, the ship was repaired, the two other ships caught up with Captain Vizcaíno's flagship, and the men prepared to continue their journey.

Scene Two

(Captain Vizcaíno and his men have left San Diego and sailed north. They are huddled near to port, looking at an island off the coast of California.)

Captain Vizcaíno: Look at that island. What a magnificent land! Let's drop anchor in that large harbor and take on more water.

Mate 1: Captain, the mapmaker wishes to know what he should call this island. Should he retain the name Cabrillo gave it?

Captain Vizcaíno: No. Since today is November 24, St. Catherine's day, we shall name it Santa Catalina in her honor.

Narrator: It took three days to maneuver the ship into harbor. Once on shore the Spaniards visited an Indian village and saw something which surprised them.

Mate 2: *(pointing)* Captain, look at that Indian woman! Do you see the Chinese silk shawl she is wearing? Where do you think she got that?

Mate 3: I know! I sailed with Captain Cermenho seven years ago. We were bringing a loaded Manila Galleon back from the Philippines. Such treasure you have never seen!

Mate 4: That's right! We had orders to map the California coastline. But as soon as we had constructed a smaller boat for exploring, our beautiful galleon crashed against the rocks. All that treasure...gone.

Mate 5: That must be part of the lost treasure. Captain, do you think these natives know where the galleon wreck is? Perhaps if they could show us where it is, we could salvage some of the riches.

Captain Vizcaíno: Good idea! Ask some of the Indian men if they would sail with us to show us where the treasure ship is. It's time to move on again.

Narrator: Two or three Indians agreed to go with Captain Vizcaíno, but as the ship was weighing anchor they changed their minds and asked to be left behind. Captain Vizcaíno, not wishing to take them against their will, agreed.

Scene Three

Narrator: The ships sailed up the coast through the Santa Barbara Channel, where they were met by an old Indian chief in a boat who tried to persuade them to land and visit his village. Since the wind was finally behind them for the first time since the beginning of the voyage, Captain Vizcaíno declined the invitation. The ships sailed around Point Conception, past the Santa Lucia Mountains, towards Point Pinos. It was now December 15, 1602.

Mate 1: *(pointing)* Look at the point ahead covered with pine trees. Could this be Point Pinos?

Captain Vizcaíno: Look carefully for a harbor now men. This is the area in which we want to build a place of refuge for the galleons. It is usually the first land they see after their long voyage from the Philippines.

Mate 2: Captain, look at those pine trees. They grow so straight and tall. They are perfect for ship masts. This would be a great place to repair the galleons.

Mate 3: I see a harbor! It is large and open to the wind, but look at that place near the river. It looks like it would be sheltered from all wind.

Captain Vizcaíno: Head for that port! We will rest on shore, explore the area, and decide what to do with the many men who are sick. Move in!

Narrator: The next day the ship was safely inside the harbor, which Captain Vizcaíno named Monterey in honor of Count Monterrey.

Captain Vizcaíno: This harbor is perfect. Look, there is water near the shore from that river which we will name the Carmelo River. Our Manila Galleons will be sheltered from the fiercest storms in this harbor. Draw maps of the area. Count Monterrey will be pleased with our discovery.

Mate 4: Captain, we have been on our voyage of discovery for seven months now. Sixteen of our men have already died.

Mate 5: Yes, and forty-five more are sick with scurvy. What shall we do to help them?

Captain Vizcaíno: The sickest must return to New Spain. They will not be able to take anymore of this strenuous journey. Prepare the San Thomas to leave immediately and return to New Spain. May God grant them safe passage. The rest of us must continue our explorations. Our orders require us to reach Cape Mendocino. After that, we may return also.

Narrator: Vizcaíno thought he had found the perfect harbor in which the Manila Galleons could be repaired and the crew refreshed. However, when the Spaniards would again visit Monterey Bay 167 years later, they would not find it so useful.

Although Cabrillo, Drake, Cermenho, and now Vizcaíno had all sailed past the best harbor, San Francisco Bay, none of them ever saw it, even though some of the ships' logs reported clear days. God kept the bay hidden. Hiding the bay was part of God's perfect plan to make California a part of the United States of America.

When one of my classes performed "The Discovery of Monterey Bay," students dressed in costume, which included checked shirts, bandanas, eye patches, sailor hats, and of course, swords. We even had our own bird—yo, ho, ho!

Class-Time Activities

The Mariners' Museum

http://www.mariner.org//educationalad/ageofex/activities.php

Not only does this website contain some great information about the Age of Exploration and the explorers, it gives students directions to make simple navigation equipment including the following:

- Box and water compass
- Astrolabe and quadrant

Hard Tack

Ship's food was very simple and needed to last for months or even years. The staple of the sailors' meals was hard tack, a hard sea biscuit. These biscuits are so hard, they needed to be soaked in coffee or stew before they were edible. Sometimes these biscuits became infested with weevils, a small type of beetle.

To make hard tack, combine

- 4 Parts Flour
- 1 Part Water
- Salt to Taste

Form into a dough. Roll on a floured sheet until about 1/2 inch thick, then cut into squares about 2 by 3 inches. Place on a baking sheet, poke holes in the top with a fork, and bake at 250 degrees for about an hour or until lightly browned.

Sea Shanties

http://www.contemplator.com/sea/index.html

Most of the work on the ships was accompanied by music, especially tasks that had to be performed in rhythm, such as pulling on a rope. This site contains the words and music to over fifty sea shanties from the British Isles and America. Listen to the tune and sing along. Pick one or two to teach your students.

Knots

http://www.animatedknots.com/

Since just about everything on a ship involved rope, every sailor need to know how to tie intricate knots. This site contains animation to show you how the knot is tied through animation. Students could make decorative knot boards or just try their hand with rope.

Semaphore

Ships could communicate with each other using flags in a system called flag *semaphore*. To give students practice in this sometimes frustrating method of communication, divide them into groups and have them send each other messages. Note: For a better diagram of this system, look up Flag Semaphore on Wikipedia.

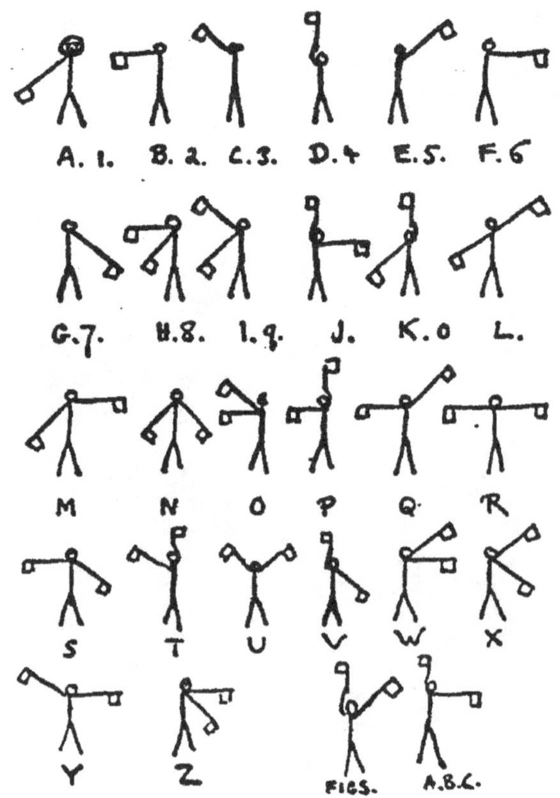

Explorer Route Maps

1. Materials Needed
   Each student will need a copy of the map which follows, colored pencils, and the textbook, *His California Story*.

2. Advance Preparation Copy maps

3. Objective
   To begin to acquaint students with California's geography by having them record the routes of the explorers.

4. Procedure
   Instruct students to label the following features on their maps. (Labels should go on the "land" side so that explorer routes can be drawn in the "ocean.")

Humboldt Bay	San Miguel Island
San Pedro Bay	Santa Rosa Island
Drake's Bay	Santa Cruz Island
Santa Barbara	Santa Catalina
San Francisco Bay	Point Conception
Monterey Bay	Cape Mendocino
San Diego Bay	

Have students read the accounts of the explorers and trace their routes using a different color pencil for each. Record the color used in the map key box.

Journey to California

To explain why it was so difficult to reach California, set your room up with objects to resemble a map of the world. Even better, find a large flat area like a parking lot, and draw large outlines of the continents with chalk (with permission, of course). Choose one or two students to be "ships" and the rest to be winds and currents—students could wear identifying placards or tags.

Students should begin their journey in "Spain," and then try to "sail" to California. They should experience difficulties all along the way including doldrums near the equator, unexpected squalls, fierce storms near Cape Horn at the tip of South America, and contrary winds and currents in the Pacific. Other students should act out these obstacles, for example twirling and whirling for storms, perhaps with long streamers. Additional difficulties they should experience include leaky water casks, spoiled food, leaks in the ship's hull, and broken masts. Students should develop an appreciation for how difficult it was to reach California.

Project Suggestions

(Any of these projects would also work well for a class-time activity. See Appendix B for a description of the class project.)

1. Prepare a report on Juan Rodríguez Cabrillo. Include a map of his voyage. Write a story about his encounter with the Indians of San Diego or San Miguel Island—what did they do, look like, and say?
2. Find out all you can about galleons and other Spanish ships. You may wish to draw pictures.
3. Prepare a report on Sir Francis Drake. Include a description of Indians he met. Perhaps visit Drake's Bay near Pt. Reyes.
4. Learn how to navigate with a compass. Set up a route for your friends or classmates. Make it your goal to have them begin and end in the same place. Can they to do it?
5. Research the art of knot-tying. Learn to tie a square knot, bowline, and half-hitch.
6. Research and write a report on scurvy or rickets. Why were sailors prone to these diseases? What were their symptoms? How were they cured? Why are these diseases no longer a problem?
7. Learn how ships communicated with each other using flags. Write a message in "flag code" (semaphore).

8. Find out all you can about anchors. How are they made, what are they used for, how can they be used to move a ship, and how are they raised? Make a report illustrated with pictures.

Oral Review Questions

Use these questions for review, to close a lesson, or for a review game like Around the World or Jeopardy.

1. Compare the explorers' ships to our ships. (small, lack modern navigational tools)
2. Name the island that Columbus first discovered in the New World. (San Salvador)
3. Why did Columbus want to reach the Indies? (carry the gospel to the ends of the earth and look for riches)
4. True or false: The Spanish king and queen felt it was their responsibility to convert their subjects to Christianity. (true)
5. What was Hernando Cortés chosen by God to do? (end practice of human sacrifice)
6. What did Cortés tell the Aztecs their human sacrifices would do? (provoke God's wrath)
7. On what land did Cortés try to start a colony? (Baja California)
8. Describe Baja California. (hostile, little water, mountainous, desert-like)
9. What was Cabrillo looking for when he found California? (Strait of Anían)
10. What is a strait? (a narrow body of water connecting two larger bodies of water)
11. Why was it so hard to travel to California? (ships had to fight against winds and currents)
12. What happened to Cabrillo on his first visit to San Miguel? (fell and broke his arm near the shoulder while trying to rescue his men from hostile Indians)
13. Why didn't Cabrillo sail past Fort Ross? (violent storms)
14. What happened to Cabrillo on his second visit to the island of San Miguel? (He died.)
15. Did the expedition return to New Spain after Cabrillo died? (No)
16. What is scurvy? (disease caused by the lack of vitamin C)
17. What is a Manila Galleon? (a Spanish treasure ship that traded with the Philippines)
18. Why did Spain want to trade with the Philippines? (to obtain goods such as silk, spices, ivory, gems, gum, and carpets)
19. What was the name of the English explorer who visited California? (Francis Drake)
20. Why did Drake visit California? (looking for the Strait of Anían to escape from the Spaniards)
21. Where did Drake land? (Drake's Bay)
22. Where was the first Protestant religious service held in the United States? (Drake's Bay)
23. How did Drake get back to England? (sailed around the world)
24. On what kind of a ship did Cermenho come to California? (Manila Galleon)
25. What happened to his ship? (It was wrecked.)
26. Where did Cermenho's ship crash? (Drake's Bay)
27. How did God save the lives of Cermenho's crew? (allowed them to find a great fish and water)
28. Who was the last major explorer to visit California? (Vizcaíno)
29. At what bay did Vizcaíno land and explore? (Monterey)
30. Why didn't the explorers find San Francisco Bay? (God's plan, wasn't there -- earthquake, limited visibility, or fog)
31. What did the Spaniards do in New Spain after the last explorer visited California? (settled and protected colonies)
32. Who built a series of missions in Baja California? (the Jesuits)

Explorer Map Routes

Name ______________________________

Map Key

Cabrillo
Drake
Cermenho
Vizcaíno

Directions:
Using different colored pencils, record the routes of Cabrillo, Drake, Cermenho, and Vizcaíno. Record the color of the pencil you used in the Map Key box. Label the location of all bays, islands, capes, and points studied so far.

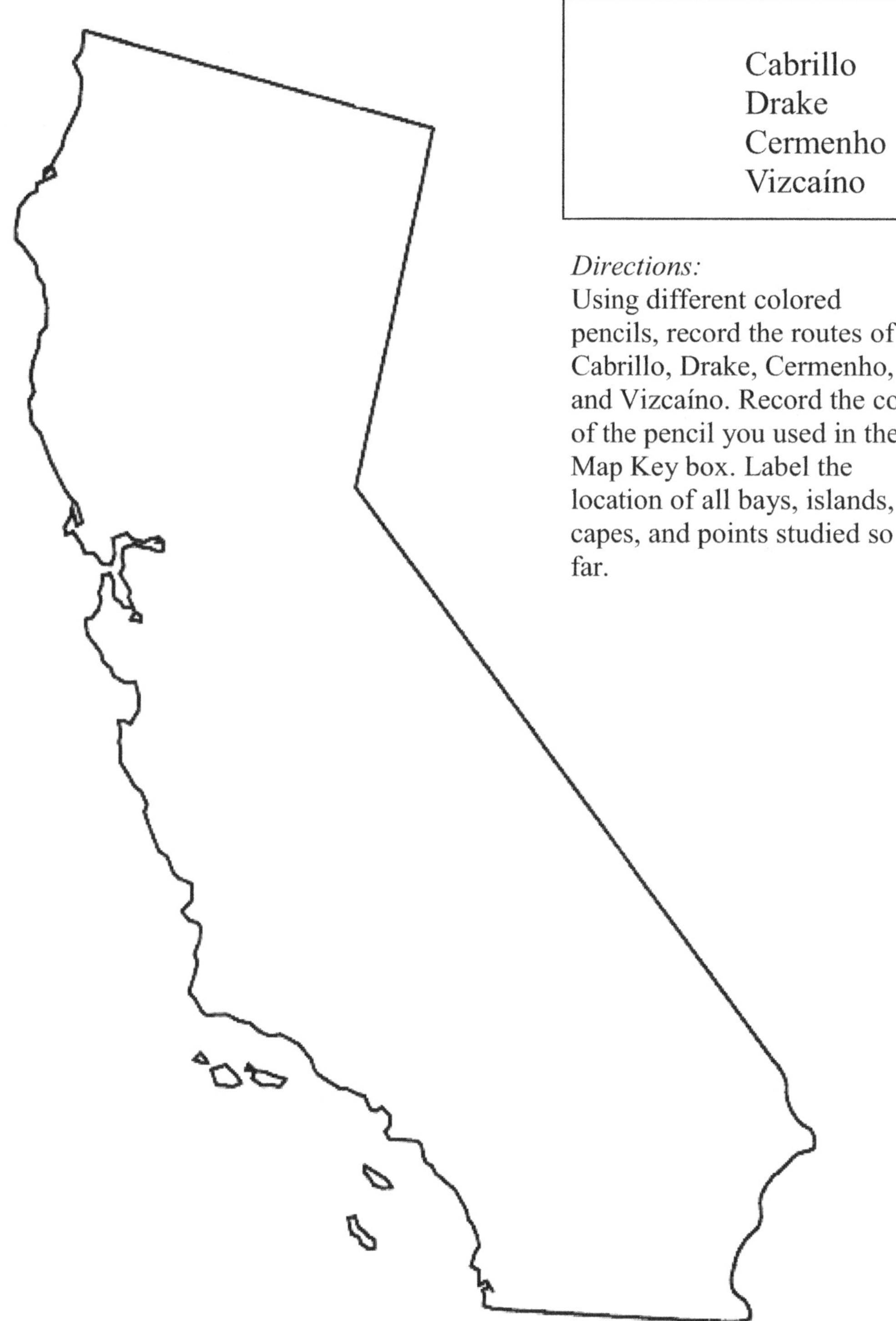

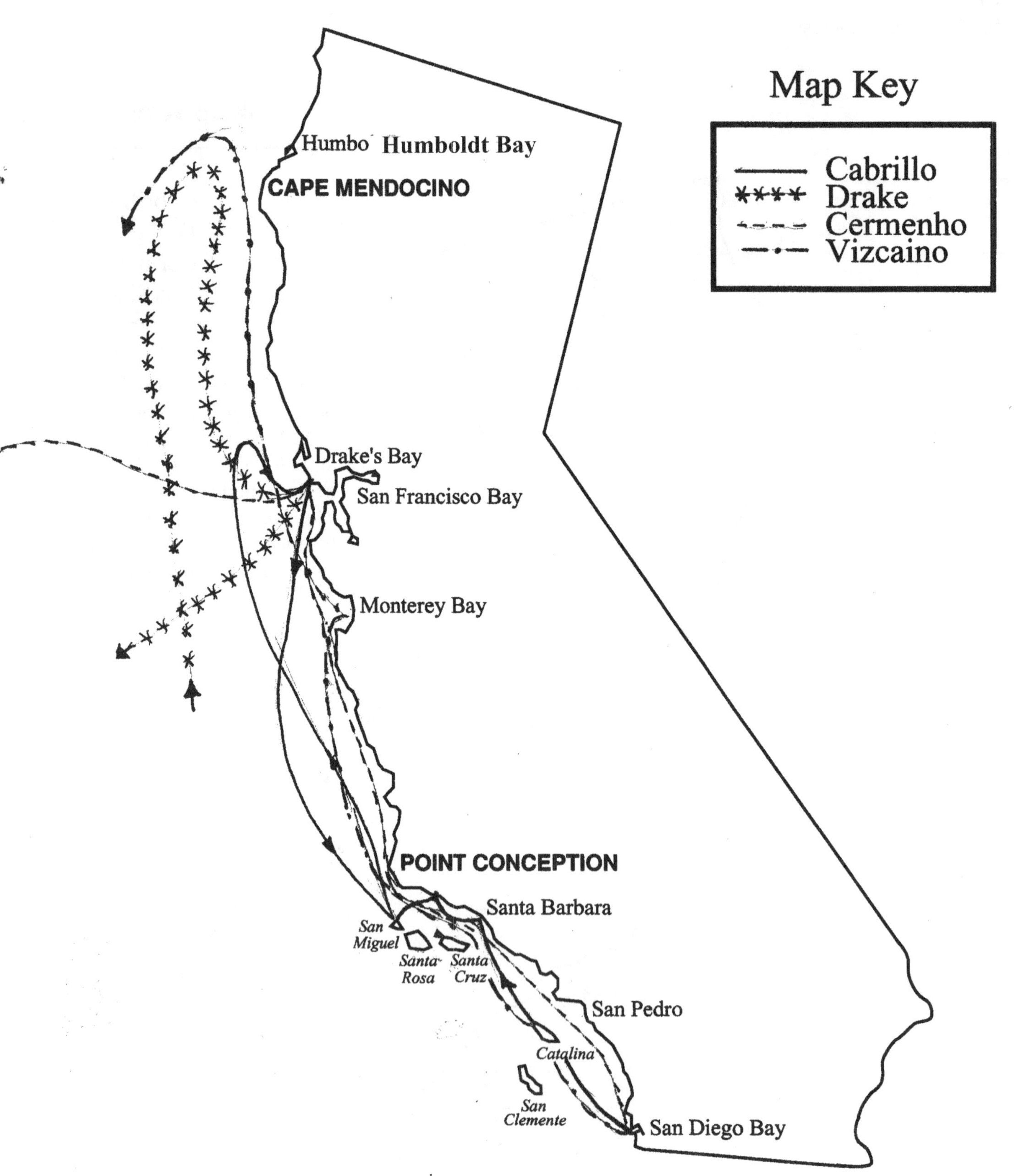
Map Key
Cabrillo
Drake
Cermenho
Vizcaino
Humbo Humboldt Bay
CAPE MENDOCINO
Drake's Bay
San Francisco Bay
Monterey Bay
POINT CONCEPTION
Santa Barbara
San Miguel
Santa Rosa
Santa Cruz
San Pedro
Catalina
San Clemente
San Diego Bay

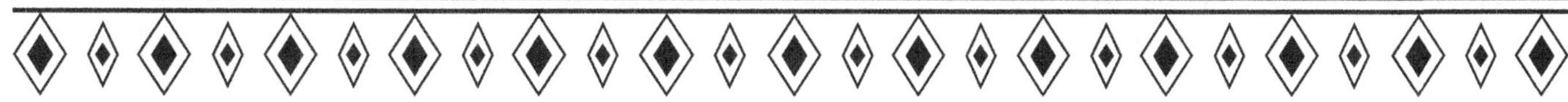

Source Documents

Ship Conditions

Charles E. Chapman, Ph.D., *A History of California: The Spanish Period*, The Macmillian Company, New York, 1921, p. 92

Conditions on board ships in the sixteenth and seventeenth centuries were quite primitive. A man named Gemelli Carei records his experiences as a passenger on a Manila Galleon in 1697:

The poor people stow'd in the cabbins of the galeon bound towards the Land of Promise of New Spain, endure no less hardships than the children of Israel did, when they went from Egypt towards Palestine. There is hunger, thirst, sickness, cold, continual watching [wakefulness], and other sufferings; besides the terrible shocks from side to side, caus'd by the furious beating of the waves. I may further say they endure all the plagues God sent upon Pharaoh to soften his hard heart; for if he was infected with leprosy, the galeon is never clear of an universal raging itch, as an addition to all other miseries. If the air then was fill'd with gnats; the ship swarms with little vermine, the Spaniards call Gorgojos, bread in the bisket; so swift that they in a short time not only run over cabins, beds, and the very dishes the men eat on, but insensibly fasten upon the body. Instead of the locusts, there are several other sorts of vermin, of sundry colours, that suck the blood. Abundance of flies fall into the dishes of broth, in which there also swim worms of several sorts. In short, if Moses miraculously converted his rod into a se[r]pent; aboard the galeon a piece of flesh, without any miracle, is converted into wood, and in the shape of a serpent. I had a good share in these misfortunes; for the boatswain, with whom I had agreed for my diet, as he had fowls at his table the first days, so when we were out at sea he made me fast after the Armenian manner, having banish'd from his table all wine, oil and vinegar; dressing his fish with fair water and salt. Upon flesh days he gave me Tassajos Fritos, that is, steaks of beef or buffalo, dri'd in the sun or wind, which are so hard that it is impossible to eat them, without they are first well beaten like stockfish; nor is there any digesting them without the help of a purge. At dinner another piece of that same sticky flesh was boil'd, without any other sauce but its own hardness, and fair water. At last he depriv'd me of the satisfaction of gnawing a good bisket, because he would spend no more of his own, but laid the king's allowance on the table; in every mouthful whereof there went down abundance of maggots and Gorgojos chew'd and bruis'd. On fish days the common diet was old rank fish boil'd in fair water and salt; at noon we had Mongos, something like kidney beans, in which there were so many maggots, that they swam at top of the broth, and the quantity was so great, that besides the loathing they caus'd, I doubted whether the dinner was fish or flesh. This bitter fare was sweeten'd after dinner with a little water and sugar; yet the allowance was but a small cocoa shell full, which rather increas'd than quench'd drought. Providence reliev'd us for a month with sharks and cachorretas the seamen caught, which, either boil'd or broil'd, were some comfort. Yet he is to be pity'd who has another at his table; for the tediousness of the voyage is the cause of all these hardships. 'Tis certain, they that take this upon them, lay out thousands of pieces of eight, in making the neces-

sary provision of flesh, fowl, fish, bisket, rice, sweetmeats, chocolate, and other things; and the quantity is so great, that during the whole voyage, they never fail of sweetmeats at table, and chocolate twice a day, of which last the sailors and grummets make as great a consumption, as the richest. Yet at last the tediousness of the voyage makes an end of all; and the more, because in a short time all the provisions grew naught, except the sweetmeats and chocolate which are the only comfort of passengers.

Religious Life of Sailors

Samuel Eliot Morison, *The European Discovery of America*, Oxford University Press, New York, 1974, p. 165-166.

Samuel Eliot Morison describes the life of a sailor with respect to religion on an early ship:

In the great days of sail, before man's inventions and gadgets had given him a false confidence in his power to conquer the ocean, seamen were the most religious of all workers on land or sea. The mariner's philosophy he took from the Vulgate's 107th Psalm: "They that go down to the sea in ships and occupy their business in great waters; these men see the works of the Lord, and his wonders in the deep. For at his word, the stormy wind ariseth, which lifteth up the waters thereof." It behooved seamen to obey the injunction of the Psalmist, "O that men would therefore praise the Lord for his goodness, and declare the wonders that he doeth for the children of men!" That is exactly what they did, after their fashion. The Protestant Reformation did not change the old customs of shipboard piety, only the ritual; Spanish prisoners on Drake's Golden Hind reported a daily service which featured the singing of psalms.

Although the captain or master, if no priest were present, led morning and evening prayers, the little semi-religious observances which marked almost every half-hour of the day were performed by the youngest lads on board, the pajes do escober (pages of the broom). This I suppose was on the same principle as having family grace said by the youngest child; God would be better pleased by the voice of innocence.

According to Eugenio de Salazar, the ritual which he describes always prevailed when venturing on unknown seas where the divine protection was imperatively needed. No pious commander would have omitted aught of these traditional observances. I repeat them here just as Salazar reports them, with a translation [Spanish version omitted here].

A young boy of the dawn watch saluted daybreak with this ditty:

Blessed be the light of day
and the Holy Cross, we say;
and the Lord of Veritie
and the Holy Trinity
Blessed be the 'immortal soul
and the Lord who keeps it whole,
blessed be the light of day
and He who sends the night away.

He then recited Pater Noster and Ave Maria, and added:

God give us good days, good voyage, good passage to the ship, sir captain and master and good company, amen; so let there be, let there be a good voyage; many good days may God grant your graces, gentlemen of the afterguard and gentlemen forward.

Before being relieved the dawn watch was supposed to have the deck well scrubbed down with salt water hauled up in buckets, using stiff besoms made of twine. At 6:30 or 7:30 the ampolleta was turned up for the seventh and last time on that watch, and the boy sang out:

Good is that which passeth,
better is which cometh,
seven is past and eight floweth,
more shall flow if God willeth,
count and pass makes voyage fast.

First Protestant Religious Service

Chapman, *A History of California: The Spanish Period*, p. 104

The chaplain of the Golden Hind, traveling with Sir Francis Drake, records their encounter with the Miwok Indians near Drake's Bay:

When they came to the top of the hill, at the bottom whereof wee had built our fort, they made a stand; where one (appointed as their chiefe speaker) wearied both vs and his hearers, and himselfe too, with a long and tedious oration; deliuered with strange and of nature, and his wordes falling so thicke one in the necke of another, that he could hardly fetch his breath againe: as soone as he had concluded, all the rest, with a reuerend bowing of their bodies (in a dreaming manner, and long producing of the same) cryed Oh: thereby giuing their consents that all was very true which he had spoken, and that they had vttered their minde by his mouth vnto vs; which done, the men laying downe their bowes vpon the hill, and leauing their women and children behinde them, came downe with their presents; in such sort as if they had appeared before a God indeed, thinking themselues happy that they might haue accesse vnto our Generall, but much more happy when they sawe that he would receiue at their hands those things which they so willingly had presented: and no doubt they thought themselues neerest vnot God when they sate or stood next to him. In the meane time the women, as if they had beene desperate, vsed vnnatural violence against themselues, crying and shrieking piteously, tearing their flesh with their nailes from their cheekes in a monstrous manner, the blood streaming downe along their brests, besides despoiling the vpper parts of their bodies of those single couerings they formerly had, and holding their hands aboue their heads that they might not rescue their brests from harme, they would with furie cast themselues vpon the ground, neuer respecting whether it were cleane or soft, but dashed themselues in this manner on hard stones, knobby hillocks, stocks or wood, and pricking bushes, or whateuer else lay in their way, iterating the same course againe and againe; yea women great with child, some nine or ten times each, and others holding out till 15 or 16 times (till their strengths failed them) exercised this cruelty against themselues: a thing more grieuous for vs to see or suffer, could we haue holpe it, then trouble to them (as it seemed) to do it. This bloudie sacrifice (against our wils) beeing thus performed, our Generall, with his companie, in the presence of those strangers, fell to prayers; and by signes in lifting vp our eyes and hands to heauen, signified vnto them that that God whom we did serue, and whom they ought to worship, was aboue; beseeching God, if it were his good pleasure, to open by some meanes their blinded eyes, that they might in due time be called to the knowledge of him, the true and euerliuing God, and of Jesus Christ whom he hath sent, the saluation of the Gentiles. In the time of which prayers, singing of Psalmes, and reading of certaine Chapters in the Bible, they sate very attentiuely: and obseruing the end at euery pause, with one voice still cried, Oh, greatly reioycing in our exercises. Yea they tooke such pleasure in our singing of Psalmes, that whensoeuer they resorted to vs, their first request was commonly this, Gnaah, by which they intreated that we would sing.

Our General hauing now bestowed vpon them diuers things, at their departure they restored them all againe, none carrying with him anything of whatsoeuer hee had receiued, thinking themselues sufficiently enriched and happie that they had found so free accesse to see vs.

Cortés

Cortez and the Conquest of Mexico by the Spaniards in 1521, Being the eye-witness Narrative of Bernal Diaz del Castillo, Soldier of Fortune & Conquistador with Cortez in Mexico, abridged & edited by B. G. Herzog, and illustrated with Six-

teenth Century Indian Drawings of the Conquest. Linnett Books, Hamden, Connecticut, 1988

The following quotes offer a different perspective than most of our modern history books on the personality of Cortes:

"To cement our friendship, the Cempoalans offered in marriage eight highborn damsels, richly adorned with golden necklets and earrings, and attended by serving maids. Cortez thanked them but explained that before we could become brothers they must abandon their human sacrifices and their idols which kept them in darkness. Each day we saw Indians butchered, their hearts offered to the idols, their arms and legs cut off and eaten as we eat butchers' beef. I even believe they sold human flesh in their markets." p. 35

"I remember that in the plaza of this town where some of their oratories stood, there were piles of human skulls neatly arranged. I estimated them at more than one hundred thousand. In another part were heaps of dead men's bones beyond counting. Also, there were large numbers of skulls strung between beams of wood, with priests keeping guard over all. Such things we saw wherever we went." p. 40

"This grim entry into the land of Tlaxcala gave us much to ponder. Cortez, however, exclaimed, 'Sirs, let us follow the holy cross on our banner and through it we shall prevail!' Then one and all we answered, 'May good fortune attend our advance, for in God lies the true strength.' Thus we continued our march." p. 41

"Cortez then through Doña Marina and Aqilar explained that our great Emperor had charged us chiefly to tell them about the one and only true God whom we worshiped, and that their own gods were in truth devils, afraid to come near our holy cross. He explained very clearly about the creation of the world and the commandments of God and how those who worship idols or sacrifice human beings would burn in Hell, and he prayed him to heed our words.

Montezuma answered that his ambassadors had told him of this, but that throughout all time they had worshiped their own gods and thought them good, as no doubt ours were, and not to trouble to speak more about them for the present. Regarding the creation of the world, they had held the same belief for ages past and for this reason took us to be those whose coming had been predicted by their ancestors. He had heard of two captains who also came in ships and said they served our great king, and were we all the same people? Cortez told him we were." p. 84

Earthquake Creating San Francisco Bay

Powers, Stephen, *Tribes of California,* University of California Press, 1976 (originally published in 1877), p. 226

According to Indian legends, the creation of the San Francisco Bay is of recent origin. The following quotes suggest that once the mountain chain was complete along the coast:

"The Liwaito relate that there was once a great sea all over the Sacramento Valley, and an earthquake rent open the Golden Gate and drained it off."

Bayard Taylor, *El Dorado*, G.P. Putnam's Sons, New York, 1879, p. 175

"The existence of these shells in the soil is but one of the facts which tend to prove the recent geological formation of this part of the coast. There is every reason to believe that a great part of the promontory on which Monterey is built, was at no very remote period of time covered by the sea. A sluggish salt lagoon, east of the Catholic Church, was not more than twenty years ago a part of the bay, from which it is now separated by a sandy meadow, quarter of a mile in breadth. According to an Indian tradition, of comparatively modern origin, the waters of San Francisco Bay once communicated with the bay of Monterey by the valley of San Jose and the Rio del Pajaro. I should think a level of fifty feet, or perhaps less - above the present one, would suffice to have effected this. The other Indian tradition, that the outlet of the Golden Gate was occasioned by violent disruption of the hills, through the means of an earthquake, is not based on natural evidence. The sloughs and marshes in the valley of San Joaquin, and around the Tulare Lakes, present every appearance of having been left by the drainage of a subsiding ocean. A thorough geological exploration of California would undoubtedly bring to light many strange and interesting facts connected with her physical features."

Teacher's Supplement

Spanish Units

Units 3 & 4

Teaching Aids—Unit 3 & 4

The Spanish Units

Teacher's Overview

THESE UNITS INTRODUCE THE STUDENT TO the Spanish period of California's history, covering Units 3 and 4 in *His California Story*. We learn about the dedicated Franciscan missionaries, including the intrepid Father Junípero Serra, who left all material comforts to bring the Catholic faith to the Indians of California.

The Settlement of New Spain

The Spaniards began to colonize California very late in the life of the Spanish Empire. We might say that California was the child of Spain, born in her old age. For 167 years after the explorer Vizcaíno visited Monterey, no Spaniards ventured to the north. Although nothing much was happening with respect to California, events in New Spain (Mexico) were progressing. Each year the frontier was pushed farther north as the Spaniards proceeded to settle the area using a combination of presidios, pueblos, and missions, the Mission System. For more information about the relationship between the Spanish church and state, please see comments at the beginning of the Explorers Unit of this manual.

At the same time the Spaniards were busy in New Spain, the Russians had discovered Russian America, the area we now call Alaska. After Vitus Bering discovered the strait that now bears his name, the Russians were attracted by the large quantities of seals and otter in the area and began a lucrative trade with the people of China and the East.

The Spanish colonization of California can be attributed to the actions of the Russians. While many history books report that the Russians were planning to colonize California and the Spaniards organized a massive effort to get there first, noted historian Charles E. Chapman records in his *A History of California: The Spanish Period* that this was a rumor started by José de Gálvez to further his own ends.

The Spaniards mounted the Sacred Expedition to California in 1769, just seven years before the Declaration of Independence was signed. The Spanish period in California's history had begun.

The Missions

The missions are the outstanding feature of the Spanish period of California's history and as such offer modern students and teachers many challenges when we try to understand this time. We hear many things about the missions that are confusing at best. For example, we hear that the Indians were forcibly rounded up from their villages and compelled to live at the missions. Although a few abuses of this nature did occur toward the end of the Mexican period, they did not generally occur during the Spanish period. Indians came to the missions of their own free will.

We also hear that the missionaries acted like tyrants and treated the Indians cruelly. As point of fact, the Spanish missionaries were pious men who sacrificed a great deal to bring the Catholic faith to the Indians. The Spanish soldiers were of another sort and caused difficulties for the missionaries. Many of the cruelties we hear from this period were performed by soldiers, not missionaries. The overwhelming majority of the Spanish missionaries treated the Indians very well.

Did the Indians Become Christians?

This question causes controversy, and although I tried to answer it in the first version of *His California Story* while writing for an elementary-age audience, my musings satisfied nobody, least of all me. To ponder this question we need to understand the differences between Catholicism and Protestantism. What do Catholics believe? What do Protestants believe? How do the two compare? I've prepared a chart—later in this section—comparing the major differences between the two faiths.

It is hard to know with certainty whether any Indians became true Christians. First, so much time has passed since the missions of California were destroyed. Second, the records that do exist record baptisms, the point at which Catholics believed salvation occurred. Although some of the Indians may have became Christians, many more came to the missions for food and security only.

Were the Indians Mistreated?

Another point of controversy that comes up in studying these units consists of the alleged mistreatment of the Indians by the missionaries. To understand this charge, we must understand that California came under the jurisdiction of the King of Spain through the provisions of the Royal Patronage, an agreement between the Spanish monarchs and the Catholic pope. This agreement gave the crown an inordinate amount of power over affairs of people in California, including where to found new missions, who could be put in charge, and over movement in general. This situation lead to a dependency on the state and a lack of self-government.

The Royal Patronage could lead to a good situation or a not-so-good situation, depending on who the king's representative was. In the West Indies, it was disastrous and thousands of Indians were enslaved and mistreated. In California, owing to the two men who served as presidents of the missions, Serra and Lasuén, it was benevolent and fatherly. It was true that the Indians became dependent on the missions. It was not true that they were enslaved as in other parts of the New World.

Some have raised concerns about the Spanish Inquisition in the New World and its effect on the Indians. However, the Indians were specifically exempt from the Inquisition, which had lost most of its power by the early 1800s anyways. It had almost no effect in California.

Another concern is use of corporal punishment on the Indians, a topic that deserves much more attention than I can give it here. The types of punishments Spaniards regularly employed, not on just the Indians but on each other, sound brutal to modern ears. These included stocks, floggings, and others we would consider inhumane. Although the missionaries insisted that corporal punishment was infrequent, we cannot condone any inhumane treatment of people, even if it was very common at the time. See the Source Documents for more information on this topic.

Worldview Clashes

The biggest problem the modern historian faces when discussing the California Missions concerns a clash of worldview. The Catholic missionaries believed they were saving men's souls. That was their primary objective and everything they did had this goal in mind. The modern secular viewpoint is that no culture has the right to impart its religion to another. One typical source says, "Despite romantic portraits of California missions they were essentially coercive religious, labor camps organized primarily to benefit the colonizers." This perspective is unfair to the Indians, who were free to choose to live at the missions or not and to become Catholics or not. Much of the criticism of the Spanish missionaries reveals an anti-Catholic if not anti-Christian bias.

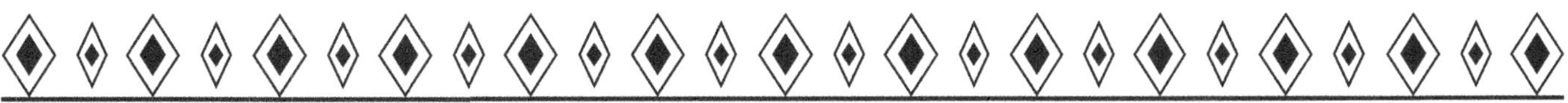

A Comparison Between Two Faiths

Catholic

Nature of the Church: Believes itself to be the only valid church and true representative of Jesus Christ. Believes the Apostle Peter invested his authority in the Catholic church and served as its first Bishop of Rome (Pope).

Authority: Catholic beliefs rest on a combination of the Bible (including the Apocrypha), on the apostolic succession, and on decisions made at church councils (such as the Council of Trent, Vatican I, or Vatican II). Peter passed his authority through the church (called apostolic succession) so that today's Catholic Church is the spiritual successor to first century Christianity. The Pope holds authority over the church and speaks with infallibility with respect to church matters (*ex-cathedra*).

Salvation: A Catholic is born again when God transforms him or her through baptism. This can occur at infancy or at some point in adulthood. Unbaptized adults go through four steps to receive salvation: 1) express desire to learn about the Catholic faith; 2) become *catechumens* and learn the catechism and doctrines of the Catholic Church; 3) undergo the *Rite of Initiation* which announces the person's intention to become Catholic. During this time the person repents and purifies him or herself; 4) *Initiation* which consists of baptism, confirmation, and first communion. At this point the person attains salvation and church membership. He or she is called a *neophyte*, new Christian, for the first year following conversion. Salvation can be lost by committing a mortal sin, and then regained by the sacrament of confession.

Sacraments: Catholics recognize seven sacraments as the means of grace; that is, the way salvation is shared with sinners. *Baptism* is administered to infants and is necessary for salvation; it forgives all sins committed prior to it. *Confirmation*, performed on children, confirms and strengthens baptismal grace. The *Eucharist* (communion) when administered by a priest becomes the physical blood and body of Christ (transubstantiation) during the Mass. In this way, Christ is not sacrificed once, but over and over. Regular partaking of the Eucharist is necessary for salvation. *Penance and Confession* occurs when a Catholic confesses his or her sins before a priest and receives absolution. *Anointing of the Sick* (also known as *Extreme Unction*), is administered to a person in immediate danger of death. It is one of the Last Rites (along with confession and the Eucharist). *Holy Orders* places a man within the apostolic succession, and sets him aside as a deacon or a priest. *Matrimony*, the

Protestant

Nature of the Church: Believes true and valid churches exist across denominational lines and must do the following:

1. Preach the true and biblical Word of God.
2. Follow the biblical administration of the sacraments: baptism and communion.
3. Faithfully execute biblical discipline.
4. Exercise strong biblical leadership (2 Tim. 4:1-4).
5. Express a heart and zeal for biblical missions.
6. Hold a right expression of biblical worship.

Churches that do not practice these six characteristics are not true churches.

Authority: The sole authority for Protestants is the Bible, which is inerrant, infallible, and divinely protected. In cases where the Bible seems to be unclear, Protestants adhere to Biblical hermeneutics and let scripture interpret scripture. The Protest Reformation was based on five foundational teachings summarized with Latin phrases: *Sola Scriptura* (by Scripture alone), *solus Christus* (by Christ alone), *sola gratia* (by grace alone), *sola fide* (by faith alone), and *soli Deo Gloria* (glory to God alone).

Salvation: Salvation begins with repentance—a true understanding of the nature of the unbeliever, who is dead in his trespasses and sins. Because all sinners are dead, they cannot save themselves. Instead Jesus Christ, who was completely without sin, paid the penalty for the sins of all believers. He ransomed them and when they receive his spotless life in place of their own (imputation and regeneration), they are spiritually renewed (born again). They receive the gift of the Holy Spirit who indwells them. The Christians' new nature gives them the ability to not sin. Although still possessing a sin nature, sin grieves Christians and leads them to confess and forsake it. Above all, salvation is a personal relationship between the believer and Jesus Christ. It is a change of heart that does not depend on any other works—it is achieved by grace alone and by faith alone.

Sacraments: Protestants recognize two biblical sacraments as symbols of grace; that is, an outward manifestation of an inward situation. *Baptism* does not save. It is either administered to infants (infant baptism) to signify the infant's special status as a member of the community of God (the covenant) and hope for future salvation, or to an adult believer (believer's baptism) to recognize a changed and saved heart (an outward expression of an inward condi-

final sacrament, establishes a permanent bond between marriage partners.

Virgin Mary: The Mother of God (the Theotokos). Believed to be born without sin and kept from sinning throughout her life (Immaculate Conception). Mary remained a virgin even after the birth of Christ and never died. She was assumed bodily into heaven (Assumption). She is to be adored and venerated, but not worshipped. She holds a position below God but above other Christians.

Saints: After death, people who lived exemplary lives go through a procedure called *canonization*. They must have performed a posthumous miracle or have been a martyr, and their lives must be examined by the church. Some saints are designated Patron Saints, who have special power in a specific area. Catholics pray to saints believing that they bring those prayers to God, that saints in heaven intercede for Christians on earth.

Afterlife: People spend all or part of their eternity in one of three places: 1) Purgatory, a place where souls are purified after death and before they are ready for heaven. 2) Heaven, a place of eternal joy where the believer is united with Christ 3) Hell, a place of fiery torment where the souls of unbelievers are forever separated from God. Although some Catholics believe that unbaptized children go to a place called limbo, this teaching has never been recognized by the Catholic church.

Good Works: Good works following baptism (where original sin is removed) are necessary for salvation and the lack of good works may cause a Catholic to lose his or her salvation. Good works must be performed while in a state of grace (i.e. by a Catholic who has not committed a mortal sin and lost his or her salvation). They are meritorious and will be rewarded in heaven.

Can Protestants Be Saved?: Catholics believe that Protestants can be saved, especially those who have been baptized. However, they believe that Protestant Christianity contains serious errors that interfere with true faith.

tion). *Communion* serves as a frequent memorial service in which the Lord is spiritually present in a true and living way. It affirms the believer's union and communion with Christ.

Virgin Mary: Mother of Jesus. She was an ordinary woman and a sinner just like all people created *imageo dei*, but devoted to God. The Holy Spirit came upon her so that she gave birth to the Messiah as a virgin. Later she had other sons and daughters. She died a natural death. She is to be esteemed as a virtuous Christian and an instrument used of God, but not as a special class of Christian.

Saints: After death, all Christians become saints, which is another name for glorified believers, those who serve the Lord in heaven and continually behold the face of Christ. Protestants believe praying to saints is ineffectual at best and heresy at worse. It detracts from the glory that is due Jesus Christ, who is the only mediator between God and man (1 Tim. 2:5).

Afterlife: At death, souls appear before Christ—absent from the body, present with the Lord—and then spend eternity in: 1) Heaven, a place of eternal joy where the believer is united with Christ or 2) Hell, a place of fiery torment where the souls of unbelievers are forever separated from God.

Good Works: Good works cannot be performed by unbelievers, only by Christians. They have no merit and are not a condition of salvation, but they are an outward expression of an inward change—the natural fruit that the tree bears. Sometimes these good works are referred to as fruits of the Spirit: love, joy, peace, longsuffering (patience), gentleness, goodness, faith, meekness, and temperance (self-control). They naturally flow from the Christian who lives in communion with his or her Lord.

Can Catholics Be Saved?: Since salvation is a personal relationship with Jesus Christ, Catholics who put their faith and trust in Christ can be saved. God saves those whom he chooses, regardless of church membership. However, Protestants believe that Catholicism contains serious errors that interfere with true faith.

Similarities

Despite their many differences, the Catholic and Protestant faiths also share many similarities. They both believe in the articles of the Apostles' Creed and the Lord's Prayer. They both believe in the Trinity—the Father, Son, and Holy Spirit—that God created the heavens and the earth, and that He is almighty. They both believe that Jesus Christ is the only savior; he was born of a virgin, lived a sinless life, was crucified for our sins, and died. On the third day after he died, he rose again and ascended into heaven. There he reigns and judges the living and the dead. In his own good time, he will return in the second coming. After death, Christians will receive a resurrected body and life everlasting. Both Catholics and Protestants believe that God has the power to forgive sin, to keep believers from temptation, and that all power and authority resides with him.

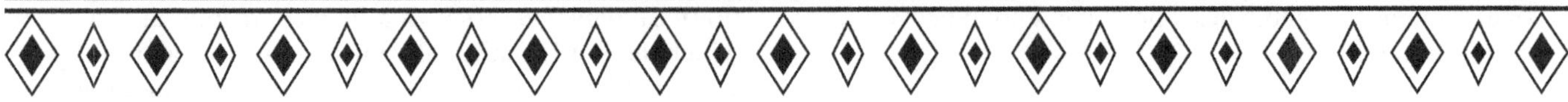

De Anza, Hancock, and the Independence Hall

SOMETIMES WHEN I TEACH CALIFORNIA HISTORY I find my students have a hard time integrating it with American history. It seems like they keep the streams of time in two separate compartments of their brain, never merging them until about high school. Most students remember 1776 as a momentous occasion on the East Coast as our nation formed out of the conflict with England, but at that same time momentous doings played out on the West Coast as Captain de Anza lead the colonizing expedition to build the first presidio (military fort) at San Francisco.

Today I'd like to recommend a way to solidify that connection, which gives me an excuse to write about one of my favorite American history attractions in California: the Independence Hall Replica at Knott's Berry Farm. It's pretty startling to see this imposing red-brick building with its white spire rise up from Buena Park's tourist attractions—the Wax Museum, Medieval Times, and Starbucks (yes, they're everywhere). I am grateful that Walter Knott felt led to give this gift to people who may not be able to travel to Philadelphia. It's completely free. When I told the parking attendant I was just visiting the replica, I didn't even have to pay for parking.

Before you go, I recommend you watch the movie *1776* with your children. It's a musical, very corny, and makes the events around the formation of our country quite memorable. I remember that the committee formed to write the Declaration of Independence nominated Jefferson to write the draft when I picture the four other members passing the quill to Jefferson on the stairwell—all to song, of course. I remember Richard Henry Lee who "positive-lee" represented Virginia and the other colorful delegates.

One caution: John Adams uses the expression "Good God" several times. At first I thought he was invoking the blessing of the Almighty, but on second thought I don't think so. When you get to the replica, ask your children if they can spot the details the movie added to the Declaration Chamber. If you can't tell, ask the docent.

Start your tour on the outside of the building by looking at the bricks. Can you see the finger and thumb prints in them? Like the ones in Philadelphia, all 120,000 bricks in this building were made by hand. Mr. Knott was interested in accuracy.

Enter the Tower Room, which contains an exact replica of the Liberty Bell. Like its original, it's cracked. Although creating a duplicate bell wasn't that hard, making the appropriate crack was. It took two weeks and several unsuccessful tries. Dry ice and a helio-torch finally did the trick.

You can hear the story of the Liberty Bell by pressing a button near the stairwell, which includes an explanation for the Bible verse written across the bell's top. However, before you do that, look for the Honesty Button, a small white button placed in the stairwell post when the building was completed and paid for, a 16th century good luck charm. According to the legend, as delegates entered the hall they rubbed the button and said a prayer asking God to help them deal honestly and fairly with their fellow congressmen.

Wander through the hall and find a copy of the lantern that Paul Revere used to signal the Bostonians that the British were coming (by sea), an original draft of the Declaration written by Jefferson, and a letter written by John Hancock, governor of Massachusetts, appointing a gentleman to the state militia.

The highlight is the Declaration Chamber, which looks like the delegates just stepped out for a moment. The delegates from the fifteen colonies were seated in desks north to south by geography, with Massachusetts in the back left corner and Georgia in the front right. The audio presentation condenses the debates into about fifteen minutes, presenting three vignettes.

We hear the motion for independence, one of Franklin's homey stories, John Adam's rousing speech (it gave me goose bumps), and the roll call which birthed our nation. After the Declaration was accepted unanimously, the presentation breaks forth with the hymn "We Gather Together." I felt like applauding. The presentation concludes by asking the poignant question, "Freedom. Can we keep it?"

The Declaration of Independence replica makes a fine family destination whenever you're in the area. If you are fortunate to live near it or are planning a trip in the future, you might be interested to know Knott's Berry Farm sponsors a variety of field trips. In addition to the Early American Heritage tour, which features Independence Hall, you can sign up for an Early California Tour or a Westward Movement Tour.

I don't know anything about these, so you're on your own. If you have participated in one, I would like to hear from you. Each tour is about $5 per student and lasts about 2 hours. Add-ons, like panning for gold, are possible and increase both the time and cost. This place is popular. The docent told me they host 200 students a day.

For more information, phone (714) 827-1776 (of course).

Travels Along the Mission Trail

Part 1 of 2

GRAVEL CRUNCHED UNDER OUR TIRES AS WE slowly drove past the remains of an Indian village towards the dilapidated mission. Dust, kicked up by the wind, stung our eyes as we beheld the rarest of California sounds: quiet.

Welcome to a re-creation of life in the 1820s along California's mission trail.

Each of the twenty-one missions founded during the Spanish period of California's history (1769 to 1821, except for Solano Mission built during the Mexican period) beckons travelers to experience the sights and sounds of the California 200 years past. I have visited seventeen of these missions and read about the remaining four. However, one stands out as a jewel, well worth a stop whenever you're near the area.

La Purisima

La Purisima, my hands down favorite, fills a small valley in the mountains near Lompac. Eleventh in the mission chain, Padre Serra's successor, Padre Lasuén, dedicated La Purisima in 1787. After an earthquake destroyed it, La Purisima moved to its present site in 1815. Several years later it again fell to ruin after Mexico abandoned the missions in the mid-1830s. Much later still, the California Department of Parks and Recreation obtained the land, reconstructed the buildings, and dedicated them on another auspicious date: December 7, 1941. Docents frequently bring this mission to life through a living history program, a spectacle I have always managed to just miss.

Begin your tour, after a stop at the obligatory gift shop, by crossing a foot bridge and walking literally in the footsteps of the padres along a portion of the authentic El Camino Real—the King's Highway—the road connecting all of the missions. Your eyes will rest on the hot pink church and you will certainly think, "Hey, I thought this was an authentic reconstruction!" Your self-guided map assures you the colors are true, matched to chunks of original plaster found in the ruins.

Several apartments and workrooms for padres, guests, and artisans (who taught mission Indians crafts such as spinning, weaving, black-smithing, and tile-making) line a long arched building along with the soldier's *cuartel* or barracks. Reconstructed out-buildings give a flavor of mission activity, including the pottery shop, grist mill, and kitchen. Each of these rooms faithfully represents mission times.

Adobe tiled apartments for about twenty Indian families, similar to the other residences, have not been reconstructed, although the map in the self-guided tour brochure notes their original location. However, the original tule dwellings of the Chumash Indians grace the area behind the mission gardens.

More than any other mission, La Purisima shows visitors the elaborate aqueduct system used to supply this thriving community of 1,500 Indians, two padres, and five soldiers. Stored in reservoirs during the rainy season, water traveled to the spring house to be filtered through sand before flowing through underground clay pipes to the courtyard fountain, ready for drinking and cooking. From here, water overflowed into the lavanderia, used for bathing and washing clothes. The now-soapy water continued to the cistern, the soap settled, and the remnant watered the mission garden.

The Parks and Recreation Department has done an excellent job of recreating the mission gardens by collecting cuttings from other missions. If you visit during the summer, your senses will be assaulted with the sights and smells of the mission era along with other native California plants. Look closely and you might spot datura, better known as jimpson weed, which Chumash Indians used in a rite-of-passage ceremony, before they came to the missions.

A trip to La Purisima Mission will definitely enhance your study of California's mission era. To obtain more information including the schedule of special events, phone (805) 733-3713 or visit www.lapurisimamission.org.

Santa Inés

While you're in the area, jet over to Solvang, a charming Danish town full of shops, Scandinavian architecture, and Danish food. Look for the smorgasbord, an all-you-can-eat collection of Danish delicacies. Solvang also holds Mission Santa Inés, a functioning Catholic church. Although smaller than its cousin, the mission boasts a gift shop (of course), museum, and displays.

At the back of the courtyard, directly opposite the gift shop, look for the plaque commemorating the legendary deed of Pasquala, who saved her mission from attack by non-mission Indians. Undoubtedly you will find a book about Pasquala's escapades in the gift shop. I'd pass it by. A better one, in my opinion, is *Pasquala of Santa Ynez Mission* by Florence Wightman Rowland (Henry Z. Walck, Inc., 1961). You might be able to find this out-of-print

book in your library, through an inter-library loan, or by searching used book sites.

Find out more about Santa Inés Mission by visiting www.missionsantaines.org or phoning (805) 688-4815.

In my next column I hope to travel further down the trail to two more missions plus suggest some ways to help you evaluate contradicting viewpoints you might hear. Until then, as the padres would say, *Amar a Dios* (Love God).

Part 2 of 2

LAST TIME IN THIS SPACE WE BEGAN TO travel along the mission trail with a preview of two of my favorite California missions. This time I'm going to continue with two more, and then discuss some worldview problems you might encounter when you visit.

San Jan Capistrano

When I was eleven, my family traveled to California from Minnesota and visited Mission San Juan Capistrano. I remember feeding the swallows that reportedly return to the mission each March 19th. Not too long ago, I found pictures from that vacation and discovered I fed pigeons! While pigeons remain, in recent years earthquake retrofitting has dislodged the swallows and naturalists are trying to entice them to return.

Mission San Juan Capistrano contains reconstructions of tanning vats, padres quarters, soldiers barracks, and various workshops. Restoration continues on the great stone church destroyed in the 1812 earthquake, which killed forty people. In my opinion, the gardens are the loveliest of all the missions, although they contain several plant varieties unknown in mission times. Ask a docent to show you the graffiti drawn by missions Indians in the plaster facing the quadrangle buildings. For a virtual tour or to learn more about San Juan Capistrano visit www.missionsjc.com or call (949) 234-1300.

Carmel Mission

At the northern part of the mission trail, San Carlos Borremo, the second mission founded by Padre Junípero Serra, sits just a few miles from Carmel-by-the-Sea. In fact, most people call it Carmel Mission. Both Padre Serra and his successor, Fermin de Lasuén lie buried beneath the altar at the front of the church. De Lasuén undertook the construction of the present stone church.

Stand in the courtyard and gaze at the window above the arched doorway and you will notice its askew star. This reminds us that Indians built the mission compound learning the principles of construction through on-the-job apprenticeship.

For me, the most intriguing part of Carmel Mission stands behind glass in one of the displays. When the Spanish explorer Vizcaíno visited Monterey in 1602, he hung bells from a huge tree to call people to Catholic Mass. When Padre Serra visited 168 years later, he hung bells in the same tree. Paintings in the museum recreate both scenes. After railroad construction destroyed this magnificent tree in the late 1800s, its trunk was filled with cement and placed behind the Royal Chapel. Two pieces survive, one at Carmel Mission and another in a case just inside the door of the Royal Chapel.

Once a part of the Monterey Presidio and now the oldest building in California, the Royal Chapel deserves a quick stop. You will find it at the intersection of Fremont and Church St. in Monterey. For more information on Carmel Mission, visit www.carmelmission.org or call (831) 624-1271.

I wish I had space to tell you of another delightful mission. San Antonio de Padua lies far off the beaten path along the original El Camino Real—the King's Highway—in the middle of the state. Check it out at www.missionsanantoniopadua.com or call (831) 385-4478.

Worldview Issues

As you visit California's missions, you might be confused by some of the information you receive. Some guidelines will help to sort it all out.

First, every mission except San Francisco Solano lived through two distinct periods. From 1769 to 1821, Spanish missionaries maintained charge over the building and administration of each mission. Each year a supply ship from San Blas in Mexico brought provisions, soldier's pay, and new missionaries. Beginning about 1811 the supply ships ceased their run. Not only did the missions bridge the gap financially by providing for the needs of the mission Indians, they also supplied the presidio soldiers, a source of continuing conflict.

In 1822, California learned it fell under the jurisdiction of Mexico as a result of the Spanish-American Wars for Independence. Relationships between missions and presidios, never good, deteriorated as presidio soldiers treated both the missionaries and mission Indians harshly. Remember these dates when you hear of Indian uprisings and other difficulties. Most problems occurred during the Mexican period, many instigated by presidio soldiers.

In addition to making no distinction between time periods, docents at the missions tend to categorize people as "the Indians" or "the Spaniards." In reality, several subcategories existed. For example "the Indians" could include faithful Catholic Mission Indians, unfaithful Catholic Mission Indians, non-Mission Indians who never had contact with a mission, and non-Mission Indians who despised these institutions. Similarly "the Spaniards" could include Spanish missionaries, highly esteemed by nearly everyone, as well as presidio soldiers, recruited for service from

Mexican jails. It is unfair and confusing to speak in such general terms, but with a bit of discernment, you should benefit from information docents and museums share with you.

Whether you visit one of my favorite missions or another closer to your home, I hope you have opportunity to experience the California of 200 years ago as you travel along the mission trail.

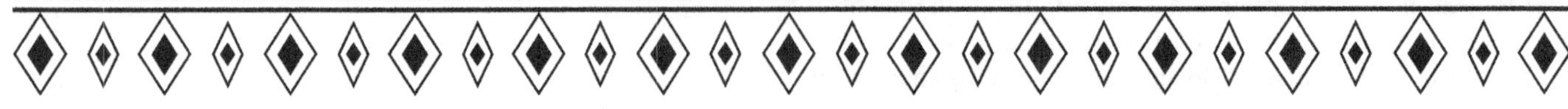

Teaching the Spanish Units

Lesson Plans

Unit 3, Spanish Colonization, and Unit 4, Spanish Days, are treated together in this manual since they deal with the same time period. In the Spanish Colonization unit, history is presented chronologically, emphasizing major events including the Sacred Expedition, the revolt at San Diego Mission, the Anza Expedition, and the Yuma Massacre.

The lifestyle of the people and the missions is detailed in Unit 4 to give students a better understanding of the past, the purpose of the missions, and what it was like to live at one. Included are short biographies of several Mission Indians, a brief discussion of an early California governor, and life at Fort Ross.

Unit 3

1. Introduction ideas:
   - If you are able, this is a great unit to begin with a field trip to a California Mission.
   - Begin with a discussion of journeys and what it takes to prepare for them. Ask students to share some of the trips they have taken. In a T-chart, compare the preparations students have made to spend several weeks away from home to the preparations the Spanish missionaries had to make to spend the rest of their lives away from their homes.
2. Teach Spain's method of colonizing new lands (cross and sword, and missions, presidios, and pueblos)
3. Teach the Sacred Expedition, the first colonizing/mission-planting trip to California and the accompanying verse from the "California Date Song." Make sure students understand the over-lapping timing of Portola's search for Monterey Bay and Serra's troubles in San Diego (Ch. 6). Do Roundup questions.
4. Do a character sketch for Father Serra.
5. Teach the Anza Expedition (Ch. 7). Do Roundup questions.
6. Do a character sketch for Juan Bautista de Anza.
7. Teach the rivers of California.
8. Teach the Yuma Massacre and the accompanying verse from the "California Date Song" (Ch. 8). Do Roundup questions.
9. Play a review game for Unit 3 using the Oral Review Questions.

Unit 4

1. Review the concept of the mission system.
2. Teach about the Spanish missions (Ch. 9). Do Roundup questions.
3. Build a small model of a mission, perhaps using the sugar cube model explained in this section. You might play some mission music as background while the students are working. Alternatively, students might make a more involved mission model, perhaps working at home. Arrange a sharing day—students should write a short description of their mission and be prepared to give a short (five minute) presentation. You might serve Mexican food—home-made or bought from a local market.
4. Show pictures or videos of a recreated mission. La Purisima's website (http://www.lapurisimamission.org) contains an excellent slide show with details of the mission and the mission grounds. Many mission gift shops (some of which are online) sell videos of all twenty-one missions. You might also check out YouTube.com. I've found several well-done videos of the missions.

5. Evaluate the missions and teach about some of the Indians who lived there (Ch. 10). Do Roundup questions.
6. Teach the valleys of California.
7. Teach about California's first lady, the Russians in California, and the accompanying verse from the "California Date Song" (Ch. 11 and 12). Do Roundup questions.
8. Do the candle-dipping or adobe brick-making activity, or both if time permits. (You could also save one for the Mexican Period, Unit 5.)
9. Play a review game for Unit 4 using the Oral Review questions.

Objectives

Objectives for Unit 3

At the completion of this unit students should:

1. Know the following major historical characters: Portolá, Serra, Anza. (If time permits, also include Bucareli and Jayme.) Students should be able to articulate the contribution of each and state some details about their character.
2. Be able to describe the circumstances under which the first colonies in California were founded. This journey was called the Sacred Expedition.
3. Be able to explain how the Yuma Massacre ended expansion efforts in California and how this worked to the advantage of the United States of America.
4. Know the following major events: Sacred Expedition, revolt at San Diego Mission, Anza Expedition, and Yuma Massacre.
5. Be able to list at least four providential events described in this unit (see below).

Objectives for Unit 4

At the completion of this unit students should be expected to:

1. Describe the Mission System and explain how it fit into Spain's plan to colonize California. This should include how missions in Mexico differed from those in California.
2. Describe the activities that took place at a mission.
3. Know how to answer the common objection to the Mission System, that it did more harm than good.
4. Describe the first contact between the Spaniards and the Russians and the subsequent establishment of Fort Ross.
5. Describe how the Spanish period ended in California.

God's Providence

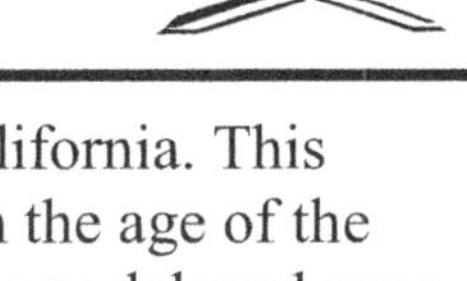

1. The decision to colonize California. This decision was made so late in the age of the Spanish Empire that had it been delayed even a few years, it would never have been accomplished, pp. 42-43.
2. The discovery of San Francisco Bay. pp. 47.
3. The protection of San Diego Mission against Indian attack shortly after the Spaniards' arrival, p. 48.
4. The arrival of the *San Antonio* so that the colony would not have to be abandoned, p. 50.
5. Viceroy Bucareli's decision to send the supply ship even when he did not think it necessary, p. 51.
6. Captain de Anza's timely arrival in California to protect the San Diego Mission, pp. 55-56.
7. The protection of the settlers from the Yuma Massacre, who were to found the pueblo of Los Angeles, pp. 58-60.

Character Sketches

(See Appendix A for further detail on character sketches)

Choose from the following:

- Portolá
- Father Serra
- Anza
- Father Jayme
- Father Lasuén
- Student's favorite Mission Indian (Lost Woman of San Nicolas, Pablo Tac, Pasquala of Santa Ines, Toypurina)
- Rezanov

California Date Song

(See Appendix C for entire song)

1769 - Beginning of the Spanish period
1781 - Yuma Massacre
1811 - Russians build Fort Ross

In seventeen hundred and sixty-nine,
Portolá crossed the Baja line,
San Francisco Bay he'd finally find,
With the Sacred Expedition.

In seventeen hundred and eighty-one,
Captain Rivera's men were stunned,
By what the Yuma Massacre had done.
The Anza trail was closed.

In eighteen hundred and eleven,
Long after Serra went to heaven,
Fort Ross was built by Russian men,
Who came to trap the otter.

Geography

(See Appendix D for further discussion of geography)

Rivers	**Valleys**
Colorado	Sacramento
Sacramento	San Joaquin
San Joaquin	Imperial
Feather	San Fernando
American	Salinas
Mokelumne	
Stanislaus	
Tuolumne	
Merced	

The Colorado River forms the border between California and Arizona. The Sacramento and San Joaquin Rivers run north and south through the Sacramento and San Joaquin Valleys. The following acronym will help the student to remember the order of all of the other rivers which begin in the mountains and empty into either the Sacramento or San Joaquin:

- For All Mount Sinai Thundered Mightily: (Feather, American, Mokelumne, Stanislaus, Tuolumne, and Merced)

(I am indebted to Karen Schachterle, a California history student, for this acronym.)

Here's another:

- Father and Mother sailed to Mexico. (Feather, American, Mokelumne, Stanislaus, Tuolumne, and Merced)

Journal

1. Do character sketches on Portolá, and Serra.
2. Do character sketches on Anza and Bucareli.
3. List examples of God's providence found in Unit 3.
4. Write an essay describing what was good and what was bad about the mission system, or write a story about a young boy or girl living at a mission.
5. Do character sketches on Father Lasuén and one Mission Indian.
6. Imagine that California became a Russian instead of an American territory. Write a story about a young person living in Russian-California today.

Unit Roundup Answers

Chapter 6

1. The Spanish colonization method used the cross and the sword. Explain what these two symbols stood for. *Cross stood for the missions and the responsibility that the Spanish monarchs felt they had to convert the people to Catholicism. Sword stood for the military forts (presidios) that protected the missions.*
2. Describe the Spanish system of colonization. Use the words *presidio*, *mission*, and *pueblo*. *Missions were built to teach the Indians Catholicism and other arts of civilization, and presidios were built to protect the Indians and the missionaries. When Indians could take care of affairs themselves, they formed pueblos, or towns, and the missionaries moved on to new challenges.*
3. Identify each of these men, and write two or three sentences describing what he did:
   - Gaspar de Portolá—*first governor of California. Lead the Sacred Expedition.*
   - Junípero Serra—*first president of the missions.*
   - Pedro Fages—*one of California's early governors. Came to California with Portolá.*
   - Captain Rivera—*one of California's early governors. Died in the Yuma Massacre.*
4. Describe the difficulties the Spaniards faced to reach California. *Students might mention long distances, hostile Indians, mountains, deserts, lack of food and water, unknown areas, and others.*
5. **Thought Question:** Would you have wanted to be a member of the Sacred Expedition? Why or why not? *Accept all answers as long as they show thought. Students should visualize the journey and infer some of the difficulties they might encounter or some of the excitement of seeing new lands.*

Chapter 7

1. Identify each of these men, and write two or three sentences describing what he did:
   - Juan Bautista de Anza—*discovered overland route to California. Brought colonists to San Francisco Presidio*
   - Viceroy Antonio Bucareli—*king's representative in New Spain. At first oversaw California, then later only sent the yearly supply ship. Authorized Anza to find an overland route to California.*
   - Tarabel—*an Indian originally from Baja California who accompanied Anza. Friend of Father Garcés*
   - Chief Salvador Palma—*Chief of the Yuma Indians. Helped Anza's groups. Massacred Riveria's groups.*
   - Father Garcés—*Spanish missionary who explored the Southwest, helped Anza find the overland route, served the Yumas, and was murdered by them.*
   - Father Jayme—*martyred missionary from*

San Diego Mission.

2. Why was it so important to find an overland route to California? Who found it? *It was very expensive to ship people and goods to California by sea. Juan Bautista de Anza.*
3. Who was María Feliciana Gutierrez, and what happened to her? *A member of the Anza expedition. She married a soldier at San Gabriel Mission.*

Chapter 8

1. What was the Yuma Massacre? *The Spaniards did not bring gifts for the Yumas and their horses trampled their crops. The Yumas became angry and murdered the Spaniards.*
2. How was Los Angeles founded? *By the families that were spared in the Yuma Massacre.*

Chapter 9

1. Describe the mission system. How did it work, and what was its goal? If you do not remember, go back and review Unit 3. *Indians were encouraged to come to the mission and learn about Christianity and various crafts. When ready, the mission would be turned into a* pueblo, *the church into a regular parish church, and the missionaries would move on.*
2. The missions were self-sufficient. What does this mean? Why did they have to be self-sufficient? *They produced almost all of the materials they needed. This was necessary because California was so far away and did not receive regular supplies.*
3. What common characteristics or features did the missions share? *Answers might include: arched hallways, central patio, work areas, bells and tower, church*
4. Describe a typical day at a mission. *Morning prayers and Mass, breakfast, work, dinner, rest, prayers, relaxing*
5. Look at the mission map. Which mission is closest to your home? Have you ever visited it? *Answers will vary.*

Chapter 10

1. What good and bad features do you see in the Spanish missions of California? *Opinion—might include: Good—teach religion and crafts; Bad—no self-government*
2. Were the Indians at the missions slaves? Why or why not? *No—came to mission of own free will, were not subject to excessive labor, sometimes could be paid*
3. Describe your favorite Mission Indian in two or three sentences. *Answers will vary between Pablo Tac, Pasquala, Toypurina, and the Lost Woman of San Nicolas.*

Chapter 11

1. Who was the Stormy Catalan? Describe him. *Pedro Fages, California's 2nd and 5th governor.*
2. Who was his wife? Describe her. *Doña Eulalia. Very contrary.*

Chapter 12

1. Why did Count Rezanov visit California? *To obtain food for the starving Sitka colony.*
2. Why was Fort Ross built? *To hunt otter, but mostly to grow food for Sitka.*
3. Why do you think God prevented the Russians from colonizing California? *Opinion—was saving it for America.*

Chapter 13

1. Describe California's part in the revolt against Spain. *Defend itself against pirates.*
2. Who was Joseph Chapman? *First American in Southern California. Deserter from the pirate ship.*
3. What might have happened to California if it had not remained a colony of Mexico after the Spanish-American Wars for Independence? *It might have become an independent nation like other Spanish colonies.*

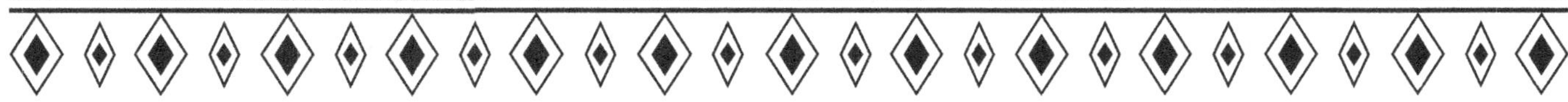

Supplemental Activities

Literature Suggestions

Mission Tales by Helen M. Roberts. Mrs. Roberts has written twenty-one short stories about each of the missions. They are absolutely wonderful. They will give the student a real feel for mission life. These are sometimes hard to find, but well worth the effort. Each mission story is published as a separate book or as one book containing three stories. Highly recommended.

Pasquala of Santa Inez by Florence Wightman Rowland. This is a great book and quite easy to read. It is based on the adventures of a young Mission Indian girl who was kidnapped from her mission. When she hears of a plot to attack Santa Inez, she escapes and runs for many days to warn the missionaries of the plot. Highly recommended.

Father Junípero Serra, The Traveling Missionary by Linda Lyngheim. A good, readable biography about the founder of California's mission system, Father Serra. Covers his life in Spain, Mexico, and California. Includes sections on the nine missions that Father Serra founded in California. While not anti-Christian, the author ignores the providential viewpoint that permeates the source documents she has used. Recommended.

Father Junípero Serra by Ivy Bolton. This is a very good biography about California's premier Catholic missionary. The author tells a lively story which accurately portrays Father Serra's love for the Indians, his piety, and his steadfastness. She also manages to describe the tension that existed between the missionaries and the military governors, while keeping the story interesting. Recommended.

The Big Ride by Dorothy Ward Erskine. A fictional story about Juan Bautista de Anza's journey to California. The main character is fictional, but we meet people who actually made the trip, including Captain de Anza and Father Pedro Font, and hear about others including Father Serra, Captain Portolá, Father Garces, Captain Rivera, Chief Salvador of the Yumas, and Tarabel, the Indian who helped Captain de Anza across the desert. *The Big Ride* is a "coming of age" story about a young boy who learns the power of forgiveness. I enjoyed getting a personal glimpse of Captain de Anza, the man so admired by the people of 1776 as well as today.

California Mission Days by Helen Bauer. See comment in the California Indian Section.

Cathedral in the Sun by Anne B. Fischer. See description in the Mexican Period Section.

Field Trips

Missions

The most obvious field trip possibilities for the Spanish period are visits to the magnificent Spanish missions. The missions were destroyed in the Mexican period (we will learn about this in the next unit) and fell into ruin. President Lincoln returned them to the Catholic Church in the

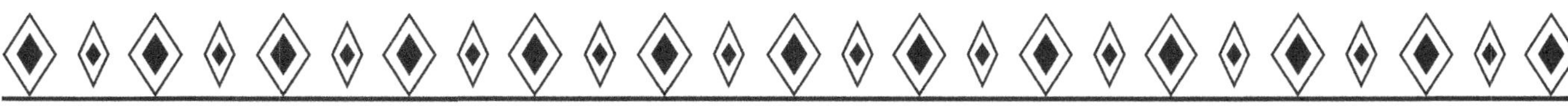

1860s. Most of these have been restored by various historical societies and the Catholic Church and are used today as parish churches.

I have visited seventeen missions and the degree of restoration varies widely, yet each has a unique story to tell. Some are little more than the chapel and a gift shop, while others include partial ground restoration. La Purisima Mission near Lompoc contains the most extensive restorations, including many of the workrooms and buildings used by the missionaries and the Indians, a lavanderia (for washing clothes), irrigation system, and extensive gardens highlighting the plants of the mission era. It is run by the California State Park system, one of the few missions not under the auspices of the Catholic church.

Each mission has its own website, all with teaching resources. If you plan on visiting a mission, be sure to check out the educational materials before you go. Additional websites include

- http://www.ac.wwu.edu/~stephan/anthony/missions.html contains an animated map of the formation of the missions, in the order they were founded.
- http://www.ca-missions.org/links.html#specificmissions, the home of California Mission Studies—lots of links to missions and places of interest.

Presidios

The four coastal presidios might be worth a field trip. I have visited the Monterey and San Francisco presidios. The reconstructed portions of the Monterey presidio are few. The San Francisco presidio was a working army base until 1994 when it was turned over to the National Park service. Its museum is filled with interesting artifacts encompassing much more than the Spanish period.

Although there were a few pueblos and ranchos in the Spanish period, a field trip to those places probably would be more profitable when studying the Mexican period.

Royal Chapel

Finally, if you are in the Monterey area, visiting the Carmel Mission, the Customs House, or any of the wonderful historical sites this city offers, be sure to visit the Royal Chapel. Not only is it the oldest building in California, it is also the longest continuously-functioning church. Further, when a Catholic bishop makes a particular church his home church, it automatically becomes a cathedral. The Royal Presidio Chapel became the San Carlos Cathedral in 1967, the smallest cathedral in the U.S. If you are in Monterey, by all means, stop by for a look. The Royal Presidio Chapel is located at 500 Church St.

Mission Images

If you are unable to visit a mission, be sure to take advantage of the numerous pictures on the Internet. Offerings will vary, but many websites have pictures with descriptions, slide shows, and videos. Also, http://virtualguidebooks.com contains some great panoramic virtual tours of several missions plus many other of California's sites.

The video *Inside the California Missions* offers a good overview of the mission system as well as close-ups of each of the twenty-one missions. Running time is fifty-eight minutes, but can be broken into smaller increments by stopping it after the description of each mission. This video is available for purchase from most mission gift shops and for loan from the library.

Crafts & Activities

Sugar Cube Missions

1. <u>Materials needed</u>
   Sugar cubes (determine number needed for

each student), white craft glue, glue containers for two students to share, cardboard for mission bases, one bell per student (available in the wedding section of craft stores), toothpicks for cross, one and one-half craft sticks per student. Plastic to protect tables, glue gun (to pre-glue crosses).

2. Advance preparation
   Cut or break one toothpick in half and glue it to a whole one to form a cross. Draw the perimeter of the mission base on the cardboard (eight cubes wide and seven deep). Cut craft sticks.

3. Objective
   To learn about mission life in early California and to make a model of the adobe missions that the Spaniards built. At first the missions were built of mud and tules, just like the Indians' huts. Later, when California was more settled, they were replaced with adobe buildings. Wood was scarce in California, so the missionaries used the materials available.

4. Procedure
   Each student should be given a group of sugar cubes, a cardboard base (it is helpful to draw a square on the cardboard to use as a guide), and some white craft glue (one for every two students). Draw a pattern on the white board for the students to follow in constructing their missions.
   a. Dip the sugar cubes in the craft glue and stack them in place.
   b. To create the open space needed for the bell tower, use the craft sticks. When the bell tower is complete, glue the cross and bell in place.
   c. After the walls and bell tower have dried, glue them together.

The sugar cube mission project takes more than an hour to complete. It can be constructed over two days, which will give the glue time to dry. Or it can be constructed in two steps, the base and bell tower. These can be glued together after the sugar cubes have dried.

Candle Dipping

1. Materials needed
   Paraffin wax, broken into small pieces so that it will melt better, coffee tin, electric skillet, string for wick (one per student), pencil to tie wick on (for dipping—one per student), newspaper or plastic to protect working surface, potholders to take coffee tin from electric skillet, plastic dish pan, and plastic to protect carpet, if needed.

1. Advance preparation
   Break paraffin wax into small pieces. Place block in a plastic bag and hit with a hammer.

2. Objective
   To learn how the Spaniards and Mexicans provided illumination in their homes and churches. We will be using paraffin, but originally the candles were made from rendered tallow (beef fat). Picture a mild, fall day with huge pots of beef fat melting in the courtyard of an adobe. Swarms of flies would hover about and the smell was terrible. The adobes smelled of beef fat throughout the winter whenever the candles were burned.

3. Procedure
   Place the wax in a coffee can and set it in the water to melt, double-boiler style. For a group of students you will need more than one coffee can of melting wax. **It is very dangerous to melt wax over an open flame!** The wax takes some time to melt so plan accordingly.

   Prepare the work area by covering the floor with plastic, taped to the carpet. Wax on the carpet is hard to remove. Be sure to also cover the table with plastic and newspaper.

   Prepare the wick by tying a piece of string to the pencil and tying a knot in the opposite end. When the wax in the coffee can has melted, remove it from the skillet and place it in a plastic dish pan filled with warm water. Now you are ready for the students.

   If you have a group of students, direct them to form a circle. Instruct each to dip the wick into the melted paraffin, then move on. At the beginning they will have to straighten out the wick so the candle will not be crooked. By the time it is the student's turn to dip again, his candle will have cooled enough to accept the next layer of paraffin. Direct students to walk on the plastic. If you have only one or two students you will need a container of ice water so that they can dip the wick in the paraffin, and then in the water to cool.

   From time to time you will have to replenish the wax at the students' work area with the wax you are melting in the electric skillet. If it cools too much, it can quickly be reheated.

   This activity takes time. The candles seem rather skinny for awhile, then they quickly get thick.

Adobe Brick-Making

1. Materials Needed
   Mud, dried weeds or grass for binding, buckets for mixing, buckets to hold water to wash

hands, rags to dry hands, brick form (optional), rubber gloves (optional), cardboard or newspaper to dry bricks on, plastic tarp to work on, broom and dustpan to clean up.

2. Advance preparation
   Obtain adobe clay (from your yard or a vacant lot, with permission of course). Obtain some dried weeds or grass (from a field or vacant lot).

3. Objective
   To show the students how adobe bricks were made. The brick I have my students make is much smaller than the ones that the Spaniards and Mexicans used. The early Californians mixed the adobe clay with their feet in a huge mud pit. Students should obtain an appreciation of the amount of work that was required to prepare the materials to build dwellings.

4. Procedure
   Direct students to mix some adobe clay with water in the buckets until it is muddy. Add straw or grass until it binds together somewhat. When of the right consistency (a thick paste), place students' cardboard or thick sheets of newspaper under the brick mold and form adobe brick. If a brick mold is not available, direct students to form the brick into a rectangle using their hands or pieces of cardboard.

   Direct students to wash off most of the mud in the buckets of water before they go to the bathroom. You want to make sure the bathrooms are not full of your mud.

The boys love this activity; the girls not so much. However, when one of my moms got the idea to use rubber gloves, the girls were happier.

To see a pictures of building being constructed with adobe bricks, go to http://www.firebudd.com/adobe/. Amazing!

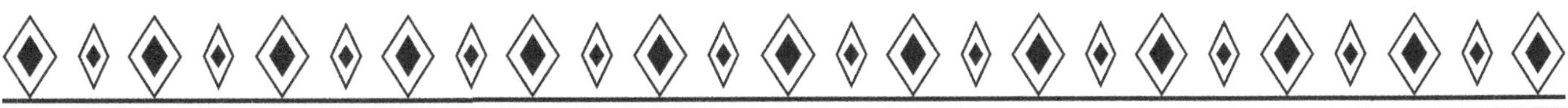

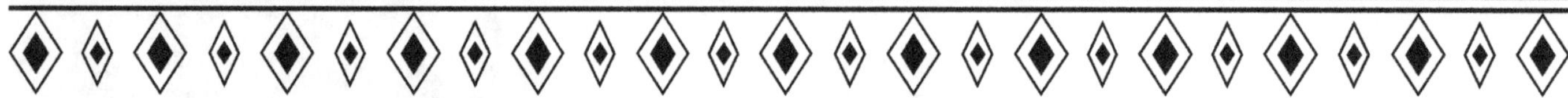

Mission Music

It might be fun to play authentic mission music while students are working on their projects. Go to http://www.californiamissions.com/music/index.html. Hear the music of the missions—links to "El Cantico del Alba," the morning hymn of praise, "The Lord's Prayer" ("Padre Nuestro"), and many others. Click on the sidebar links for information about each mission.

Oral Review Questions

Use these questions for review, to close a lesson, or for a review game like Around the World or Jeopardy.

1. Name the three methods the Spaniards used to colonize California. (mission, presidio, pueblo)
2. What was the Sacred Expedition? (first overland expedition to California)
3. What happened to the three ships that traveled to California on the Sacred Expedition? (one vanished, the other two arrived in very poor condition)
4. Describe the character of Father Serra. (pious, loved the Indians, dedicated, humble)
5. What did Governor Portolá find when he reached San Diego? (hospital tents and scurvy)
6. What did the Indians do after San Diego Mission was founded? (stole, wouldn't eat food, attacked Spaniards)
7. What bay did Governor Portolá discover on his first journey north of San Diego? (San Francisco Bay)
8. Why didn't Governor Portolá find Monterey Bay on his first expedition? (Vizcaíno exaggerated quality of the bay, climate changed, or God wanted him to find San Francisco Bay)
9. What happened in the Canyon of the Bears? (great bear hunt to avert a famine)
10. What did Viceroy Bucareli want to find to make it easier to send supplies to California? (overland route)
11. Who is Juan Bautista de Anza? (Discoverer of the overland route to California. Also brought colonists to establish a presidio and mission at San Francisco)
12. Why was de Anza's second arrival in California providential? (rescued San Diego Mission)
13. What was happening in the United States when the San Francisco presidio was being built? (Declaration of Independence)
14. How did Jose de Galvez stop the colonization of California? (appointed new viceroy, Teodoro de Croix)
15. What caused the Yuma Massacre? (the wrath of the Indians set off by Spaniards destroying crops)
16. What effect did the Yuma Massacre have? (closed the Anza trail and halted colonization)
17. What is the Mission System? (Indians gathered on missions to learn the Catholic faith and useful crafts)
18. Why did the missionaries insist that the Indians stay at the missions after they were baptized? (if left mission would suffer temptation to return to old ways)
19. How long would missions be needed in California? (until the Indians became Spanish citizens and Catholics and learned useful crafts)
20. Describe a mission. (adobe, church, workrooms, Indian village)
21. What is adobe? (mixture of clay and straw. Used to make bricks)
22. What did Indians learn at the missions? (masonry, pottery, mill-making, carpentry, blacksmithing, candle-making, soap-making, reading, writing, singing. Indian women: sewing, cooking, weaving)
23. Who was Father Lasuén? (President after

Serra)
24. How did the Fathers persuade an Indian to visit a mission? (food, trinkets, clothing, and other gifts which were called "the bait of spiritual fishing")
25. What were some of the ways the Fathers taught the Indians? (songs, pictures, and simple plays)
26. Who was Pedro Fages? Describe his character. (California's second and fifth governor. Stormy but lovable. Devoted to children.)
27. Who was Doña Eulalia Fages? Describe her character. (Pedro Fages' wife. Temperamental. Used to getting own way.)
28. Who was Rezanov? (Ambassador from Russia)
29. What happened to Rezanov in California? (fell in love)
30. What part of the Spanish American Wars for Independence took place in California? (California was attacked by privateers)
31. What happened as a result of the war? (California became a Mexican province)
32. Who was Joseph Chapman? (First American in Southern California. Was a member of Bouchard's crew)

Project Suggestions

(See Appendix B for a description of the class project)

1. Draw an "event map" (words or pictures illustrating what happened along the way) of Portolá's march to San Diego and Monterey. Record what happened at each place. Pretend you are Portolá and write a letter to place under the cross at Monterey. Record the most important things that have happened in your journey. Discuss the reason you are returning to San Diego.
2. Do a study of the La Brea tar pits from a creationist point of view. Find out how the Indians used the tar. What else was found in the pits? What does this tell you about California's past?
3. Compare San Francisco Bay as it was when originally discovered to the area today. What parts were filled in and why? What is there now? (Downtown San Francisco!)
4. Draw an "event map" of the Anza Expedition. Research Juan Bautista de Anza.
5. Research and report on the California sea otter. What was its habitat? Why and how was it hunted? What was its fur used for? Now that it is a protected species, how is it doing? What would it be like if sea otters were as abundant as they were originally? (Their voracious appetites would cause abalone and other seafood to be scarce along the coast.)
6. Research and report on the grizzly bear. Find out more about the bear hunt at El Cañon de los Osos (near San Luis Obispo). Describe a bull and bear fight. Do you think this was cruel? Are you glad grizzlies do not live in California anymore? Describe their temperament and habits. Write a fictional account of a person meeting a grizzly. Find out more about Jedediah Smith's meeting with a grizzly.
7. Report on Doña Concepción and Count Rezanov (several authors have written fictional accounts of this romance. See Gertrude Athernon in the adult section of the library). How did their different religions cause problems for them?
8. Make some adobes. Make a large adobe brick (clay mixed with straw or large pieces of dried grass put into a form) or several small ones. Perhaps make a model of an adobe home. Describe how the Spaniards made their adobe homes. Why did they coat them with limestone? Why did the San Jose Mission, and other missions, add tar to the adobes when they reconstructed them? (So they wouldn't "melt" in the rain.)
9. Learn how to do some of the things Mission Indians would have done such as carding and

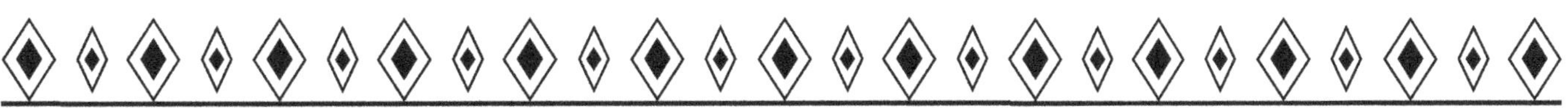

spinning wool or weaving cloth.

10. Do a report on the Russian colony at Sitka, Alaska. What was the people's religion? Who were the Aleuts? What did the Russians do at Sitka?
11. Do a report on any of the missions. Build a model using sugar cubes and egg white icing or glue. You could also build a model from Styrofoam. What took place at the mission? Perhaps paint or draw pictures of some of these activities.
12. Make a map showing the location of all 21 missions. Perhaps draw pictures or make models of some of these. Visit as many as you can, take pictures, and build a display.
13. Dress up as Pasquala and tell the exciting story of your kidnap, escape, and dangerous journey to save Mission Santa Inés.

Helpful Links

http://www.ca-missions.org/links.html#specificmissions
California Mission Studies—lots of links to missions and places of interest.

http://www.californiahistory.com/parks.html
Links to California state parks.

http://www.californiahistory.com/museums.html
Links to California historical societies and museums

http://teams.lacoe.edu/documentation/classrooms/angie/california/teacher/teacher.html
Angie's Teacher's Corner—lots of educational links.

Source Documents

A Letter From Father Serra

Antonine Tebesar O.F.M. editor, *The Writings of Junípero Serra*, Academy of American Franciscan History, Washington D.C., 1955 pp. 133-139.

Father Serra wrote many letters to his superiors in New Spain detailing his progress in California. The letters in the student's book have been paraphrased from the originals. A sample of Serra's original correspondence from July 3, 1769 follows.

Hail Jesus, Mary, Joseph!

Very Reverend Father Guardian Fray Juan Andres Venerable Father and my dear Sir:

I am writing this letter in this Port and new Mission-to-be of San Diego, some hundred leagues within the heathen land of California. Here I have with me Fathers Crespi, Viscaíno, Parron and Gomez all in good health, thank God, and at the orders of Your Reverence, as our father and lord.

We came together here in separate groups, a few at a time. Fathers Viscaíno and Gomez came first, arriving by the packet boat *San Antonio*; then Father Parron in the *San Carlos*, which, starting a month and a half before the *San Antonio*, arrived twenty days after it. The third on the list was Father Crespi, with the first part of the land expedition; and I was the last to join them here, the day before yesterday, with the Governor and the rest of the said expedition.

As regards the missions already in existence, Father Professor Palou who is now their President, as I wrote in my last letters to Your Reverence before beginning this journey—which fact appeared to confirm to me why Your Reverence had nominated him as President—no doubt will report to Your Reverence the state of affairs and all that has happened since the visit of His Most Illustrious Lordship to Loreto. He was still expected to come when I left.

Before starting, I drew up a memorandum putting down all the matters that, in my mind had to be laid before the said gentleman so that everything might be in good order. I was informed before leaving Christian parts that all my suggestions were approved of. Blessed be God.

As regards our present undertaking: the expedition by sea was a disaster. As a matter of fact both ships landed at this port, but neither of them is in condition to proceed to Monterey. Owing to the faulty condition of the barrels, the *San Carlos* suddenly found itself without water. They put in to the coast and procured some water but of poor quality. The crew took sick with scurvy—or Loanda sickness—and since their arrival at this port, they all died, with the exception of one sailor and a cook.

Of the volunteers, or Migueletes, from Catalonia, three died, and many are sick with little hope of recovery. The worst of all was that the crew of the *San Antonio*, which was ready to sail from here to Monterey, arriving here in good health, went to the assistance of the *San Carlos* and were themselves infected, and eight of their number died. Therefore the gentlemen here came to the decision that the said *San Antonio*, also called *El Principe*, must return to the Port of San Blas and that from there it should bring a double crew, so that on returning, both ships may be manned and continue their voyage.

The third packet boat, the *San Joseph*, we

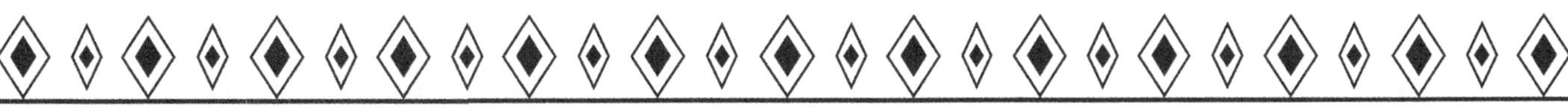

imagine must have already set sail for the same destination. On it comes Father Murguia; that is on the supposition that his mission at Santiago de los Coras was placed by His Most Illustrious Lordship in the care of Father Baeza, a secular priest, and nephew of Father Fray Buenaventura. If the ship lands here in good condition, and ready to go ahead, although it was the last to leave, it will be the first to get to Monterey.

I regret that my time is all too short to write more extensively. Arriving the day before yesterday, about noon, after a tiresome journey, I am being pressed by the report that the boat sails this very night. That is why I am not sending to Your Reverence the diary of my journey which lasted among the infidels a little less than one month and a half. We met with no hostile demonstrations, in fact just the reverse. On many occasions we were regaled by the gentiles—reversing the proverb, "The stingy man gives more that the naked," because these naked Indians gave us more than many stingy men would have given us.

Naked indeed are all the males among the gentiles, be they children or adults, throughout all this country, without any exception. They go just as their mothers brought them into the world. And they have given us, on many occasions, food—not that we needed it, since, thank God, we came with plenty. Father Crespi and his companions of the expedition, by the way, experienced dire hunger on the road. They arrived at this port emaciated, and five of their Indians died on the way from extreme want.

On the first opportunity that presents itself after this, I will send you the said diary. In the letter enclosed with this, I promise our Father Commissary General a copy of the diary, on condition that if I cannot have it duplicated here, I will ask Your Reverence to order a good transcript to be made there. Not that it is worth anybody's attention, but it may help to a knowledge of these lands that had never before been trodden by a Christian foot. It will show how rich is the harvest of souls that might easily be gathered into the bosom of our holy Mother the Church, and it would appear, with very little trouble.

I asked them in different places if they would like me to stay with them and their answer was always yes.

Here there are no Apaches, and no enemies other than the spiritual ones. Thus with apostolic zeal and the grace of God, it seems to me that we may work to our hearts' content, and our Lord God will accomplish the promise made to our Seraphic Father Saint Francis that, at the mere sight of his sons, in these last centuries, the gentiles will be converted. It was fulfilled in what happened at the new mission of San Fernando de Velicata, to which Father Campa is appointed, as I wrote to Your Reverence, I think, in my last letter.

And so, my Reverend Father Guardian, we need ministers and more ministers, now that God Our Lord has put in the hands of our holy College the care of so bounteous a harvest.

Of those who are up here three have asked me repeatedly to be returned to the College. They are Fathers Villumbrales, Medinaveytia, and Basterra. It seems to me advisable that permission be granted in order not to spread their discouragement to others. As to poor Father Moran, he richly deserves the rest that his age requires.

Of the five that are here, within a few days Fathers Crespi and Gomez will both set out to accompany the expedition; I will stay here for some time, and wait and see if I will take ship from here in the *San Joseph*. My intentions are to rest a little after my continuous journeyings—the distance from here to Loreto is about 250 leagues—and also to give a helping hand to these good Fathers in the foundation and organization of the new mission here. We will start work on it as soon as all the excitement caused by the setting out of the land expedition subsides.

Land here is plentiful and good, and a river goes with it. Although not long ago it had flowing water, at present—this being the driest part of the year—there is no water running in it.

But there are still large and good pools. And so as regards the material side of things it seems that quite a good mission can be established. Besides there are so many vines grown by nature and without human help that it would mean little expense to follow the example of our good father Noe [Noah].

There are roses of Castile and trees in abundance; above all a large population of gentiles, both in this locality and in the surrounding country. They visit us frequently, but first they put aside their bows and arrows. May God grant both us and them His holy grace so that soon they may all become Christians.

To sum it all up, my intention is that as ministers of the mission here, Fathers Murguia and Parron, should remain; for the Mission of San Buenaventura, that has to follow this, Fathers Gomez and Viscaíno; and for Monterey Mission, Father Crespi and I.

Here it is quite cold, and my tunics—well, they are both about falling to pieces. Although on the way up here I took particular care to mend them. So I ask you especially that, at the first opportunity, you assist us in this matter. The tunics should be made of the thickest sackcloth that can be found.

As regards anything more, thanks be to God, I want for nothing but the prayers of many, that His Divine Majesty deign to grant me pardon for my numerous and great sins and enable me to become a worthy minister of the Holy Gospel. And so I ask for the prayers of our holy Community both for myself and for all my brethren here. You in turn I will always remember in my own poor and lukewarm prayers.

Those who are assigned to come to this country should be sure to bring with them good blankets. With regard to those who come to missions already established, blankets will be superfluous. In this way it seems to me that blankets should be specified more for the missions than for the missionaries, that is if they are not already earmarked for a specified destination. And I am referring here to the missions yet to be founded, when our numbers are increased, and when the older missions are furnished with a second minister, for they have been too long with only one.

I intended to speak of many other things to Your Reverence; but there is no time for more. This however I will add: I consider that the missions to be founded in these parts will enjoy many advantages over the old ones, as the land is much better and the water supply is more plentiful. The Indians especially of the west coast seem to me much more gifted; they are well set up, and the Governor looks upon most of them as likely Grenadier Guards because they are such stoutly built and tall fellows.

To sum up, those who are to come here as ministers should not imagine that they come for any other purpose than to put up with hardships for the love of God and the salvation of souls. In a desert like this it is impossible for the old missions to come to the help of the new ones. The distances are great and the intervening spaces are peopled by gentiles. In addition to this, the almost complete lack of communication by sea makes it necessary that they endure, especially at the beginning, many and dire hardships. But to a willing heart all is sweet, *amanti suave est*.

Much more beyond compare, did these poor Indians cost my Lord Jesus Christ. May His most holy Majesty keep Your Reverence, and all of you, and every one of the members of your holy Community—to whom I recommend myself with much affection—or many years in health and in His holy grace.

From this port among the infidels, and the projected Mission of San Diego, in California, July 3, 1769.

Kissing the hand of Your Reverence,

Your most affectionate and devoted subject and servant in Jesus Christ,

Fray Junípero Serra

The California Missions

Rupert and Jeannette Henry Costo, *The Missions of California, A Legacy of Genocide*, Indian His-

torian Press, San Francisco, 1987.

Although this book offers little more than emotion to the discussion of the Indians in California, its appendix contains interviews with many modern California history professors and scholars. These conversations shed much light on the missions of California. The following quotes have been summarized into five areas:

1. ***Why do modern scholars have such a negative perception of the California missions?***

Dr. David Hornbeck, Professor since 1972, Department of Historical Geography, California State University, Northridge; Ph.D. University of Nebraska, 1974. Ibid pp. 6-7:

A great deal of this stems from an attempt in the 1890's to romanticize everything Spanish in California. You begin to get an attitude in California that Spain, oh boy, that was great. You could love Spanish architecture. It was very romanticized. After that a growing number of people just naturally got involved in looking at agriculture, the missions, Indians, etc. The problem is, the people who were doing the research weren't good researchers. They weren't skilled at what they were doing. As a consequence, they took whatever analogy they possibly could. It's an easy analogy, now, to know about slavery, to know about plantations, to know about the abuses that occurred on the plantations, and to simply make the association that missions were like plantations. So, therefore, you don't have to do much research on missions, you simply take everything that you know, or that you've read, maybe documented or undocumented, and you transplant these ideas to the missions, then you begin to write about missions . . . .

Actually, you have two things occurring at the same time. The romanticizing of the missions, and also a very negative image appearing. The two don't work well together if you think about it, but they're still there. Over a period of time, the romanticism sort of died, but the negative image of the missions never goes away because nobody's ever gone out and done any real research on how many Indians there were, what in fact was the death rate, what happened, how did the system work. All those questions that were not asked.

In the 1920's, 1930's, and 1940's people were more interested so you got not the romantic literature, that's fairly easy to spot, but all of a sudden you have an article over here or a book over there that talks about the very negative image of the missions. You get that worked into the school textbooks, and it perpetuates. You have the persistence of error. That's where we get this idea the missions were located one day's journey apart. Because you simply look at a map, it's very obvious that's exactly what Father Serra did, you write it down, and it's stayed with us now for almost a hundred years.

There's one thing you can ask people about the missions, as a fact, they'll tell you, almost to a person—one day's journey apart.

Dr. Harry Kelsey, Chief Curator of History since 1971, Los Angeles County Museum of Natural History; Ph.D. University of Denver, Colorado, 1965. Ibid p. 18:

Bigotry is part of it, an anti-religious attitude, maybe an anti-Christian attitude. Maybe an assumption that Serra's religion disqualifies him from being able to do anything that's very good. I think that you'd have to at least investigate that idea.

2. ***Were the missions little more than death camps where European diseases killed thousands?***

Dr. Doyce B. Nunis Jr., Professor since 1968, Department of History, University of Southern California; Ph. D., University of Southern California, 1985. Ibid p. 28:

Nobody understood the germ theory. The germ theory was not hypothesized until 1841, not proven until 1870. So, the missionaries didn't know about infectious diseases.

Rev. Francis F. Guest, O.E.M., Director, Santa Barbara Museum Archive-Library; Member, Academy of American Franciscan History. Ibid pp. 37-39:

One is held responsible for the harm that one foresees will follow from a course of action that one deliberately chooses. But did not the Franciscan missionaries, because of the experience they had had, first in the Sierra Gorda Mountains of Mexico among the Pames Indians, and then among the rapidly diminishing native population of Baja California, have some previous knowledge of the disastrous effect missionization could have on the aboriginal inhabitants of virgin mission territory? Were they not aware of the Spanish saying so common on the frontier, "The shadow of the Spaniard means the death of the Indian?" Why, then, did they come?

First, of all, let us consider this question from the standpoint of medicine. In Serra's day, in California, missionized Indians, when taken seriously ill with some disease that could prove fatal, would almost invariably refuse the administration of Spanish medicines, whether by a surgeon or by the padres, and have recourse instead to the remedies provided by their native doctors. They put their confidence in the medical science to which in their culture, they were accustomed. And they continued to follow this policy for generations, even though their experience told them that these remedies were not dependable . . . .

Secondly, let us consider the question posed above from the standpoint of religion. Christ, in the final verses of St. Matthew's Gospel, laid upon his apostles the obligation to make disciples of all men, an injunction the Franciscan missionaries interpreted as a solemn duty to Christianize the Indians. Furthermore, they held fast to the supremacy of the spiritual over the temporal, the supernatural over the natural, salvation and holiness over material health and well being...

The decline of the mission Indian population in California, then, if it is to be understood, should normally be studied in the light of this broad experience which covered approximately half the globe. If, because of the death-rate at the missions, one applies unpleasant epithets to the Franciscan missionaries of Hispanic California, how is one to describe physicians who had the misfortune to live out their careers before Louis Pasteur, Joseph Lister, and Robert Koch established and developed the modern science of bacteriology? Previous to the formulation of the germ theory by these three eminent scientists, the death-rate caused by contagious diseases in large European and American cities was no compliment to the medical profession. And the friars were no more capable of preventing or curing diseases than were the doctors of the pre-Pasteur period . . . .

3. Were the California Mission Indians slaves?

Rev. Francis F. Guest, O.E.M., Director, Santa Barbara Museum Archive-Library; Member, Academy of American Franciscan History. Ibid p. 34:

Thirdly, let us now consider the accusation of enslavement. Why did the missionaries insist on keeping these wards of theirs, these neophytes, in residence at the mission instead of allowing them to live at will in their native villages? The missionaries followed this policy for two principal reasons, one theological, the other juridical. Let us take the theological reason first.

In their native habitat the non-Christian Indians followed a number of customs and observances which did not conform to Christian morality as the missionaries understood it. For example, the Indians not only practiced divorce and remarriage; they commonly allowed casual cohabitation. Again, as mission documentation

makes clear, they were accustomed to punish injury with death. The missionaries, in their interpretation of Catholic theology, found it necessary to keep their converts in residence at the mission, not only because they thought it essential to instruct them in Christian doctrine twice a day, but also to protect them against the proximate occasion of grave sin which prolonged visits by individuals or small groups to their native villages would inevitably entail. Once a year, for a period of five or six weeks, the Catholic Indians went in a body to visit their parents, relatives, and friends in their native villages. Good example, prayer, mutual support, advice, counsel, encouragement, vigilance, prudence—all this rendered the proximate occasion sufficiently remote to permit this limited visit by a large group. This was the general line of reasoning, followed by the missionaries with respect to their wards, the Indian converts.

Taking its stand, in part, on this theological foundation, the Spanish government, on February 4, 1604, enacted a law which required that Indian converts be kept in residence at the reduction (mission) to which they were attached. And if the neophytes, as was perfectly natural for them, tired of mission life after a while and wanted to return to the cultural ways of their forefathers, they were supposed to be recovered by the missionaries and brought back to the mission, just as children in Spain who had run away from home would be restored to their parents by civil authorities. Some scholars have mistakenly criticized as enslavement this practice which can easily be explained by a simple reference to Spanish theology and Spanish law.

4. *Did the Indians come to the missions by choice?*

Dr. Harry Kelsey, Chief Curator of History since 1971, Los Angeles County Museum of Natural History; Ph.D. University of Denver, Colorado, 1965. Ibid p. 17:

The Indians were delighted to come into the missions. They had been living on the bare edge of existence. Until they came to the missions, they didn't know from one month to the next or one day to the next what they were going to eat, or how they were going to cure themselves from an illness, or what they were going to do in the event of some dire tragedy. And there was constant warfare.

California Indians lived in very circumscribed areas. They competed with people in adjoining areas for food and firewood and water and everything else. This idea that they lived in a sort of pastoral Eden, in perfect peace with one another, is just the greatest malarkey. There's absolutely no truth to it at all.

There are records as far back as 1542, when the first explorers came here, that the Indians fought continually with one another, and also that many times they were on the verge of starvation.

I don't know why the critics of the missions don't do their research. In all fields of history, there's an awful lot of discussion and considerably less research.

Dr. Doyce B. Nunis Jr., Professor since 1968, Department of History, University of Southern California; Ph. D., University of Southern California, 1985. Ibid p. 29:

Today we live in an age when people talk about born-again Christians, and there are an awful lot of them out there. Has it ever dawned on anybody that many of these California mission Indians may have truly accepted with joy, and great happiness and great fulfillment, the new religion? . . . .

Life was very hard. Very hard. They simply had to really grub for a living. And that living meant just eating and staying alive. We don't even know the mortality rate among the Indians prior to white contact. People always assume the moment the Spanish came in, death came. Well, that's absurd. Death was always there.

5. ***Did the Spanish missionaries treat the Indians cruelly?***

Dr. Michael Mathes, Professor since 1966, History Department, University of San Francisco; Ph.D. University of New Mexico, 1965. Ibid p. 21:

I've seen no documentation that indicates anything in this regard about Father Serra, or in fact most of the other missionaries. There were a few who were problems we know—and Franciscan historians have very openly discussed these people. We had a couple of alcoholics, and a couple of friars that had some really heavy psychological problems that they just couldn't stand the pressure of being alone. Some would hit the sacramental wine bottles and things of this sort. When they were found out, they were removed and sent back.

Rev. Francis F. Guest, O.E.M., Director, Santa Barbara Museum Archive-Library; Member, Academy of American Franciscan History. Ibid p. 42:

In the opinion of the present author, the methods of discipline employed by the Franciscan missionaries of Hispanic California are to be viewed through the lens of eighteenth-century European culture. In Hispanic households of that period it was customary for parents to impose whippings, not only on younger children who had misbehaved, but also upon children who had reached adulthood and were still living under the parental roof. The step from punishing adult children in a Spanish home to punishing adult wards in a Spanish mission in Upper California was not, for Spaniards of that time and culture, a long one to take. Abuses sometimes occurred, to be sure. Sometimes there were friars, like Father José Pedro Panto at Mission San Diego, who went to excess in punishing neophytes for their deficiencies. Not all the Franciscans who attempted missionary life were well suited to it. Some Indian family traditions keep alive memories of Franciscan harsh treatment. It would be surprising if these departures from the virtues of justice and charity had not occurred. On the other hand, however, the same kind of traditions recorded as sworn depositions in the 1940s , reveal that, among Indian as well as non-Indian families, Junípero Serra's reputation for holiness of life was firmly upheld.

In 1801 Lasuén wrote that at Mission San Francisco 130 non-Christian Indians suddenly presented themselves for baptism. In 1817 Father Jose Senan, head missionary at Mission San Buenaventura, wrote, "We now have 55 non-Christian Indians quartered here. They came to us from a considerable distance, but are quite happy to be here, and would like very much to have a mission in their own territory." These quotations and others like them are difficult to reconcile with the frequently heard complaint that, at the missions, the treatment of the Indians was universally harsh.

Teacher's Supplement

Mexican Units

Units 5 & 6

Teaching Aids—Unit 5 & 6

The Mexican Units

Teacher's Overview

CALIFORNIA WAS UNDER THE JURISDICTION of Mexico for a very short time, only twenty-five years, yet these years were filled with momentous changes. First, California's isolation ended with the abrupt arrival of Jedediah Smith at San Gabriel Mission. Mountains and deserts, which the Spaniards had thought were impassable, had been breached. Second, the missions were destroyed, causing incredible hardship and degradation to the Indians. Third, American settlers began to make their way to California, establishing an American presence and example in California. Finally, the unstable Californio government fell, allowing California to become an American territory.

The Mexican Republic

The Mexican period of California's history began with Mexico declaring its independence from Spain. The paternalistic, authoritarian government of Spain was to be replaced with a republican form of government similar to the United States'. However, instead of prospering under the new form of government, as the Americans did, the Mexicans, and consequently the Californians, suffered massive unrest, revolutions, and counter-revolutions. The reason for this is quite simple: the Mexicans had not been trained to govern themselves. Instead, they were trained to rely on the government to supply their every need. They were heavily influenced by the ungodly, humanistic ideas of the French Revolution prevalent at the time. The Americans, on the other hand, had a long history of Christian self-government, using the Bible as their guide.

Secularization

The Spanish government never expected the missions to be a permanent feature in California or in any of its colonies. In Mexico, the missions were to last no more than ten years, while the Indians learned the rudiments of Catholicism and how to take care of their own affairs. In California the ten years had to be extended because the Indians had the lowest level of civilization of any of the Indians of North America and a great deal to learn to become Spanish citizens. This was compounded by the problem of the Spanish-American Wars. As Mexico fought for its independence, California was neglected. Supply ships did not arrive, so the missions had to become the basic economic units of California. This necessity undoubtedly distracted the missionaries from pursuing their objective of preparing the Indians for independence. Additionally, the power of the missionaries was severely curtailed during the Mexican period so that they were not always able to meet their goals.

Ultimately, the missions were not secularized; that is, they were not turned into parish churches, and the land was not distributed among the Indians. Instead, most of the land was confiscated by Californios who were more interested in their own gain than in the welfare of the Indians.

Coming of the Americans

American settlers began to follow the trails of the fur trappers as they made their way to beautiful California. Once there, the Americans prospered. They worked hard and became influential and respected citizens. Dissatisfaction with the unstable Mexican government increased as more Americans made California their home. They and some Californios began to work toward the goal of becoming a territory of the United States. This goal was finally realized when Mexico declared war on the United States over a dispute involving Texas. Often we are told that the Americans acquired California through unjust means, but this is not true. The Americans paid a fair price for the territory and made sure that the citizens were treated justly.

Did the U.S. Steal California?

A FEW YEARS AGO, WHEN I WAS DOING SOME research for my book, our family spent a weekend in Monterey. We visited the Customs House where sea captains, mostly Americans, paid an import tax to the Mexican government on goods brought to California. The Customs House was staffed by a docent who was explaining about life in the Mexican period of California's history.

"Of course the Mexican period ended after only 25 years," she lamented. "The United States came in and stole the land from the Californians. They just *took* it!"

I had read enough of California's history to doubt the veracity of this statement and started to argue, but to no avail. The conversation began to get a little heated and my husband decided to end the argument by escorting me from the room.

Did the United States steal California from Mexico? Absolutely not!

California Purchased

California became a part of the United States at the conclusion of the Mexican War in 1846. At the conclusion of the war, Northern Mexico and Baja California were returned to their rightful owners, the Mexicans, while the California territory was purchased. That's right—purchased. The sales price was $18.5 million in cash and forgiven debts, a price that sounded more generous in the days before rampant inflation.

Much confusion followed the war. Land, which did not have much value during the Mexican period, since it was only used to raise cattle, suddenly became very valuable in the eyes of the Americans. The treaty ending the war guaranteed that land would not be confiscated from those who had rightful title to it. It fell to the newly formed Land Commission to determine which titles were lawful.

The Land Commission

The Land Commission had a considerable challenge. Much of the Mexican period was a time of great lawlessness in California. Often Mexican law was not followed with respect to land grants.

In order for a ranchero to have legal title to his land, at least three requirements had to be met. First, the land had to be granted by someone who had the authority to do so. Second, the person who received the land was required to live on it for at least a year, build a house and a corral, plant a crop, and raise cattle. Finally, a map of the land grant, a *diseño*, detailing the boundaries of the property, had to be prepared and sent to the governor of California.

Many grants were declared invalid, including those conveyed by departing Mexican governors to repay political favors after their authority had expired. Pio Pico, the last Mexican governor of California, issued grants copiously after the Americans raised the flag at Monterey. Some were nullified because the Californians had not fulfilled Mexican law. Others were disputed because boundaries had been negligently marked with markers, such as a cattle skull or a branch in a crook of a tree, that easily disappeared with the passage of time. If two neighbors claimed the same area, the Land Commission did its best to determine the rightful owner.

The Gold Rush brought prosperity to the California rancheros. As cattle prices increased, many became wealthy. This new-found wealth was spent prodigiously on luxuries and extravagant living. When cattle prices fell after 1855, many rancheros found themselves in debt and were forced to sell some of their land to clear their obligations.

About one-fourth of all the land grants brought before the Land Commission were negated. When these were appealed to the Supreme Court, thirty-two were found invalid. Mistakes undoubtedly were made and some land was unjustly taken from its rightful owners, but the most frequent accusation is that the process just took too long.

Sometimes it took years to sort out the problems as cases were referred from the Land Commission to the courts. As lawyers got involved expenses rose. We must remember, however, that these problems were many times the consequence of the Californios not following their own government's laws.

The final act that caused the ranchos to be broken up and sold to Americans had little to do with the Land Commission, titles, *diseños,* or courts—it was an act of God. Between the 1862 and 1863 a two-year drought occurred, where it rained only once. After the drought, the rain poured and caused severe flooding. Cattle died by the thousands. Rancheros, heavily in debt because of extravagant living, were forced to sell their land. The rancho period had effectively come to an end.

It's easy to look 150 years or so into the past and find fault with the people of the time. It's easy, but not right. Some in the United States government made mistakes and some of the Californios neglected to follow their own laws, but there was no wholesale conspiracy to cheat the people out of their land, and there was certainly no theft.

Mighty Mountain Man

The Story of Jedediah Smith

IN THE 1820S, CALIFORNIA, ALONG WITH MOST of the West, was a vast area of white space on the maps of North America, where no white men had ever traveled. Outside of the Spanish domains, little was known of this rich and fertile area. More than anyone else, one man named Jedediah Strong Smith opened this area to the eyes and hearts of American immigrants. Not only did his exploits allow him to behold wonders never before revealed to the eyes of white men, they have earned for him a well-deserved place in the annals of California history.

Responding to an ad for 100 "Enterprising Young Men," Smith began an adventurous career as a mountain man, hunting and trapping beaver, which was used in men's fashions, especially hats. In very short time he became a leader, a partner, and then co-owner of his own trapping business. Time and again his exploits became fodder for nightly campfire discussions among the mountain men—harrowing escapes from Indians, perilous encounters with grizzly bears (one of which left him scarred for life), and exciting discoveries, including the South Pass through the Rocky Mountains. Exploring much of the Southwest, Smith eventually ventured to California.

Three Firsts

The year was 1826, while California was under the rule of Mexico. One bright morning, Smith and his men presented themselves to the missionaries at San Gabriel Mission. Although they were warmly welcomed with a great show of Spanish hospitality, their presence shocked the authorities. Between California and the territories of the United States, lay a vast, thought to be impenetrable, desert. Smith shattered that perception and became the first white man to enter California from the east.

California's governor accused him of spying for the Americans, but with difficulty, Smith assured him he was a simple trapper, eager to buy supplies and continue on his way. The governor finally was persuaded, and leaving some men in California, Smith made his way over the treacherous Sierra Nevada to rejoin his partners at the yearly rendezvous in what now is Utah. Unknown to him, he had accomplished another feat: the first white man to cross this mountain barrier.

Promptly Jailed

The next year Smith returned. Most of his men were massacred by Mojave Indians near the Colorado River, but Smith managed to rejoin his men in the Sacramento Valley. With no provisions, he was forced to apply to the hospitality of San José Mission. He was promptly jailed! American ship captains arranged for his release and Smith made plans to leave California for good. But, which way should he go? The southern route was not an option because of the Mojave's treachery. The mountains would be too hazardous for the horses Smith had purchased. Following the only other option, Smith headed north and left his name upon Jedediah Smith State Park, and Smith River. Additionally, he was the first white man to travel what is now the length of the state.

The Bible-Toter

Smith's exploring adventures, which opened the state to other fur trappers and eventually settlers, are sufficient to leave an imprint on the pages of history. Christians however, find a delightful surprise as they pursue their study of the intrepid explorer. Jedediah Smith was a steadfast, fellow believer, who was always careful to give glory and honor to his Lord and Savior, Jesus Christ. Carrying his Bible with him on all his journeys, Smith earned the nickname Bible-Toter. Until recently, most history books recorded this appellation.

From the writings of other mountain men, we hear of the powerful prayers Smith spoke over the graves of departed friends, prayers so mighty that they moved the coarse men to tears. From his letters to his brother, we learn that he used his wealth to supply the needs of his family, church, and even strangers. From the descriptions of his closest companions, we see his Christian character, constantly tested by trials and temptations, shine as a brilliant light in the wilderness.

Encountering any Christian on the pages of California's history brings joy. Not only are our children encouraged, their faith is strengthened as they learn of Christians who strove to be worthy of their calling. To that end Jedediah Smith's story is pure pleasure to read.

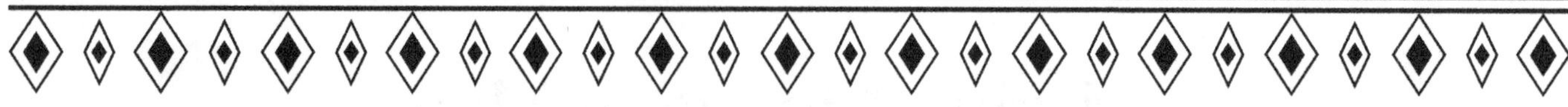

Teaching the Mexican Period Units

Lesson Plans

Unit 5

1. Introduction ideas:
   - Go to http://www.californiaweekly.com/ca_ranchos.htm to determine if the students' homes sit on what used to be a California rancho. See if you can find some information about the ranchero.
   - The diseño activity might serve to open this unit.
   - Do some research on the California Trail, the 2,000 mile route to California. Start here: http://www.nps.gov/cali/historyculture/index.htm. Discuss the difficulties people encountered on their way to California in the days before cars, trains, and airplanes.
2. Introduce the Mexican period of California's history. Teach the beginning or the Mexican (independence) verse (1821) of the "California Date Song."
3. Teach about the mountain men (Ch. 14). Do Roundup questions and teach the Jedediah Smith verse of the "California Date Song."
4. Do a character sketch on Jedediah Smith.
5. If you have time, do the Mountain Man Lingo activity, discussed in the Class-Time Activities section. You might also explain how beaver hats were made to explain the importance of the fur trade. See http://www.whiteoak.org/learning/furhat.htm (excellent explanation) or http://people.ucsc.edu/~kfeinste/felting.html (pictures).

   I purchased a beaver hat at an antique store to use as a teaching prop and wanted a beaver pelt as well so that I could explain the process. Beaver pelts are available on eBay (as is most everything else), but they were too expensive. I poked around, found a forum for fur trappers (I've long since lost the URL), and posted a message along the lines of "California history teacher desires beaver pelt to teach students about the Northwest fur trade." I got scores of responses in prices ranging from not-so-much to outrageous. I picked one, placed my order, and added another piece of relia to my collection.

   Finally, Jedediah Smith is a favorite with students. Sometimes I dress in costume, pretend I'm his sister, and tell his story. I spend a lot of time on the grizzly bear and Smith's ear. The boys love it. The girls not so much.
6. Explain how the missions were destroyed (Ch. 15) and do Roundup questions. Emphasize the difference between *freedom*, especially freedom in Christ, and *slavery*.
7. Do a character sketch on Mariano Vallejo.
8. Teach the lakes of California.
9. Teach and describe the typical way of life on a rancho (Ch. 16) and do Roundup questions.
10. If time permits, do one or more of the class-time activities.
11. Play a review game for Unit 5 using the Oral Review Questions.

Unit 6

1. Teach about early wagon trips to California (Ch. 17). Do Roundup Questions and teach the John Sutter (1839) and John Bidwell (1841) verses of the "California Date Song."
2. Explain how California became a United States military territory (Ch. 19). Do Roundup questions.
3. Make Bear Flags—see Class-Time Activities for directions.
4. Do character sketches on the three (or four) Johns: John Sutter, John Bidwell, and John

Charles Frémont (and perhaps John Marsh).
5. Teach the deserts of California.
6. As time permits, choose other activities from this section.
7. Play a review game using the Oral Review Questions for Unit 6.

Objectives

Objectives for Unit 5

At the completion of this unit students should be able to:

1. Explain the importance and consequences of Jedediah Smith's visits to California.
2. Explain how the Parable of the Talents applied to Mexican California.
3. Describe how and why the missions were destroyed (secularized), what impact this had on the Indians, and why the Indians did not become self-sufficient as was hoped.
4. Articulate what life was like on a California rancho.
5. Know the following historical characters: Jedediah Smith and Mariano Vallejo.

Objectives for Unit 6

At the completion of this unit students should:

1. Be able to describe the first wagon trip to California, the Bidwell-Bartleson party, and understand the hardships that the immigrants faced.
2. Explain who John Sutter was and what his contribution was to the settlement of California.
3. Describe the relationship between California, Mexico, England, and America towards the end of the Mexican period.
4. Articulate the impact of the following with respect to California's becoming an American territory:
    a. The efforts of Vallejo and Larkin
    b. Commodore Jones' mistake
    c. The Mexican War
    d. The Bear Flag Revolt
    e. Frémont
    f. The California Battalion
5. Be able to list two providential aspects of California's becoming an American territory.
6. Understand how Sloat's proclamation would have reassured the Californians.
7. Know the three Johns: John Sutter, John Bidwell, and John Charles Frémont. (You could add John Marsh to make it the four Johns.)

God's Providence

1. Mexican-California's many failures at self-government allowed it to eventually become a part of the United States rather than a separate country, p. 88, 97.
2. Just when the Bidwell party's supplies and spirits were almost exhausted, the men reached California, p.112-113.
3. A plan to allow 3,000 immigrants to come to California failed because it was finalized after California became an American territory, p. 121.
4. Commodore Sloat raised the flag at Monterey just before the British Admiral Seymour arrived, p. 122.

Character Sketches

(See Appendix A for further detail on character sketches)

Choose from the following:

- Jedediah Smith
- Mariano Vallejo
- John Bidwell

- John Marsh
- John Sutter
- John Frémont

California Date Song

(See Appendix C for entire song)

1821—Beginning of the Mexican period
1826—Jedediah Smith visits California
1839—John Sutter immigrates to California
1841—First overland wagon trip (Bidwell)

In eighteen hundred and twenty-one,
Mexican independence was won,
For California it was no fun,
The poor, neglected province.

In eighteen hundred and twenty-six,
A man blazed trails west through the sticks,
Of beaver pelts he took his picks,
Bible-totin' Jed Smith.

In eighteen hundred and thirty-nine,
John Sutter left his debts behind,
To settlers he was always kind,
And he built a fort in the valley.

In eighteen hundred and forty-one,
The first wagons rolled toward the setting sun,
They met John Marsh when the trip was done,
John Bidwell's seven-month journey.

Geography

(See Appendix D for further discussion of geography)

Students should continue to review previously learned geographical features while adding the following:

Lakes	**Deserts**
Goose	Mohave
Shasta	Death Valley
Lake Almanor	
Tahoe	
Clear Lake	
Mono Lake	
Salton Sea	
Honey Lake	

Journal

1. Do character sketches on Jedidah Smith and Mariano Vallejo.
2. Write a short essay discussing why the missions were destroyed. Was this good or bad?
3. Write two paragraphs discussing whether or not you would like to live on a California rancho.
4. Do character sketches on the four Johns: John Sutter, John Bidwell, John Charles Frémont, and John Marsh.
5. Write a paragraph or two describing the circumstances under which California became a military territory of the U.S.

Unit Roundup Answers

Chapter 14

1. Describe the changes in California's land between the days of the frontier men and today. Do you think these changes are good or bad? *Travel easier, less wildlife, greater control of resources. Many people have greatly benefited from these changes.*
2. What problems did Mexico have after it

became a republic? How did the Mexican republic differ from the American republic? *Was not able to govern itself and governors sent from Mexico were often corrupt. Americans governed themselves using the Bible as their standard.*

3. What evidences of Jedediah Smith's Christianity can be seen in his adventures? *His care for his men, his strong moral character, and his reliance on God.*
4. Jedediah Smith accomplished three "firsts" in his travels to California. What were they? *First to enter California from the east, first to cross Sierra Nevada, and first to travel what is now the length of the state.*
5. Who were James Pattie and Joseph Walker? *Fur trappers who came to California just after Smith.*

Chapter 15

1. What is the difference between freedom and slavery? *This question will be difficult for students, but use it to discuss the difference between freedom to sin and freedom not to sin.*
2. Why were the missions destroyed? *Greed. The Californiaos wanted the land. Also ungodly influence of French Revolution.*
3. What happened to the Mission Indians? *They lost their homes and became destitute.*
4. Do you think the destruction of the missions was good or bad? Give your reasons. *Opinion. Answers will vary.*
5. This chapter says that the Mexicans neglected the Californios. What does this mean? Give examples. *Neglect means to ignore, to give no attention to. Mexico did not send the supply ships and did not pay the soldiers salaries. Students may list other examples.*
6. How did California become a prison colony? *Mexico sent convicts to the presidios.*
7. Who was General Mariano Vallejo? Write two sentences about him. *See the biography on page 109.*

Chapter 16

1. Describe two things that appeal to you about California ranchos and two that do not. *Opinion. Answers will vary, but should include specific details about rancho life.*

Chapter 17

1. Briefly describe the first immigrant wagon train to California. *It was hard, rugged mountains to climb, shortage of water and food. Scenery was beautiful.*
2. How would John Bidwell travel from St. Louis to California today? *On an airplane, by car, bus, or train. The trip would be easy.*
3. What were some of the hardships that people on the early wagon trips encountered? *Could not bring wagons over the mountains, had to discard some of their goods, faced sickness and death.*
4. Who was Nancy Kelsey? *Only woman to continue the journey to California. Ruth 1:16.*
5. How does the saying, "It's always darkest before the dawn," apply to John Bidwell's arrival in California? Can you think of a Bible verse that applies? *When their strength and supplies were almost exhausted, they arrived in the Sacramento Valley. Gal. 6:9.*
6. Write one or two sentences describing the following immigrant wagon trains:
    a. Chiles-Walker. *Tried to bring sawmill parts to California.*
    b. Stevens-Murphy. *First to bring wagons over the mountains. Moses Schallenberger had to stay with the wagons during the winter.*
    c. Donner. *Trapped in the mountains for four months. About half of the party (forty-one people) died.*
7. Describe John Sutter. How did he help settlers come to California? *See biography on page 127.*

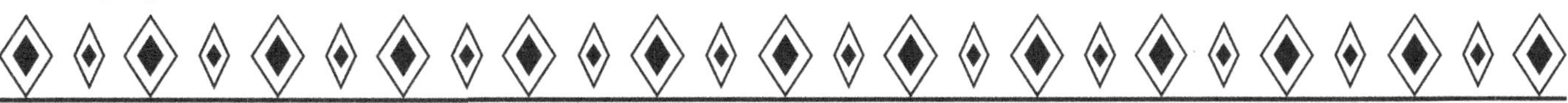

Chapter 18

1. Who was Mariano Vallejo and what country did he want California to be ruled by? *California's military governor. The United States.*
2. What was Commodore Jones' mistake? *Took possession of Monterey thinking that Mexico had declared war on the United States.*
3. How did the Mexican War begin? How did it affect California? *The war began when Mexico declared war on the United States. California became an American military territory.*
4. What was the Bear Flag Revolt? *American settlers near Sonoma took possession of the town and declared California an independent republic.*

Chapter 19

1. What was Sloat's Proclamation? List at least two of its features. *A message to reassure the Californios that they would be treated with kindness. Some features: Choosing their own local rulers, worshipping God in the way they wished, keeping land if they had lawful title to it, no taxes on goods sent from the U.S.*
2. What was providential about the U.S. conquest of California? *Two plans to secure California, one for the British (Admiral Seymour) and on for the Irish (Father McNamara) narrowly failed.*
3. Was the American conquest of California right or wrong? Defend your answer. *Answers will vary but should be defended.*
4. How might Daniel 4:17 apply to the American conquest of California? *Because God is in control of all earthly kingdoms, He gives them to whomever He pleases. If it was against God's will for America to have California, it would not have happened.*

Biblical Allusions

You will need to make sure students understand what a biblical allusion is (a subtle reference to the Bible—a verse, story, or passage) and its purpose (to make an association between the subject being discussed and the Biblical story). You might want to explain it as talking in code, but not a secret code—the reader needs to understand the Bible before he or she can understand the allusion.

1. *To Ruth's dedication to her mother-in-law and her mother-in-law's God.*
2. *To the prodigal son as he finally comes to his senses.*

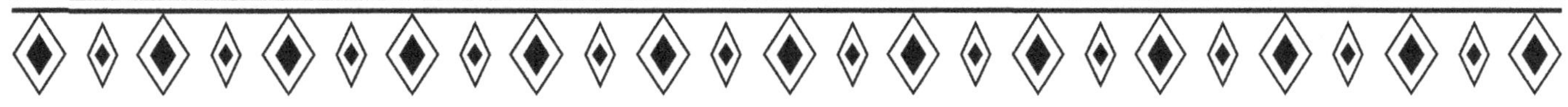

Supplemental Activities

Literature Suggestions

Two Years Before the Mast by Richard Henry Dana. Dana took some time off from his studies at Harvard College and traveled to California on a hide-trading ship. This book chronicles his adventures. The original is great, but hard to read because of some of the "nautical language." There is an abridged version, available in the Adult Basic Education section of some libraries, which would be more suitable for fourth through sixth grade. Both are highly recommended.

Cathedral in the Sun by Anne B. Fisher. This novel begins in the Spanish period with the story of a Mission Indian named Juan. Juan lives through the unstable times of secularization when the missions were destroyed. The story continues with his daughter's adventures during the Mexican period. This book is highly recommended for very strong readers or adults.

Vallejo—A California Legend by Alexander Hunter. This booklet is available from Vallejo's home in Sonoma. It would be a good supplement for a student doing a report on Vallejo.

Trappers of the West by Fred Reinfeld. A generally good book. It describes mountain men and early beaver trappers. The first few chapters are a bit dull, but filled with good information. I especially liked the chapter entitled "Mountain Men" and the biographies of John Coulter, Old Bill Williams, Jed Smith (who is properly identified, in passing, as a Christian), Jim Bridger and Kit Carson. Indians are treated fairly and realistically. From the Landmark series. Recommended.

The Forts of Old California by Michael Chester. A good explanation of Spain's, Mexico's and Russia's military fortifications, including the San Diego and Monterey presidios, Fort Ross, and Sutter's Fort. Good treatment of Mexican period-personalities including Castro, Vallejo, Sutter and Alvarado. Frémont is treated quite harshly. You might want to skip that chapter. This is part of the Sagas of California series. Recommended.

Jedediah Smith, Fur Trapper of the West by Olive Burt. A good and highly readable book about one of the greatest of all mountain men. Includes his journey to California on the Southwest expedition. Highly recommended.

God's Mountain Man by Esther Loewen Vogt. A bit easier to read than the above book by Olive Burt, but also lacking a bit in color. Recommended.

The Southwest Expedition of Jedediah S. Smith, 1826-27. This is Smith's actual journal, which chronicles part of his journey to California. Should be used by very strong readers or adults. Helpful notes make it easier to follow Smith's travels.

California Rancho Days, by Helen Bauer. See description in California Indians section of his book.

Flag of the Dreadful Bear: The Story of the Republic of California by Robert West Howard. A delightful account of the latter part of the Mexican period, 1837 to 1846, leading to the Bear Flag Revolt. Describes the time of lawlessness

and revolution that existed in California before it became an American territory. Vividly portrays the roles of Captain Frémont Thomas Larkin, General Vallejo, and William Todd. John Sutter, John Marsh, and John Bidwell are described accurately as is Bidwell's journey to California. The book is well-written and exciting. Part of the Sagas of California series. Highly recommended.

Kit Carson and the Wild Frontier by Ralph Moody. This book is part of Random House's Landmark series. One of the chapters is entitled "The Hand of the Almighty." It describes a situation where the Lord intervened to save the life of Carson and his men. The author describes Carson's early days as a mountain man, including the two expeditions where he acted as guide for Captain Frémont. It covers Carson's part in the California Conquest, and his later days as an Indian agent in New Mexico. Carson's humbleness and devotion to duty are emphasized. Highly recommended.

Kit Carson's Autobiography. Kit Carson did not learn to read and write until he was an adult. He dictated the story of his life to an acquaintance, who transcribed it into manuscript form. It remained unpublished for many years. Strong readers and adults will enjoy reading about this very famous mountain man.

First Wagons to California by Michael Chester. This book tells the story of the first emigrant train to California that was successful in bringing its wagons over the mountains—the Stevens-Murphy party. Five wagons were pulled over the mountains, but the remainder could not be moved before winter arrived. Seventeen-year-old Moses Schallenberger must spend several long months in a cabin east of the Sierra Nevada, guarding the remaining wagons. The book describes the journey and Schallengerger's lonely winter vigil. Highly recommended.

Patty Reed's Doll by Rachel K. Laurgaard. This is a great little book about the story of the Reeds' and the Donner's arduous journey to California, as told by Patty Reed's doll. When Patty was rescued by her father, she slipped the little wooden doll into her dress and carried it with her to California. The doll has been preserved at Sutter's Fort in Sacramento. This book is very suitable for young children. I read it to my daughter when she was seven. It will give students an appreciation for the hardships the settlers faced in coming to California. Highly recommended.

Note: There is a great unit to accompany *Patty Reed's Doll* available at http://www.sdcoe.k12.ca.us/SCORE/patty/pattytg.html. Unfortunately, several of the links are broken, but plenty of ideas remain to keep you and your students busy.

John Charles Frémont by Olive Burt. A fair biography of Frémont, balanced in its treatment of the controversial explorer. It covers Frémont's life from his teen years to his death. His four exploring expeditions, including his two to California, are covered in great detail. Frémont's involvement in the Bear Flag Revolt, his subsequent court martial and pardon, his short career as a California Senator and his gold mine at Mariposa are described. The narrative is fast-paced and should hold the interest of a fourth-grader.

I have two problems with this book. First, the author insists on calling Captain Frémont "Charley," even when she is describing the adult. I found this annoying. Second, she implies that Frémont worshipped nature. Little is known about Frémont's spiritual condition. Some people claim he was a Christian, although I have been unable to verify this. He did attend the Episcopal church in San Francisco with his wife (it was built around 1850). If Frémont was a Christian, these statements seem out of place. I have found no historical basis for them. Recommended with reservations noted.

Field Trips

Ranchos, horses, cows, and pueblos are the attractions for the Mexican period of California's history. Many ranchos have been reconstructed and turned into state or regional parks. If you are fortunate enough to live near one of these, it would be well worth your while to visit. My classes visited Petaluma Adobe for several years. The rooms in this reconstructed adobe have been furnished so that students can see how the adobe would have operated during the Mexican period.

Sutter's Fort in Sacramento played such an important part in California's history. If you can manage it, go! The rooms have been reconstructed and are especially fun to visit on one of the park-sponsored living history days. Even better, school groups may arrange to stay overnight at the fort and live in the 1840s for a short time.

San Diego, Los Angeles, and San Jose all contain reconstructions of their original pueblos, along with scenes from the early American period.

Rodeos & Cattle

If you do not live near any ranchos or pueblos, there are still ample opportunities for field trips. Try to visit a rodeo. The early Californians were expert horsemen. Some of their exploits can be imagined while at a rodeo.

If you live near the country, you might try to set up a tour of a cattle ranch. The cattle in the Mexican period were quite a bit smaller than the cattle of today, but students can still get an appreciation for the kind of work that the rancheros and vaqueros performed.

Sonoma

If you visit Sonoma, be sure to stop at the several attractions in the Sonoma State Historic Park, including the magnificent gift shop. Attractions include Mission San Francisco Solano de Sonoma (the only mission built during the Mexican period), Sonoma Barracks, Bear Flag Monument in the plaza, Toscano Hotel, Vallejo's home La Casa Grande (only the servant's quarters remain), and Vallejo's last home, Lachryma Montis—tears of the mountain, and one of my favorite historical homes. For more information on this and other attractions near Sonoma, visit http://www.parks.sonoma.net/default.htm.

Monterey

Monterey is a wonderful place to visit, since it was the capital of California during the Mexican period. Attractions include the Customs House where American hide traders would arrive, the home of Thomas Larkin, and Colton Hall, which was used for California's first constitutional convention.

Donner Memorial State Park

If you can visit the mountains near Tahoe, Donner Memorial State Park is an absolute must. For information and a video, go to
http://www.parks.ca.gov/?page_id=503
It's sobering to stand outside the Emigrant Trail Museum and view the monument that shows how deep the snow was during that fateful winter. You can view the location of the Schallenberger cabin and the Murphy's cabin as well as other memorabilia in the museum. I really like this museum because instead of focusing on the nefarious problems of the Donner Party, it explains the situation facing all emigrants. Although it's been a few years since I've had the pleasure of visiting, I thought the introductory video was extremely well done.

After your visit, continue down Hwy. 40 to a pull-out for China Wall. This is the last remaining part of a wall built by Chinese laborers for the transcontinental railroad. Above the wall are two old railway tunnels, No. 7 and 8, and some snowsheds to protect the trains from the elements. Visit http://cprr.org/Museum/Tunnels.html#Chinese_Wall for a picture.

Mountain Men Rendezvous

If you can find a mountain man historical reenactment near your home, even if you cannot take your class, by all means go. Not only are the activities fun, and you may be able to transport some to your classroom, you can pick up all sorts of replica mountain man equipment. Over the years, I've accumulated a good-sized box. Search for "mountain man rendezvous" or "mountain man historical reenactment."

Class-Time Activities

Report Covers

1. Materials Needed
   11 by 17-inch assorted color construction paper, tempera paint, potatoes (one per student plus some extras), cutting board, knife (to cut potatoes), kitchen knives and potato peelers for each student, plastic covers for tables, and small paper plates for paints.

2. Advance Preparation
   None

3. Objective
   To produce an artful cover for students' end-of-term reports and for thank-you notes to be sent to field trip docents. Additionally, to discuss how cattle were branded during the rancho days of California's Mexican period.

4. Procedure
   Cut potatoes in half and give one-half to each student. Student will make a "brand" by carving the potato using his potato peeler and kitchen knife. Remind student to cut away the part of the potato that should not be stamped while leaving the part that should. Additionally, remind student that letters of the alphabet should be carved backwards so that when they are printed they will be correct. See page 101 in *His California Story* for brands, although students will probably be more successful if they design more angular brands—perhaps their initials. You might draw some samples of ways to join letters or symbols.

   Give each student a piece of construction paper and direct him to fold it in half. Have him make a design on the front for his report cover. Dip the potato in the paint and make the design. Some creative students are not satisfied with decorating only the front and want to decorate the back as well.

   Have the students make extra covers to be used to make booklets of thank-you notes for field trip docents. Sometimes when I find a particularly creative design, I ask the student to make several copies of it so I can have my choice when selecting thank-you-note covers.

Bear Flags

1. Materials Needed
   Sheets (hemmed, if desired, 17.5 by 21-inch—white or off-white), tempera paint (brown, red, and black), paint brushes, small

paper cups for paint, stencils for bear and star, stencil brush, yardstick or ruler, pencils, plastic to cover tables, paper towels.

2. <u>Advance Preparation</u>
   Cut sheet into rectangles and if desired, hem. Each finished rectangle should be 17.5 by 21 inches.

3. <u>Objective</u>
   Introduce students to the Bear Flag Revolt and have them make a replica of the Bear Flag. The original flag was destroyed in the fire following the 1906 earthquake. In 1911 it became the model for our state flag.

4. <u>Procedure</u>
   Have students work from the top of their flag down, otherwise they will end up with their forearms in wet paint.

Using the star stencil or the tracing pattern, make a red star and a brown bear at the top of the flag. Write the words "California Republic" under the star and bear using a black marker, like a Sharpie. See page 120 in *His California Story* for a picture of the Bear Flag. Draw a line about three inches from the bottom of the flag and paint a red border.

Mexican Adobe Model

1. Materials Needed
   A square box (if a square box is not available you can make one out of cut pieces of cardboard), a piece of cardboard about one inch longer and wider than the box—to be used for the roof, six to eight long straight twigs that are about 2 inches longer than the width of the box, elbow macaroni, salt dough mixture for each student (one cup flour and one-half cup salt), glue, tape, and tempera paint (white, red, and brown), paint brushes and scissors. (An x-acto knife can be used under close supervision.)

2. Advance preparation
   None

3. Objective
   To make a model of a Mexican adobe. Discuss the features and construction of the adobe: the mud-brick walls covered with limestone, which made the adobe warm in the winter and cool in the summer, the stick and tile roof, and the few windows and doors.

4. Procedure
   Cut the cardboard for the back of the house about an inch or more lower than the front. Cut the sides between the front and the back so that they will slant. With a pencil, mark openings for one window and a door. Cut these out. Make sure the window is small and square. Using a pencil, punch holes in the front and back of the adobe about one half inch from the roof. Insert the twigs for the rafters through these holes. Let them stick out about one inch on either end. Glue or tape the roof to the top of the adobe.

   Mix the salt dough mixture using two parts flour to one part salt. Add water until mixture is the consistency of bread dough. Cover the roof with the mixture, then top with rows of macaroni to resemble roof tiles. Cover the remainder of the adobe with the salt dough mixture. Use extra salt-dough to make beehive ovens.

   When the paste is dry (perhaps in conjunction with the report cover activity above), paint the roof red and the rest of the adobe light brown. White paint can be mixed with brown to create a light tan color.

Diseño

1. Materials Needed
   Paper, pencils, markers, rulers, compass (optional), long piece of rope for a reata (optional).

2. Advance Preparation
   You might want to have several examples of diseños on hand, which can be found at the following websites:

- http://content.cdlib.org/ark:/13030/hb4q2nb276/?brand=calcultures
  Diseño de Rancho San José de Buenos Ayres
- http://content.cdlib.org/ark:/13030/hb100002x8/?docId=hb100002x8&brand=calisphere&layout=printable-details
  Rancho El Ricon Santa Barbara and Ventura Counties

Alternatively, you might look for a diseño of a rancho in your area. To find the name of a rancho near you, go to http://www.californiaweekly.com/ca_ranchos.htm. Then search for the name of the rancho and the word diseño, for example "Monte del Diablo Diseno."

3. Objective
To give students some experience in mapmaking and orienteering. Additionally, to build some schema so that students will understand how difficult it was to determine who owned what land, and the land's boundaries, when it became valuable during the American period.

4. Procedure
Explain to the students that to receive a grant of land, Californios needed to draw a diseño and send it to the governor, who approved the grant. Then within a year, the owner needed to build a house and a corral, plant a crop, and bring in cattle. If he did not do all of these things, according to Mexican law he did not have proper title to the land.

Diseños were maps that marked the boundaries of each rancho. Since land was plentiful and cheap in California, they were usually sketchy and boundaries were defined by a stream, hill, tree, clump of cacti, dead tree stump, pile of rocks, or an object placed in a tree.

Ask students to draw a map of their home, neighborhood, or school. The map should be oriented north ("up" on the map). Use a compass to determine north or just explain the directions to the students. Encourage students to draw their maps to scale. They may use any landmarks—natural or not—to draw their boundaries.

An optional extension to this activity is to measure distances using a *reata*, which was a 40-50 foot rope made of braided leather or horsehair. (You may choose to use thick rope from the hardware store.) Vaqueros tied a pole to each end of the reata. One drove his end into the ground, while the other rode ahead until the reata was stretched tight and drove his pole into the ground. Then the vaqueros switched places with the first one going ahead. They kept count of the number of times they stretched the reata to measure the land.

Using your measure of rope (which may be shorter than 50 feet), have pairs of students measure distances between their landmarks. One student stands still and holds one end of the rope/reata, while the other walks forward until the rope is taut. Then they switch places and record their measurements. Record distances on the diseño.

When diseños are complete, share some of them with the class and discuss what would happen if some of the markers were moved (a backpack or a car for example) or deteriorated (a tree stump or a pile of rocks). Ask students if they had any difficulties measuring distances with their "reatas." Although these maps were entirely sufficient in a country where land was plentiful and people were few, they lacked precision and caused difficulties for the American land commission when it tried to establish proper titles.

Other Ideas

Mountain Man Lingo

The mountain men had their own jargon or language that they used to talk to each other. Two glossaries of mountain men terms are at http://www.coon-n-crockett.org/cnc~glos.htm and http://www.xmission.com/~drudy/amm/gloss.html. Choose ten or so interesting words and ask students to write a dialogue between two mountain men using all ten words.

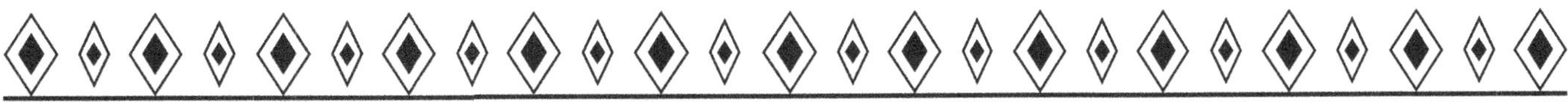

Period Music

To listen to music of the time, go to http://sdcml.homestead.com/music.html. (For more choices, search on "mountain man music."

Oral Review Questions

A fun game to play using these questions involves collecting supply cards for a covered wagon trip to California. Cut out the accompanying supply cards and mount them on colored paper—a different color for the food and household equipment sets. Divide students into groups of no more than three. Teacher asks the question and gives everyone a moment to write down their answer, keeping it secret from the other members of the group. If the student whose turn it is answers it correctly, he or she draws a supply card of their choice. If the answer is incorrect, the student to the left gets to try. (Note, this student also gets to take his or her normal turn.) The objective of the game is to collect as many supply cards as possible and to become familiar with some of the supplies a family would need to make the trip to California by covered wagon.

1. What one word best describes the way Mexico treated California? (neglect)
2. How long was California a part of Mexico? (25 years)
3. Who was called the Bible-toter? (Jed Smith)
4. Why was Jedediah Smith called the Bible-toter? (He carried his Bible with him always.)
5. What were the circumstances under which Jed Smith came to California? (He used up all of his supplies in the desert.)
6. What did Governor Echeandia think Jed Smith was? (a spy)
7. Under what circumstances did Jed Smith return to California the second time? (Half of his men were killed by the Mohave Indians.)
8. Name one other fur trapper who came to California between the two visits of Jed Smith. (Pattie or Walker)
9. What three historic firsts did Jed Smith accomplish? (first white man to enter California from the east, first to cross Sierras, and first to travel the length of the state)
10. What did the people of California want to do with the missions? (divide up the land for themselves)
11. Did the Indians want to leave the missions? (No)
12. Why didn't the Indians build their own pueblos after the missions were destroyed? (not self-governing)
13. What happened to the Indians after the missions were destroyed? (A few built pueblos, some worked at ranchos, and some sold land for liquor and became idlers or thieves.)
14. What did Mexico do with its criminals? (shipped them to California)
15. What was a fandango? (fiesta or party)
16. What happened at a rodeo? (Cattle were rounded up and branded.)
17. What can you say about the Californians' horsemanship? (superb)
18. What insect was (and still is) prevalent in California? (flea)
19. Where did the Californians get their manufactured goods during the Mexican period? (U.S.A.)
20. What did John Bidwell do before he came west? (taught school, farmed)
21. What were some of the difficulties the Bartleson-Bidwell party experienced on its way to California? (no trails, smoke blocked vision, mirages, hunger, and thirst)
22. What was the name of the only woman who stayed with the Bidwell party? (Nancy Kelsey)
23. At whose rancho did the Bidwell party arrive? (John Marsh)
24. What difficulties did the Chiles-Walker party experience in coming to California? (could not bring wagons over mountains and had to

leave sawmill parts)
25. What did the Stevens-Murphy company accomplish? (first to bring wagons over the mountains)
26. What difficulties did the Donner party experience? (trapped by winter snows)
27. What did Patty Reed bring with her to California? (her doll)
28. What did John Sutter build in California? (Sutter's Fort)
29. Why did John Sutter come to California? (escape debts and build an empire)
30. What countries were competing to obtain possession of California? (France, England, and U.S.A.)
31. Which country did General Vallejo want to have California? (U.S.A.)
32. What was Commodore Jones' mistake? (taking possession of Monterey when there was no war)
33. Why did Frémont come to California? (scientific exploration)
34. What is the Bear Flag? (flag made in honor of the Bear Flag Revolt before Californians heard of war with Mexico)
35. What did the Mexican War have to do with California? (the war, which began in Texas, spread to California)
36. What did Sloat's Proclamation say? (Californian's would be treated fairly)
37. What providential event saved California from becoming an English territory? (Sloat arrived in California before the British Admiral Seymour)
38. Why did California have to re-conquered? (Los Angeles revolted after Gillespie treated it harshly)
39. How much did the U.S. pay Mexico for the California territory? ($15 million)

Project Suggestions

(See Appendix D for a description of the class project)

1. Find out all you can about the hide and tallow trade. Draw a map to mark the routes followed by the hide ships to Boston, California, and Hawaii. What routes did the English ships follow? How were hides prepared for the trip? How were they loaded on board ship? What kinds of things did the Mexican-Californians trade their hides for? (*Two Years Before the Mast* by Richard Henry Dana has a good description of this trade.)
2. Research the old California rodeos. What kinds of activities took place? How were cattle roped? What kinds of social activities took place? What were bull and bear fights? What kinds of horses were used? How were the horses ornamented? Illustrate with pictures or build a model of a rodeo. What is a vaquero? (cowboy)
3. Find out how tortillas were made in Mexican-California. Try to make one. Grind the corn by hand on a *metate* or similar surface. Learn how to make bread as the early Californians did. What other kinds of food can you think of to make? Perhaps make a display and offer samples.
4. Make a model of a pueblo. Perhaps choose the Los Angeles pueblo. Search the Internet for information on Los Angeles Pueblo State Park, a reconstruction of the original pueblo in downtown Los Angeles. Or prepare a report on the San José Pueblo. Visit Kelley Park in San Jose. You could illustrate your report with pictures of activities that took place in a pueblo. What was the plaza used for?
5. Find out more about frontier men such as Jedediah Smith or Kit Carson. Draw maps of their expeditions. What procedures did they use to trap? What did they trap? What kinds

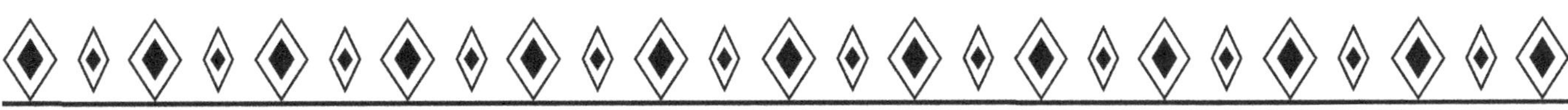

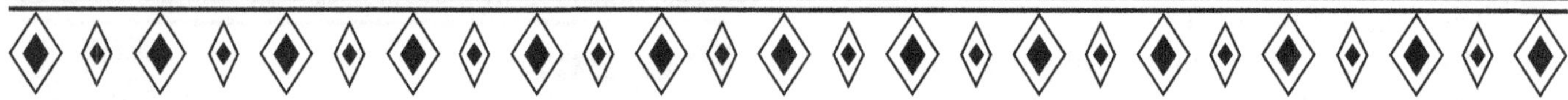

of experiences did they have with Indians?

6. Research beavers. Where do they live? What are their habits? Why were they trapped? How was their fur used? Would it be good to have a quantity of beaver near civilization today? (The forest service usually relocates beavers to remote areas because their dams create problems with water supplies.) Could you find a beaver dam?
7. How were covered wagons made? How were wagon trains assembled? How were captains selected? What happened at night? What trails were used to get to California? What difficulties did travelers faced? Research specific wagon-train parties such as the Stevens-Murphy party (*First Wagons to California* by Michael Chester) or the Donner Party. What kinds of landmarks did the pioneers look for? (Courthouse Rock, Chimney Rock, Independence Rock.) Where are they located?
8. Make a model of Sutter's Fort. Prepare a report on John Sutter. Where was he from? How did he build his fort? What activities took place there? Perhaps visit the reconstructed Sutter's Fort in Sacramento.
9. Research whales. How was the whaling trade important to California? Where did the whalers go? (The Sandwich Islands, as Hawaii was called.) Research William Richardson, who lived in what is now Sausalito. How did he help the whalers? (Through trade). How was whale oil obtained? What was it used for? Illustrate with pictures and maps. Find out what whaling ships looked like.
10. Draw pictures of some of the costumes worn by rancheros during Mexican California. Make costumes for dolls, clothespin people, or yourself. Where did the clothes come from? Learn how to embroider or do needlework like the California women did.
11. Find out which Mexican ranchos existed in your area. Find out all you can about some of the founding families. Draw a map of the ranchos. Are there any adobes that you can visit in your area?
12. Make Patty Reed's doll from a clothespin and pipe cleaners. Dress it as Patty would have. Find out how Patty and her family were rescued by their father when the Donner party became trapped in the winter of 1845-46.

Food supply cards for Wagon Trip to California game (see Oral Review p. 98).

150 lbs. flour	10 lbs. tea	50 lbs. salt
50 lbs. sugar	100 lbs. coffee	40 lbs. bacon
100 lbs. dried fruit	10 lbs. cornmeal	100 lbs. split peas
8 lbs. oatmeal	25 lbs. vinegar	50 lbs. pickles
25 lbs. dried beef	5 lbs. salt pork	5 lbs. assorted spices
5 lbs. vegetables	50 lbs. sugar	50 lbs beans

Equipment supply cards for Wagon Trip to California game (see Oral Review p. 98).

coffee grinder	clock	bedding
mirror	Dutch oven	butter churn
table and 4 chairs	piano	baby cradle
wooden bucket	lantern	butter mold
rocking chair	pitcher and bowl	cooking stove
cooking utensils	stool	spinning wheel

Source Documents

Definition of "Secularization"

From *Noah Webster's First Edition of the American Dictionary of the English Language,* 1828:

The act of converting a regular person, place or benefice into a secular one. Most cathedral churches were formerly regular, that is, the canons were of religious or monastic orders; but they have since been secularized. For the secularization of a regular church, there is wanted the authority of the pope, that of the prince, the bishop of the place, the patron, and even the consent of the people.

Decline of the Missions

Alfred Robinson, *Life in California*, Peregrine Press, Santa Barbara, 1970, (originally 1891, first published 1846).

Robinson was an American who lived in California during the Mexican period. He saw these events first hand.

Now commenced the downfall of the Missions! Echeandia retreated to St. Juan Capistrano, where he sought the co-operation of the Indians. His promises of liberty and land were sufficient to entice all from their labors, and caused the subsequent abandonment of their former pursuits. Rapine, murder, and drunkenness were the result; and, in the midst, revelled the Mexican chieftain. p. 85

Echeandia had retired to San Diego, to prepare for his return to Mexico. What a scourge he had been to California! What an instigator of vice! "Hombre de vicio," as he was called. The seeds of dishonor sown by him will never by extirpated so long as there remains a Mission to rob, or a treasury to plunder! If Mexico, in her zeal for the welfare of her territories, had been more circumspect in the choice of officers for California, she would not have experienced the humiliation that she has borne, nor incurred the expense of so many expeditions to reconquer it. Her own people have been in all cases the fomenters; and here, as has been frequently done in Mexico, they have aimed at the removal of certain governmental officers, not so much for the desire of reform, as for the division of the spoils! This is the pretended patriotism of all Mexicans who have taken active part in revolutionizing their own country, and which has been disseminated by them amongst the Californians, till, like themselves, they have become "Patriotas de bosla"! p. 99

For several years past a few evil-minded persons had sought the ruin of the missions in California, by dividing their possessions among the Indians. Various decrees had passed the Mexican Congress relative to their secularization, which were afterwards made null by counter resolutions. Here, in the territorial department, as I have before observed, the same eagerness was also manifested for their entire destruction; and rumors were afloat that the determined spirit of Sr. Padres, and the love of enterprise in Sr. Bandini, the representative of California to the Mexican Congress, had formed another more effective scheme, for the ruin of these rich and flourishing establishments. The administration of Gomez Farias, as President of the Republic, was favorable to the plan; and the powerful influence of Padres procured from his Excellency his sanction to an act of the Mexican Congress, passed on the

17th of August, 1833, entitled, "An Act, for the secularization of the Missions of the Californias; for the colonization of both territories; for the appointment of Sr. Don Jose Maria de Hijar 'Gefe politico' de la Alta California, y Director de la Colonizacion." This movement would have been political as well as advantageous, had it not been for other views, which time disclosed. The Government, actuated by motives of interest for the progress and welfare of California, had taken the grand enterprise under its protection; and "Padres," delighted to see the realization of his favorite scheme so near its fulfillment, procured for himself the appointment of "Sub Director"!

This intelligence, together with the instructions to Governor Hijar relative to colonization, &c., had been published in 'El Diario del Govierno,' and circulated throughout the Missions. It was sufficient to rouse the spirit of the holy missionaries, who had labored the greater part of their lives in fostering the interests of the Indians, and they determined to defeat, if possible, the scheme. If the property were to be destroyed they resolved that the natives of the country should reap its benefits as long as it lasted, and from this time the work of destruction went on.

At many of the establishments, orders were given for the immediate slaughter of their cattle; contracts were made, with individuals, to kill them and divide their proceeds with the Missions. At St. Gabriel, the ruin was more perceptible than at other places, owing to the superiority of its possessions. Thousands of cattle were slain, for their hides only, whilst their carcasses remained to decompose upon the plains. In this way, a vast amount of tallow and beef was entirely lost. The rascally contractors, who were enriching themselves so easily, were not inclined to avail themselves of this opportunity of so doing, to the fullest extent; but, as it was, they secretly appropriated two hides for their portion, to one on account of the Mission. A wanton spirit of destruction seemed to possess them, co-equal with their desire for plunder, and they continued to ravage and lay waste. In like manner, other interests of the establishments were neglected by the missionaries, and gradually fell to decay. His Excellency, the Governor, was soon officially apprised of the appointment of Senor Hijar to the civil command in California, and that a multitude of persons, of both sexes, were to accompany him as colonists to whom the pay of half a dollar a day was assigned till their arrival, with a free passage, and maintenance during the voyage. pp. 110-111

Many men who were appointed to look after the temporal affairs of the missions desired these appointments so that they could enrich themselves with the spoils. Many that were poor soon became wealthy, and possessors of farms, which they stocked with cattle. p. 117

Criticism of Frémont

Allan Nevins, *Frémont Pathmarker of the West* Longmans, Green and Co., New York, 1955.

Frémont is accused of acting without specific authority and, of course, that charge is true. He was six months' travel by a dangerous and difficult route from Washington; through Gillespie he had received news and letters which made him feel it was his duty to assume a certain independent responsibility. He did just what a long line of officers of the English-speaking race have always done in emergencies. The British Empire owes half its territory to subalterns, generals, ship-captains, and merchants who have acted without authority and been applauded later. Andrew Jackson had no authority in 1818 to invade the Spanish territory of Florida and seize Pensacola, but he did it. Commodore T.A.C. Jones had had no authority in 1842 for the occupation of Monterey, but he occupied it. Frémont doubtless believed that an officer who will not go beyond out-of-date and insufficient orders in an emergency, who will not use his own discretion, is not worth his salt. Admiral Sloat was such an officer, and the Administration in Washington regarded

Sloat's timidity and vacillation on the Pacific Coast as a national misfortune, making that fact quite clear to everybody.

Frémont has been accused, again, of taking action which, orders or no orders, was not justified by the facts of the California situation, or his knowledge of the general wishes of the Federal Government. But to this he could have answered that the position of the American settlers in the Sacramento Valley, as he found it on his return to that region, warranted him in the "precautionary" measures of which he wrote to Montgomery on June 16th. And so far as it went, this would have been a good answer. It is useless to deny that the fear of an Indian attack was general; Sutter himself feared it. It cannot be denied, moreover, that Castro was acting in a way which filled the American settlers with apprehension for their property and personal safety—his own orders and proclamations prove that —or that Frémont had some reason for fearing a sudden British proclamation of some form of protectorate. p. 281

Revere's Report of the Junta

Joseph Warren Revere, *Naval Duty in California*, Biobooks, Oakland, CA, 1947.

Revere records a meeting of Californios, called to discuss whether to stay under the jurisdiction of Mexico, or affiliate itself with England, France, or America.

We arrived at Monterey at a very interesting time. A Junta was in session, composed of some of the leading Californians, who had met to take into consideration what line of conduct should be adopted in the existing state of affairs. The Californians had just succeeded in getting rid of Micheltorna, the last Mexican satrap sent to plunder them and mal-administer the affairs of the Province. They had shipped him, and as many of his fustian officers and scarecrow soldiery as they could lay hands on, back to Mexico, and had elected a native of the Province, by name Jose Castro, as their commander-in-chief. The civil governor was Don Pio Pico, and the views of these two worthies entirely corresponded, both being in favor of annexation to an European power. I have been favored, by an intelligent member of the Junta, with the following authentic report of the substance of Pico's speech to that illustrious body of statesmen: "Excellent Sirs! to what a deplorable condition is our country reduced! Mexico, professing to be our mother and our protectress, has given us neither arms, nor money, nor the material of war for our defense. She is not likely to do any thing in our behalf, although she is quite willing to afflict us with her extortionate minions, who come hither in the guise of soldiers and civil officers, to harass and oppress our people. We possess a glorious country, capable of attaining a physical and moral greatness corresponding with the grandeur and beauty which an Almighty hand has stamped upon the face of our beloved California. But although nature has been prodigal, it cannot be denied that we are not in a position to avail ourselves of her bounty. Our population is not large, and it is sparsely scattered over valley and mountain, covering an immense area of virgin soil, destitute of roads, and traversed with difficulty; hence it is hardly possible to collect an army of any considerable force. Our people are poor, as well as few, and cannot well govern themselves and maintain a decent show of sovereign power. Although we live in the midst of plenty, we lay up nothing; but, tilling the earth in an imperfect manner, all our time is required to provide proper subsistence for ourselves and our families. Thus circumstanced, we find ourselves suddenly threatened by hordes of Yankee emigrants, who have already begun to flock into our country, and whose progress we cannot arrest. Already have the wagons of that perfidious people scaled the almost inaccessible summits of the Sierra Nevada, crossed the entire continent, and penetrated the fruitful valley of the Sacramento. What that astonishing people will next undertake, I cannot say; but in whatever enterprise they embark they will be sure to prove successful. Already are these

adventurous land-voyagers spreading themselves far and wide over a country which seems suited to their tastes. They are cultivating farms, establishing vineyards, erecting mills, sawing up lumber, building workshops, and doing a thousand other things which seem natural to them, but which Californians neglect or despise. What then are we to do? Shall we remain supine, while these daring strangers are overrunning our fertile plains, and gradually outnumbering and displacing us? Shall these incursions go on unchecked, until we shall become strangers in our own land? We cannot successfully oppose them by our own unaided power, and the swelling tide of emigration renders the odds against us more formidable every day. We cannot stand alone against them, nor can we creditably maintain our independence even against Mexico; but there is something that we can do which will elevate our country, strengthen her at all points, and yet enable us to preserve our identity and remain masters of our own soil. Perhaps what I am about to suggest may seem to some, faint-hearted and dishonorable. But to me it does not appear so. It is the last hope of a feeble people, struggling against a tyrannical government which claims their submission at home, and threatened by bands of avaricious strangers from without, voluntarily to connect themselves with a power, able and willing to defend and preserve them. It is the right and the duty of the weak to demand support from the strong, provided the demand be made upon terms just to both parties. I see no dishonor in this last refuse of the oppressed and powerless, and I boldly avow that such is the step I would now have California take. There are two great powers in Europe, which seem destined to divide between them the unappropriated countries of the world. They have large fleets and armies not unpractised in the art of war. Is it not better to connect ourselves with one of these powerful nations, than to struggle on without hope, as we are doing now? Is it not better that one of them should be invited to send a fleet and an army, to defend and protect California, rather than we should fall an easy prey to the lawless adventurers who are overrunning our beautiful country? I pronounce for annexation to France or England, and the people of California will never regret having taken my advice. They will no longer be subjected to the trouble and grievous expense of governing themselves, and their beef, and their grain, which they produce in such abundance, would find a ready market among the newcomers. But I hear some one say, "No monarchy!" But is not monarchy better than anarchy? Is not existence in some shape better than annihilation? No monarchy! and what is there so terrible in a monarchy? Have we not all lived under a monarchy far more despotic than that of France, or England, and were not our people happy under it? Have not the leading men among our agriculturists been bred beneath the royal rule of Spain, and have they been happier since the mock republic of Mexico has supplied its place? Nay, does not every man abhor the miserable abortion christened the Republic of Mexico, and look back with regret to the golden days of the Spanish monarchy? Let us restore that glorious era. Then may our people go quietly to their ranchos, and live there as of yore, leading a merry and thoughtless life, un-troubled by politics or cares of State, sure of what is the own, and safe from the incursions of the Yankees, who would soon be forced to retreat into their own country."

Fortunately for California, and, as the sequel proved, for the views of the government of the United States, which already embraced the acquisition by treaty or purchase of that important territory, with its fine seaports, so essential to the interests of our growing commerce in the Pacific, a man was found at this crisis whose opinions were more honest and enlightened than those of the military and civil rulers of his country. Like a true patriot, he could not endure to see the land of his birth traded away to any European monarchy, and he rightly judged, that although foreign protection might postpone, it could not ultimately avert the "manifest destiny" of California. Possessed at the time of no political power, and having had few early advantages, still his position was so exalted, and his character so highly respected by both the foreign and native population, that he had been invited to participate in the deliberations of the Junta. This man was Don Mariano Guadalupe Vallejo. Born in California, of Mexican parents, he commenced his career in the army as an "alferes," or ensign, and in this humble grade, he volunteered, at the suggestion of the Mexican government, with a command of only fifty soldiers, to establish a colony on the north side of the bay of San Francisco, for the protection of the frontier. He effectually subdued the hostile Indians inhabiting that then remote district, and laid the foundation of the reputation for integrity, judgment, and ability, unequalled by any of his countrymen. Although quite a young man, he had already filled the highest offices in the province, and had at this time retired to private life near his estates in the vicinity of the town of Sonoma. He did not hesitate to oppose with all his strength the views advanced by Pico and Castro. He spoke nearly as follows:

"I cannot, gentlemen, coincide in opinion with the military and civil functionaries who have advocated the cession of our country to France or England. It is most true, that to rely any longer upon Mexico to govern and defend us, would be idle and absurd. To this extent I fully agree with my distinguished colleagues. It is also true that we posses a noble country, every way calculated, from position and resources, to become great and powerful. For that very reason I would have had her a mere dependency upon a foreign monarchy, naturally alien, or at least indifferent, to our interests and our welfare. It is not to be denied that feeble nations have in former times thrown themselves upon the protection of their powerful neighbors. The Britons invoked the aid of the warlike Saxons, and fell an easy prey to their protectors, who seized their lands, and treated them like slaves. Long before that time, feeble and distracted provinces had appealed for aid to the all-conquering arms of imperial Rome; and they were at the same time protected and subjugated by their grasping ally. Even could we tolerate the idea of dependence, ought we to go to distant Europe for a master? What possible sympathy could exist between us and a nation separated from us by two vast oceans? But waiving this insuperable objection, how could we endure to come under the dominion of a monarchy?—for although others speak lightly of a form of government, as a freeman, I cannot do so. We are republicans—badly governed and badly situated as we are—still we are all, in sentiment, republicans. So far as we are governed at all, we at least profess to be self-governed. Who, then, that possess true patriotism will consent to subject himself and his children to the caprices of a foreign king and his official minions? But it is asked, If we do not throw ourselves upon the protection of France or England, what shall we do? I do not come here to support the existing order of things, but I come prepared to propose instant and effective action to extricate our country from her present forlorn condition. My opinion is made up that we must persevere in throwing off the galling yoke of Mexico, and proclaim our independence of her for ever. We have endured her official cormorants and her villainous soldiery until we can endure no longer. All will probably agree with me that we ought at once to rid ourselves of what may remain of Mexican domination. But some profess to doubt our ability to maintain our position. To my mind, there comes no doubt. Look at Texas, and see how long she withstood the power of the united Mexico. The resources of Texas were not to be compared with ours, and she was much nearer to her enemy than we are. Our position is so remote, either by land or sea, that we are in no danger from a Mexican invasion. Why, then should we hesitate still to assert our independence? We have indeed taken the first step, by electing our own governor, but another remains to be taken. I will mention it plainly and distinctly: it is annexation to the United States. In contemplating this consummation of our destiny, I feel nothing but pleasure, and I ask you to share it. Discard old prejudices, disregard old customs, and prepare for the glori-

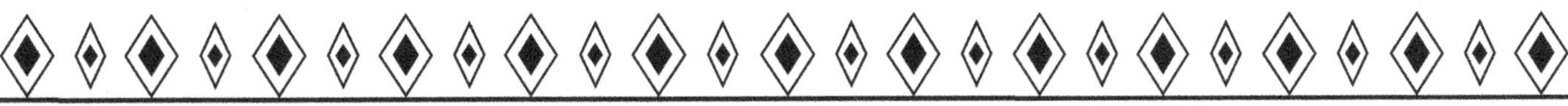

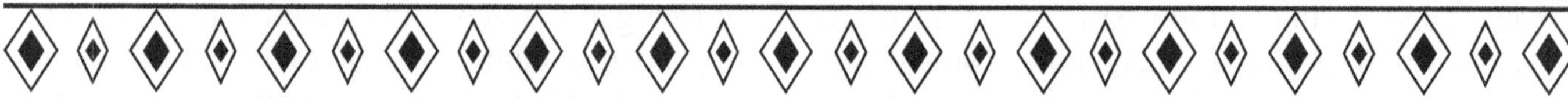

ous change which awaits our country. Why should we shrink from incorporating ourselves with the happiest and freest nation in the world, destined soon to be the most wealthy and powerful? Why should we go abroad for protection when this great nation is our adjoining neighbor? When we join our fortunes to hers, we shall not become subjects, but fellow-citizens, possessing all the rights of the people of the United States, and choosing our own federal and local rulers. We shall have a stable government and just laws. California will grow strong and flourish, and her people will be prosperous, happy, and free. Look not, therefore, with jealousy upon the hardy pioneers who scale our mountains and cultivate our unoccupied plains, but rather welcome them as brothers, who come to share with us a common destiny." pp. 19-23

Californios' Reaction to American Conquest

Walter Colton, *Three Years in California*, Stanford University, Stanford, CA, 1949 (original 1850).

Walter Colton, a Naval Chaplain, served as an alcalde *for three years after the conquest of California.*

Wednesday, March 17. I met a Californian today with a guitar, from which he was reeling off a merry strain, and asked him how it was possible he could be so light-hearted while the flag of his country was passing to the hands of the stranger. Oh, said the Californian, give us the guitar and a fandango, and the devil take the flag. This reveals a fact deeper than what meets the eye. The Californians as a community never had any profound reverence for their nominal flag. They have regarded it only as an evidence of their colonial relation to Mexico; a relation for which they have felt neither affection nor pride. p. 191

The Bear Flag Revolt

T. J. Schoonover, *The Life and Times of Gen. John A Sutter*, Johnson & Co., Printers, 1985.

After [the capture of Vallejos when] Morpheus had folded them in his gentle embrace the sleepers were approached by a band of desperadoes, under the leadership of Juan de Padilla, an outlaw, who cautiously crept to where they lay, and informed General Vallejo that he had a strong force of well armed rancheros who could surprise and kill the Americans before they could fly to arms.

Vallejo, outranking Padilla, instructed him to banish from his mind so foul a plot, which, if carried into execution, would imperil the lives of their families and strengthen the cause of the foreigners. He told Padilla he should go with his captors, and hoped for good treatment. Valor and magnanimity, he said, go hand in hand, and no people who are as brave as the Americans are can fail to be generous.

The prompt action of the patriots, which eventuated in the capture of Sonoma, is entitled to the commendation of humane, loyal and brave men. Their determination to protect themselves, their homes and their friends against unprovoked and brutal violence was cool in its inception, mild in its execution and beneficent in its tendency. A plan had been matured by the enemy to visit an immigrant train with robbery, hardship and distress. Had the Americans acted with indifference of inertly pending this plan to pillage a helpless train of their countrymen, their friends and their kindred, they would have sullied the record of American courage and patriotism. Besides this threat, those in position to grant passports to those wishing to travel through the province had refused to do so. The commander-in-chief, as we have noticed, had ordered every foreigner out of the country, under pain of death should the order be disregarded. These insults the Americans were neither prepared nor disposed to endure.

They had been lured to California by the

promise of land and the promise of protection. The land had been withheld, and instead of being protected the government was directing its arms against them. They, as well as all other Californians by adoption, had grown tired of such injustice. This fact appeared evident from the unsettled state of affairs which had existed more than twenty years prior to the Bear Flag war.

While the spirit of revolution was known to be spreading throughout the province, many were apprehensive of results prejudicial to the interest of foreigners from premature and indiscreet action. The ignorant and narrow-minded class of native Californians were jealous of the Americans, who, they claimed, were steadily encroaching upon their domain, and who, through habits of push and economy, were increasing their riches. pp. 96-97

Meanwhile, Castro sent out a proclamation calling on all good Californians to unite, and in one bold effort fall on and kill the bears of Sonoma, and then return and kill the whelps afterwards. This murderous proclamation aided greatly in increasing the garrison.

Incensed by the barbarous threat of Castro, the foreigners who had hitherto been neutral or conservative took on bolder conditions, and resolved to stand by the Americans, and on the 19th of June, the garrison of Sonoma was reinforced. p. 98

Teacher's Supplement

Gold Rush

Units 7 & 8

The Gold Rush Units

Teacher's Overview

IT IS ABSOLUTELY AMAZING TO SEE WITH historical hindsight the hand of God in the formation of the state of California. In 1846, California became a possession of the United States by military conquest. Just two years later, the treaty with Mexico was signed in which the United States purchased the California territory for $15,000,000 plus $3,500,000 in forgiven debts. This treaty was signed only nine days after the discovery of gold on California's soil, leaving no possibility for word to reach Mexico before the treaty was consummated. Clearly, God saved the discovery of gold for the Americans.

The Greedy Gold Miners

To celebrate the sesquicentennial (150th anniversary) of the Gold Rush, museums hosted displays highlighting this rich time. However, most of the exhibits contained some very disparaging remarks concerning the greedy Americans who discriminated against Chinese and Mexican miners by taxing them or running them out of the gold fields. While in no way condoning violence against any person, and recognizing that abuses did occur during this unsettled time, let's look at this situation from a slightly different perspective.

Let's postulate a discovery of gold in Russia, China, or any other foreign nation. If Americans, enticed by the riches to be had, were to rush to these fields, would they be welcomed with open arms? Hardly. The governing authorities of that nation, exercising their sovereignty, would have every right to dispel the Americans from their soil. Should they allow the Americans access to their fields, they would have every right to tax them. (By the way, the idea for a gold miners' tax originated with Chinese miners and their representatives.) Every nation has the right to control its borders, and California as an American territory was no different.

Changes, Changes, Changes

The discovery of gold brought rapid and eventful changes to California: law and order (and later lawlessness), prosperity, inflation, gambling, and most importantly, the gospel. The mission boards of many churches looked upon California as a fertile field filled with hordes of gold seekers from many foreign lands. If they could be converted in California, they would bring the gospel back to their own countries, and it would be spread even further. Many dedicated men and women made the journey to tell the Californians about the Lord. William Taylor is my favorite.

Statehood

The discovery of gold and the subsequent influx of 49'ers allowed California to become a state the following year (September 9, 1850). The state basically skipped the territorial stage, in which Congress was supposed to provide a territorial government, and proceeded directly to statehood. When California was admitted as the thirty-first state, the balance between free and slave states in the U.S. Senate was upset and the stage was set for the War Between the States.

The End of the Ranchos

The great drought of 1862-63 fundamentally ended the rancho period in California. Many rancheros were heavily in debt, partly because of unexpected lawyer fees but mostly from improvident living. The prosperity of the Gold Rush was enjoyed by the rancheros. Instead of saving some of their new wealth for the future, they spent it on lavish living, often incurring large debts. When their cattle died in the drought, they lost their source of income, and they had to sell their land to pay their debts.

The Decline of the Indian Culture

The population of the Indians in California had been steadily declining during the Mexican period. At the time of the Gold Rush, reports of the day place the Indian population at 20,000 to 30,000. Today we hear that the Americans murdered the Indians and dispossessed them of their land; however, the population had drastically declined before the Americans came. Problems continued after California became a territory and a state. Many evil men came to California as a result of the Gold Rush, who treated the Indians harshly. What we almost never hear today is how the Indians treated the settlers. Indians frequently stole from and murdered the early pioneers. It was the army's job to protect them from the Indians. Fort Humboldt, where Ulysses S. Grant served as a captain, was built to protect the settlers from the Indians of Northern California.

The U.S. government, along with many individuals such as John Bidwell, assumed the responsibility of caring for the Indians by building reservations. These were very similar to the missions set up by the Franciscan missionaries. At first Christian doctrine was not taught, but when Grant became president, he turned the administration of the reservations over to churches so that the Indians could hear about Christianity.

Gold Rush Units

Unit 7, The Gold Rush and Unit 8, Beginnings and Endings are treated together in this manual because they deal with the same time period. The Gold Rush details how gold was discovered at Sutter's Mill and the many events that followed. Thousands of people poured into California from all over the world until there were enough people living in the land to allow California to apply for statehood. Beginnings and Endings describes the events that followed, including how Christianity tamed San Francisco in just seven years, the end of the ranchos after the Great Drought, and the decline of the California Indian culture.

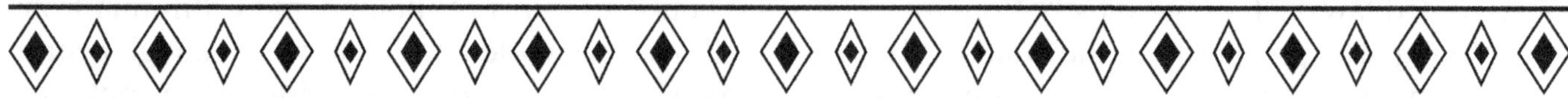

California's Constitution—A Short History

THE NOVEMBER ELECTIONS ARE APPROACHING AND you will have the opportunity to vote on proposed amendments to the state constitution. You may wonder as I did why we frequently amend California's constitution, yet rarely amend the United States Constitution. If we look at the events surrounding the formation of our state constitution, we will gain a better perspective.

California's first constitution was written in 1849. The U.S. Congress was supposed to provide a territorial government for California, yet for political reasons they delayed. (Some things never change!) Self-governing Californians took matters into their own hands and called for a constitutional convention.

Delegates from all over the state traveled to Monterey to set a course for the soon-to-be state. They included the politician William Gwin, who immigrated to California so he could become its first senator but later fell under the specter of treason. The old *Californio* families were represented as well as Americans who had become Mexican citizens, including Able Stearns (affectionately called "Horseface"). The colorful Swiss immigrant John Sutter and many newly arrived American gold seekers also made the journey to Monterey.

Chaplains were appointed so that each session would begin with prayer. These predominately young men (their average age was only thirty-six) produced a short document which defined and limited the power of the state. It was accepted almost unanimously by the Californians.

The first constitution had some interesting features. No paper money was allowed, only gold or silver coin. Californians had experienced so many problems with inflation, as gold expanded the money supply, that they wanted to prevent similar problems caused by printing paper money. No lottery was allowed and debt was strictly regulated. Additionally, legislators could not raise their own pay. Any proposed pay hike would take effect only after the voting legislators had left office.

California's first constitution had problems that became evident as the population increased. Rather than address them, delegates met in 1879 and wrote a new constitution. It is the one we operate under today.

It was not considered a total success at the time. Parts were declared invalid, and others were called an unwarranted expansion of governmental authority. California's compulsory school attendance law was instituted along with the stipulation that sectarian (which has since been defined as all Christian) materials could not be used in public schools.

The document was perceived as a move towards socialism. It even caught the attention of the father of the political system known as socialism, Karl Marx, who reported that he was watching events in California closely.

In the 1920s the Progressive political party arose, determined to break the iron grip the Southern Pacific Railroad had exercised in politics for several decades previous. The progressive candidate Hiram Johnson, who traveled the campaign trail in a red car rather than use the railroad, was elected governor.

The Progressives made significant changes to the constitution allowing direct actions by citizens. These modifications included the referendum, initiative, and recall. By gathering a certain percentage of signatures on a petition, citizens could bypass the legislature and place before the voters measures designed to overturn a law, institute a new law, or recall an elected official.

These changes signified a move away from a representative form of government in which godly men carefully formulated law. As Christians abandoned the political realm in the early 1900s, non-Christians began to expand the role of civil government.

Our constitution has been amended numerous times since its inception, and it is now a unwieldy document. The ponderous constitution is just one sign that our society has moved away from its Biblical moorings. God instituted three spheres of government for society: the family, church, and state. As Christians abandoned their responsibilities in the first two spheres, the third grew.

Recently, Christians have worked hard in politics to reverse this effect. While we support, applaud, and work along side our brothers and sisters in the political sphere, over the long run we will reclaim our government by working in the spheres of family and church.

One of the best ways to participate in the November election, in addition to studying the issues and voting, is to continue what you are doing—raising godly children. Teach them their heritage and the principles of Christian government. Who knows, you may be raising tomorrow's governor!

Road Kill History

I LOVE TO PERUSE USED BOOK SALES, ESPECIALLY THE free tables. At our group's last used book sale I picked up two books on California history, one written in 1991 and the other in 1949. Both were secular and written for public schools, but their presentation of California's story were as different as Mt. Shasta and Death Valley.

I must admit I felt a pang of jealousy as I picked up the newer book and cracked its inviting hard cover. Full-color illustrations leaped off the page giving a visual panorama of California's history. The friendly format invited students to dig in and feast as special features dotted the pages, allowing students to savor details along the way. Impressive author credentials filled two pages. Then I read the book. That cured my envy. In fact, it took me three days to read this book, and I had to force myself to continue. It was like eating cardboard.

The older book was much plainer and easy to overlook in a pile of freebies. Its line drawings and Spartan typeset functioned, but did not invite. However, I've read enough old books to realize that appearances can deceive and opened the faded and torn cover. What a rich banquet! I devoured this book in an afternoon; in fact, I couldn't put it down.

The contrast between the old and the new was so marked I had to ask myself what made the one so inviting and the other so distasteful? I found a number of differences.

The new book was written according to a formula I've seen many times before. First we learn a bit about geography, beginning with the world and funneling down to California and its natural resources. Then it's on to a chronological examination of history beginning with the California Indians (and I was surprised to hear them called "California Indians" rather than native peoples, but perhaps that change came after 1991) and continuing to the present time. The book ends with a look to the future and the many problems we as a state need to overcome, especially with respect to the environment. It's a lot of ground to cover in 350 pages.

And that's this book's biggest problem as far as I'm concerned—it covers the ground too fast. It's like students are barreling down the highway of history and see something interesting on the road ahead. But the car doesn't slow enough for a closer look. Instead it runs over the event leaving students wistfully looking back at it in the rear view mirror. I call this Road Kill History. Instead of appreciating California's rich heritage, the past becomes a confusing blend of litter.

The older book skipped the geography lesson, but included some maps labeled with the places the students would read about. Also chronological in approach, it began with the California Indians, but instead of hearing a dry recitation of what they ate, drank, and wore, we learned about these items and more through stories of three different tribes in northern, central, and coastal California. Although these stories were short on plot, they accurately described the three Indian villages and included some action and dialogue, making them more memorable.

The books differed in other ways as well. The new book goes out of its way to portray women in non-traditional roles. When discussing the ranchos in the Mexican period, we read an account of men measuring land for a Señora's rancho and another of a vaquera (cowgirl) at work. While there were rare vaqueras and rancheras in old California, the older book is more accurate when it says, "The girls were taught embroidery and sewing and how to manage a house. The boys followed their fathers in raising horses and cattle."

Times have changed and women of our time do have more opportunities than those who lived before us. However, it is misleading to read a feminist agenda back into the past. The old book, characteristic of most books of that time, concentrates on stories of men, omitting almost all mention of women, which is just as wrong. We need to hear about women in history, but in their true roles, not in what someone of our times thinks their roles should have been.

Finally, the newer book misleads. When speaking of Gold Rush times it says, "These Americanos, as the Californios called them, acted if California were all theirs." Wait a minute—wasn't it? At the conclusion of the Mexican War in 1848, weren't conquered Baja and Northern California returned to the Mexicans and the California Territory purchased? Didn't the Treaty of Guadalupe Hidalgo seal the purchase and transfer? While providing safeguards for the Californios already living in coastal and central California, didn't the treaty state the mountainous Gold Rush area belonged to the United States?

As I finished my comparison, I thought about the students who learn about California's history by reading the new book. Not only are they getting an incomplete flavor of the time, they are being starved. History doesn't have to be anemic. It's full of a rich blend of people and their stories. It's time to stop the car and savor the true historical moments.

Teaching the Gold Rush Units

Lesson Plans

Unit 7

1. Introduction ideas:
   Both of these activities work well to introduce the Gold Rush units—one simple and one complex.

- When the Rev. William Taylor came to California to minister to the gold miners, he asked them a very important question: "For what is a man profited, if he shall gain the whole world, and lose his own soul? or what shall a man give in exchange for his soul?" (Matthew 16:26). You might begin this unit with a devotion. Ask your students the same question. Explain the allure of gold and the difference between treasure in heaven and treasure on earth (Matthew 6:19-21).
- Turn your room into a gold mining camp. (For more ideas about this project, see *Tales and Treasures of the California Gold Rush: Hands-on History*.)
  a. First, select a colorful name, similar to the names of actual Gold Rush towns: Hangtown, Poverty Hill, Dry Town, Volcano, Angel's Camp, Rough and Ready, Liar's Flat, and Slumgullian. Divide students into groups and ask each to select a name and make up a story that explains the name. Let them present their idea to the other students, and then let the students vote on a name.
  b. Decorate the town. Obtain large pieces of butcher paper and draw one or two typical buildings found in a mining camp: a bank, store, recorder's office. Fill the room with signs: the name of town and its population, distances from it to other towns, perhaps some Wanted Posters for local bandits.
  c. Determine laws for your town. How will miners mark a claim or abandon it? How will laws be enforced?

2. Introduce the Gold Rush period of California's history (Ch. 20). Teach the gold discovery verse (1848) of the "California Date Song." Do Roundup questions.
3. Do a character sketch on James Marshall. If students have previously done a character sketch on John Sutter, ask them to add information to it.
4. Teach about the different routes to California (Ch 21). Trace the routes on a map and discuss the pros and cons of each. Do Roundup questions.
5. Teach the different mining methods.
6. Do the gold-panning activity.
7. Teach about life in the mines (Ch. 22) and do Roundup questions.
8. Teach the results of the Gold Rush (Ch. 23) and do Roundup questions.
9. Do the Inflation Demonstration.
10. Teach the statehood verse (1850) of "The California Date Song."
11. Play a review game for Unit 7 using the Oral Review Questions.

Unit 8

1. Explain Christianity's effect on San Francisco (Ch. 24). Do Roundup questions.
2. Teach "The Royal Proclamation."
3. Do the Letters to Home activity.
4. Do character sketches on the two Williams: William Taylor and William Coleman.
5. Teach the Vigilance Committee (1856) verse of "The California Date Song."
6. Explain how the ranchos lost their influence

and became smaller farms (Ch. 19). Do Roundup questions.
7. Teach the great drought (1862-63) verse of "The California Date Song."
8. Teach the mountains of California.
9. Discuss the decline of the California Indians (Ch. 26) and do Roundup questions.
10. Play a review game using the Oral Review Questions for Unit 8.

Objectives

Objectives for Unit 7

At the completion of this unit students should:
1. Be able to describe the circumstances under which gold was discovered in California.
2. Articulate why the presence of gold might have been kept a secret during the Spanish or Mexican periods.
3. Describe the providential aspects of the discovery of gold.
4. Understand what inflation is and what it causes.
5. Articulate the Christian missionaries' opinion as to why God caused the Gold Rush.
6. Explain why Congress was reluctant to provide a territorial government for California.
7. Describe at least one interesting feature about California's first constitution.

Objectives for Unit 8

At the completion of this unit students will be expected to:
1. Describe early life in San Francisco and how Christianity was able to tame it.
2. Identify at least two Christian missionaries who came to minister in California and describe their work.
3. Explain why the citizens of San Francisco felt the need to organize a Vigilance Committee, describe its purpose, and discern whether these actions were right or wrong.
4. Describe some of the problems that the Land Commission had as it tried to determine the lawful owners of the land.
5. Articulate the effect of the great drought on the Californios.
6. Explain what happened to the California Indians' way of life.
7. Describe John and Annie Bidwell's work among the Indians of California.
8. List some ways in which the Indian culture benefited from contact with the American Christian culture.

God's Providence

1. Gold was discovered on January 24, 1848, just nine days before the Treaty of Guadalupe Hidalgo was signed (February 2, 1848), in which California was purchased by the United States. Since communication was slow, there was no chance for word of the discovery to reach Mexico, p. 132.
2. Although small amounts of gold had been known to exist in California prior to 1848, God did not allow these discoveries to be exploited until California was securely a part of the United States, p. 132.
3. The discovery of gold, along with American possession, allowed Christian missionaries to bring the gospel to California, p. 142.
4. A rapid increase in population along with self-governing Christians who formed a state constitution, allowed California to become a state without passing through the formal territorial stage, p. 144.
5. According to William Taylor, the many fires that San Francisco experienced were a judgment on the wicked city. They were a warning sign from God, which the city heeded as it repented, p. 157.

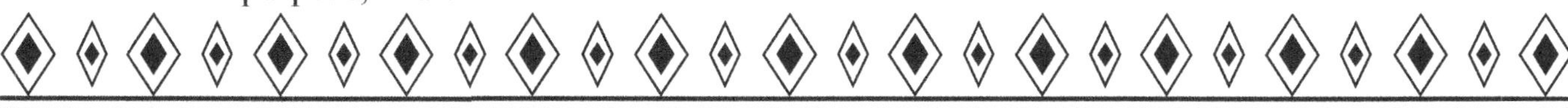

6. After sending one of the wettest winters on record, God sent a drought which dried up all of the wild grasses. This caused cattle to die by the thousands, and consequently, the ranchos had to be sold to pay off debts. The rancho period ended, although provident Californios prospered under American rule, pp. 162-163.
7. Christian work was able to begin again among the Indians of California as missionaries and Christian workers began to share the news that Jesus Christ died to save the Indians from their sin, p. 166.

Character Sketches

(See Appendix A for further detail on character sketches)

Choose from the following:

- James Marshall
- John Sutter (make additions if previously chosen)
- Lewis Manly
- Isaac Owen
- William Taylor
- William Coleman
- John Bidwell (make additions if previously chosen)

California Date Song

(See Appendix C for entire song)

1848 - Gold discovery
1850 - Statehood
1856 - Vigilance Committee
1862-63 - Great Drought

In eighteen hundred and forty-eight,
James Marshall found a shining bait,
Soon men would flood the Golden Gate,
In the California Gold Rush.

In eighteen hundred and fifty years,
Congress overcame its fears,
And a thirty-first star appeared—
California joined the Union.

In eighteen hundred and fifty-six,
San Francisco's Coleman was called to fix,
Its crimes and murders and corrupt politics,
With the Vigilance Committee.

In eighteen sixty-two and three,
First flood, then drought, oh mercy me!
Dead cattle led to bankruptcy,
And the end of the old ranchos.

Geography

(See Appendix D for further discussion of geography)

Review and add the following:

Mountains:

Mt. Shasta
Mt. Lassen
Lava Beds
Mt. Whitney
San Gorgonio
San Jacinto

Journal

1. Do character sketches on James Marshall and Lewis Manly. Add to your character sketch on John Sutter.
2. Find one Bible verse regarding what the

Bible says about gaining wealth or riches.
3. List at least two reasons the Gold Rush was providential.
4. Write an essay describing how God planned and guided California from the time of the Indians until statehood in 1850.
5. Do character sketches on the two Williams: William Taylor and William Coleman.
6. Write a short essay describing the actions of the Vigilance Committee and discussing whether these actions were right or wrong.
7. Describe how Christianity was able to tame San Francisco in just seven years.
8. Read Matthew 25:14-30. Does it apply to this time period?
9. Read Deuteronomy 28. Does it apply to this time period?

Unit Roundup Answers

Chapter 20

1. Describe the way gold was discovered in California. Who made the discovery? *James Marshall discovered gold while digging a channel for Sutter's sawmill.*
2. Explain why gold might have been found during the Spanish or Mexican periods but kept secret. *In the Spanish period it was kept secret so that it would not affect the work of the missions; in the Mexican period so that people would not lose their land.*
3. What was providential about the timing of the gold discovery? *It was not discovered until California was secure as an American territory (nine days before the treaty was signed).*

Chapter 21

1. Describe the three ways people traveled to California. Which way would you choose and why? *Around the Horn, across the Isthmus of Panama, and across the plains. Opinion, answers will vary.*
2. Why should Lewis Manly and John Rogers be considered heroes? *Even though they had made it to safety, and even though their journey had taken much longer than anticipated, they risked their lives to rescue the rest of their party stranded in Death Valley.*
3. Why are the people who rushed to California called "forty-niners"? *It took almost a year for word of the gold to reach the rest of the world and for people to travel to California. Most arrived in 1849.*

Chapter 22

1. Describe different ways to pan for gold. *Panning, cradle, and long tom or sluice.*
2. Why do you think Mrs. Phelps made more money selling apple pies than her husband did mining for gold? *Because there were so few women in the mines, and apple pies were in high demand.*
3. How was Rev. Anthony rewarded when he obeyed the fourth commandment? *He kept the Sabbath holy even when his partners did not and was blessed by finding gold the next day.*

Chapter 23

1. What is inflation and what does it cause? *An increase in the supply of money (gold) which causes prices to rise.*
2. Why did the first Christian ministers come to California when gold was discovered? *They followed their congregations to minister to them.*
3. Describe the hardships of the Owen family. *All of their belongings were lost in the Sacramento River, their house in Sacramento was destroyed by a flood, and their baby daughter died.*
4. How was law and order a result of the Gold Rush? *Self-governing Americans came to California and instituted courts and systems*

of law.

5. The Christian ministers believed God caused the Gold Rush for what reason? *To spread the Gospel.*
6. Why didn't the U.S. Congress provide a territorial government for California? *If California were to become a territory and then a state, the balance of power between the slave and free states in the senate would be destroyed.*
7. Describe California's first Constitutional Convention. *Congress had failed in its duty to provide a government; therefore forty-eight delegates got together from all of California to write the constitution. Sessions began with prayer.*
8. On what day did California become a state? What do we call this holiday? *September 9, 1850. Admission Day.*

Chapter 24

1. Describe early (1850-1856) life in San Francisco. *Wild. Crime and gambling flourished.*
2. Name the first Christian ministers to come to San Francisco and describe how they helped to tame the city. *Rev. T. Dwight Hunt, Rev. O.C. Wheeler, William Taylor, and Isaac Owens. They faithfully preached God's Word.*
3. How many men listened to William Taylor's first sermon on Portsmouth Square? How many men do you think would listen to him today? What does this tell you about modern San Francisco? *One thousand men. Opinion, answers will vary.*
4. Why were there so many fires in early San Francisco? *Some set deliberately, lack of fireproof buildings, and according to William Taylor, perhaps a judgment from God.*
5. Why was the Vigilance Committee formed and what did it do? *A group of men who tried to help stop crime. The people took the law away from corrupt officials and enforced it.*
6. Do you think the actions of the Vigilance Committee were right or wrong? Explain your answer. *Opinion. Answers will vary.*

Chapter 25

1. What were some of the problems the Land Commission experienced with California property? *Boundaries or ownership overlapped, boundary marks were not permanent—they disappeared with the passage of time, people took land that they thought was vacant, some did not build homes and do other things as required by law, and some got land by fraud.*
2. How did the Gold Rush affect the Californios? *They became wealthy because the price of land and cattle increased.*
3. What providential event caused the break-up of many ranchos? *The Great Drought of 1862-63.*
4. Read Matthew 25:14-30 and tell how it applies to the Californios. *They didn't handle their wealth wisely or plan for the future. Instead they spent money on frivolous things.*

Chapter 26

1. Write two or three sentences describing the conflicts between the settlers and the California Indians. *Horse thefts and raids, Indians hard to employee, killings on both sides, reservations run by corrupt officials (at first), Christian missionary work on reservations.*
2. How did Annie Bidwell minister to the Indians of Rancho Chico? *Taught them—reading, sewing, arithmetic, home-making. Worked with the General to teach them Christianity.*
3. In what way did the California Indians benefit from contact with the Americans? *Food, shelter, comfort, education, women's rights, Christianity.*

Supplemental Activities

Literature Suggestions

The Rush for Gold by Frank L. Beals. This book is actually a biography of John Bidwell, one of the members of the first wagon train to travel to California in 1841. It follows his life in California through the Gold Rush. Bidwell worked for Sutter when gold was discovered. If circumstances had turned out a little differently, he would have gone down in history as the discoverer of gold. Recommended.

By the Great Horn Spoon by Sid Fleischman. When young Jack learns of his aunt's financial problems, he joins the rush to California's gold fields with his aunt's butler, Praiseworthy. The two meet adventure at every step, from the time they stow away onboard ship, to their arrival in California, to their adventures in the gold fields. Newberry Medal winner. Students love this book. Highly recommended.

They Rode the Frontier by Wyatt Blassingame. Contains a story called "William Taylor and the California Gold Rush." This is a great short story about William Taylor, San Francisco's first street preacher. Rev. Taylor worked himself out of a job. It only took seven years for Christianity to subdue San Francisco, so Taylor moved on to other missionary fields. This story is about his early years in San Francisco. Recommended.

The Gold Discovery by William C. Dillinger. This colorful booklet has great photos and pictures to illustrate the California Gold Rush. It would be a good resource for a student doing a project on the discovery of gold in California.

The Gold at Sutter's Mill by Conrad Stein. A good, fast-paced, short book about life among the miners during the Gold Rush. Covers events from the discovery of gold until about 1855. A Cornerstones of Freedom book. Recommended.

The California Gold Rush by May McNeer. Excellent description of early Gold Rush days. Author uses facts and source documents to weave a readable tale. Accurate flavor of the time. Omits the fact that Walter Colton was a chaplain in the Navy and a Congregational minister. Part of Random House's Landmark series. Highly recommended.

California Gold Days by Helen Bauer. See description in the "California Indians" section.

The Story of San Francisco by Charlotte Jackson. Part of Random House's Landmark series. This easy-to-read, fast-paced book describes life in San Francisco and the men who lived there from the days before the Gold Rush until after the 1906 earthquake and fire. Like most of the Landmark books, it is excellent. Highly recommended.

Other Landmark books for this period include:
The Panama Canal by Bob Considine
Clipper Ship Days by John Jennings

A Frontier Lady by Sarah Royce. Sarah Royce records her recollections of the Gold Rush and life in early California. Mrs. Royce was a Christian who had a spiritual experience in the desert, which drew her even closer to her Lord. She describes churches in California and mining camp

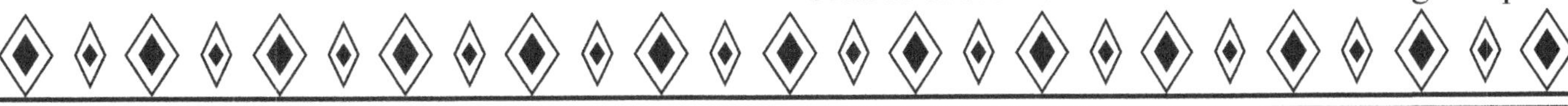

life. A very good book. Recommended for strong readers and adults.

Excerpt from *Roughing It* by Mark Twain. Available at http://www.glittering.com/letters/mtwain.html. A colorful and engaging account of the men who made their way to California. Short. Recommended for strong readers and adults.

"The Discovery of Gold in California" by Gen. John A. Sutter. Available at http://www.sfmuseum.org/hist2/gold.html. Originally printed in *Hutchings' California Magazine* November 1857, this is Sutter's account of the gold discovery. Recommended for strong readers and adults.

Field Trips

A visit to the gold country might be a profitable and enjoyable venture at this time. Columbia State Park has been reconstructed as a period Gold Rush town, and a video is available on the California State Parks website. Students can pan for gold in the park. When I organized a field trip to this park several years ago, I learned of an actual gold mine that our group got to tour. It's worth checking out.

Jamestown and Sonora also provide opportunities for gold panning, along with a gold rush flavor. Coloma, where James Marshall discovered gold, has been turned into a state park, with a video available online. Empire Mines in Grass Valley was once a working gold mine. Today visitors can preview it through a state park video, or see the restored cottage, peer into the mine shafts, and view an extensive model of the mine. Empire Mines is especially fun to visit during one of its living history days. Although it takes some time to travel to, Malakoff Diggings shows the results of hydraulic mining—huge, bare hillsides denuded before this destructive mining method was outlawed. If you can't make it, the state park website contains numerous pictures in their photo gallery.

When studying California's entrance to the Union, a visit to the state capitol is almost a requirement. Tours can be arranged for groups of students in addition to the tours that are open to the general public. If you live some distance from Sacramento, you might consider an overnight camping trip, which would allow you to visit the capitol, Sutter's Fort, the State Indian Museum, the California State Railroad Museum, the Crocker Art Museum (where the painting "Sunday Morning in the Mines" hangs), the Governor's Mansion, and perhaps a side trip to Coloma. If camping is not your thing, there's a great hostel in Sacramento, a restored mansion. And if traveling is not your thing, you can watch several videos on the parks' website.

Finally, if you live in Northern California, a visit to Bidwell's Mansion near Chico is a real treat. If you don't, you may watch a video showcasing the mansion and the Bidwells' lives on the California State Parks website.

Nothing beats visiting the sites in person, but if that is not possible, several other video clips are available on the Internet. In addition to the above, other state park videos worth checking out include Bale Grist Mill and Bodie (preview first—ghost stories). Another website that offers panoramic views of various sites (Gold Rush and others) is www.virtualguidebooks.com.

Working Gold Mines

Several working gold mines offer tours. Not only are these informative, there is something mysterious in actually seeing the gold in the earth. To find a gold mine near you, search the Internet for "California working gold mine tours."

Class-Time Activities

Panning for Gold

This is my students' favorite activity.

1. Materials Needed
   A pan with sloping sides (a pie pan without ridges or a gold pan purchased from a museum gift shop, a state park gift shop, or online), sand (sandbox sand is fine as long as it doesn't contain a lot of extra debris), a larger container with a flat bottom to hold the sand and water, and the gold. To find gold flakes, search online for "gold vial." Small vials of gold flakes are also available at several state parks and museums. You might also order some small vials for each student so they can store the gold they find. It's a very inexpensive gesture that gives a lot of pleasure.

2. Objective
   To allow students to experience gold-mining techniques as well as the joy that accompanies a strike.

3. Procedure
   I usually do this activity in conjunction with another so that I don't have to set up multiple

panning stations or purchase multiple gold pans. Allow students to work in pairs. Place some sand and water in the pan and demonstrate the panning motion—side-to-side to let the gold sink to the bottom of the pan and then circular to let some of the sand mixture escape over the side to reveal the gold at the bottom. (For a more complete explanation of how prospectors pan for gold along streams, search the Internet for "How to pan for gold.") Let students practice these motions for a time.

Next, fill the pan with a small amount of sand, place a gold flake on the sand, fill the pan with water and shake gently. The heavier gold flake should sink to the bottom of the pan, but should still be visible when students gently swirl their sand.

Several state parks and gold mining attractions have gold mining stations where gold is mixed with sand in a long trough. Students dip their pans in the trough, scoop out some sand, and try to find the gold. I don't pour my vial of gold flakes into my sand because I tend to lose the gold. Placing a flake in each pan assures that each student will be successful in striking it rich.

Inflation Demonstration

Because inflation is a very difficult concept to understand, even for adults, I have used the following demonstration to make it easier for students to comprehend. It is just a little more complex than the example in the book.

1. Materials Needed
   "Pieces of gold" (I've used gold foil-covered chocolate candy, or pennies)
   An object to buy (a notebook, toy, or pencil box—whatever is handy)
   Four students: the gold mine, the gold miner (shopper), the storekeeper (seller), and the supplier.

   Note: This demonstration can also be illustrated with one student and a parent. The pieces of gold can be placed at the "gold mine," and the role of the supplier can be explained. (For example, the storekeeper can talk out loud and say, "Oh no! The price of this toy has gone up to fifteen pieces of gold. Now I am making the same profit as I did before!")

2. Objective
   To understand the following:
   - Definition—Inflation is an increase in the supply of money.
   - Effects—Causes prices to rise.

3. Procedure

Demonstration One

a. The storekeeper starts with five pieces of gold. (Give the rest of the gold to the student who will be the gold mine.) The storekeeper goes to the supplier and buys a toy for five pieces of gold, and then brings it back to his store.
b. The storekeeper sets the price for the toy at ten pieces of gold and opens for business.
c. The gold miner goes to the gold mine and finds ten pieces of gold (student portraying gold mine gives these to him).
d. Next, the gold miner goes to the store and buys the toy for ten pieces of gold. Explain that everyone is satisfied with the transaction. The gold miner has his toy, and the storekeeper and supplier have both made a profit.

Demonstration Two

a. The gold miner goes to the gold field and finds twenty pieces of gold. He is happy because now that his supply of money has increased, he can buy two toys.
b. The storekeeper realizes that the gold miner has more money now, so he increases the price of the toy to twenty pieces of gold.
c. The gold miner tries to buy two toys, but finds that even though his supply of money has increased, or inflated, he cannot buy more goods. He again buys the one toy, but this time for twenty pieces of gold.
d. At this point the students will think that the storekeeper is the winner in this demonstration. Have the storekeeper go to the supplier and buy another toy. The supplier realizes that the storekeeper's money supply has been inflated, so he increases his price to fifteen pieces of gold.
e. At the end of the transaction no one is better off. Even though the gold miner found twenty pieces of gold, he was able to buy only one toy. Even though the storekeeper increased his price, his profit did not increase because the supplier increased his costs. Inflation, an increase in the money supply, did not bring more prosperity; it only caused prices to rise.

Objections

a. Students will think that the supplier was the winner in the second demonstration. Explain that in the real world his costs would have been increased as well so that his profit would remain the same.
b. Perceptive storekeepers, once they realize that they can set the price for the toy, will try to set it as high as they can, often higher than twenty pieces of gold. Let them, and then explain that the gold miner cannot buy the toy since he only has twenty pieces of gold. Prices cannot rise unless the money supply is increased.

After this demonstration, you might explain that inflation usually accompanies large finds of gold, but it can also be caused by governments, like our own, which print paper money. Do not expect students to fully understand this concept; however, by being introduced to it at an early age, they will have a foundation upon which to build when they study more complex economic issues.

For a more complete description of inflation and its effects, see *Whatever Happened to Penny Candy?* by Richard J. Maybury.

The Royal Proclamation

The song that Rev. William Taylor used to "sing up a crowd" before he preached in early San Francisco follows. Teach it to your students. (Next page.)

Letters to Home

Look at some of the letters at this site, http://www.glittering.com/letters/index.html, that the 49ers sent to their families at home. Choose several and share them, or parts of some of them, with your students. Analyze them with your students, and make a chart of their features. Are there ideas that recur in the letters? What is life like in the gold fields? What difficulties do the miners face? What do they seem to miss the most?

After spending some time discussing the miners' letters, ask students to assume the persona of a gold miner (pretend he or she is a gold miner) and write their own letter to their families.

To the Gold Fields Game

This activity requires quite a bit of advanced preparation, but might be worth it. Create a game for groups of students to play that teaches what a 49er might experience as he or she travels to the gold fields. Players should have the choice of several routes. One example of a game is at http://tinyurl.com/2uf95b. You might use some of this game's ideas to make your own.

Oral Review Questions

1. How was gold discovered at Sutter's Mill? (noticed while digging the channel under waterwheel of sawmill)
2. How did Sutter react to the discovery? (asked that it be kept secret)
3. Did Sutter prosper from the discovery? (no)
4. True or false: The gold discovered at Sutter's Mill was the first gold ever found in California. (false)
5. Why didn't God allow gold to be discovered while the Spaniards or Mexicans ruled California? (Providence, missionaries afraid would affect work of missions, Californian's thought might lose land)
6. How did the people of California react to the news of the gold discovery? (skepticism at first, then everyone dropped everything and raced to the mines)
7. What were the three methods of travel used to get to California? (around the horn, across the plains, and by way of the isthmus)
8. What is Lewis Manley famous for? (going for help and returning to rescue a party stranded in Death Valley)

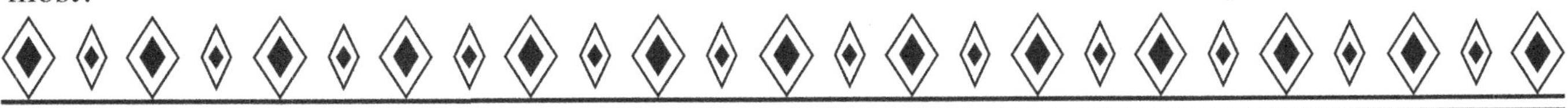

Royal Proclamation

1. Hear the roy - al pro - cla - ma - tion The glad tid - ings
2. See the roy - al ban - ner fly - ing Hear the her - alds
3. Ho! ye sons of wrath and ru - in Who have wrought your

of sal - va __ tion Pub - lished now to ev - ery crea __ ture
loud - ly cry __ ing Reb - el sin - ners roy - al fa __ vour
own un - do __ ing Here are life and full sal - va __ tion

To the ru __ ined sons of na __ ture.
Now is of __ fered by the sav __ iour.
Of __ fered to __ the whole cre - a __ tion.

refrain

Lo! He reigns, He reigns vic - to - ri - ous

ov - er hea - ven and_ earth, most glo - ri - ous Je - sus reigns.

4th Verse:

Here are wine and milk and honey
Come and purchase without money;
Mercy like a flowing fountain,
Streaming from the Holy Mountain.

5th Verse:

For this love let rocks and mountains,
Pushing streams and crystal fountains
Roaring thunders, lightning blazes
Shout the great Messiah's praises.

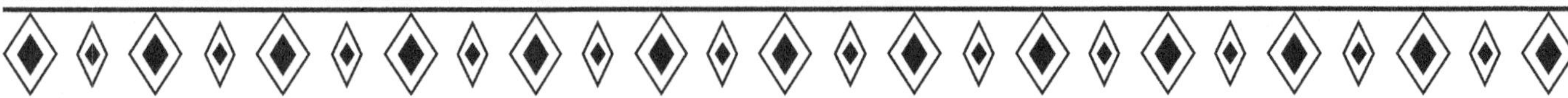

9. What were the three common methods of water (gold) panning? (pan, cradle, long tom)
10. What did men do on Sundays while they were at the mines? (rested, worshipped, read Bible, wrote letters, mended clothes, various recreation, gambled)
11. Was it easy to pan for gold? (No, it was hard work.)
12. Name some consequences of the Gold Rush. (inflation, gambling, Christian ministers, law and order, and prosperity)
13. Describe the hardships of the Owen family. (hard trek across plains, lost all possessions as boat sank to bottom of Sacramento River, home destroyed in a flood, daughter died)
14. We say the miners in the early mining camps were self-governing. What does this mean? (obeyed Bible willingly instead of having to be forced)
15. How many states were already in the Union when California joined? (30)
16. What happened to the Union when California became a state? (balance between slave and free states forever destroyed)
17. Name one of the provisions found in California's first constitution (see p. 145)
18. When did California become a state? (September 9, 1850)
19. What was San Francisco called at first? (Yerba Buena)
20. Where did the men of early San Francisco live? (tents or boarding homes)
21. Who was San Francisco's first street preacher? (William Taylor)
22. Describe William Taylor's first preaching at Portsmouth Square. (What will a man profit if he lose his own soul...)
23. How did the early San Francisco ministers work with each other? (in unity and harmony)
24. What did William Taylor do when a shark was sighted on his way to California? (continued to read his Bible)
25. Name some of William Taylor's missionary efforts in California. (street preaching, hospital, Bethel)
26. What did William Taylor do after he left California? (Brought gospel to every continent. Crossed equator 37 times)
27. Why did San Francisco suffer such severe fires? (God's judgment, poor construction, set as diversions for crime)
28. What was the Vigilance Committee? (group set up to restore law and order in San Francisco)
29. Were the actions of the Vigilance Committee right or wrong? (Opinion. Answers will vary)
30. What do we know about William Coleman? (head of Vigilance Committee, millionaire, worked to pay debt)
31. Why did the Americans have such a hard time trying to determine who lawfully owned the land in California? (marked with boundary marks that could easily disappear over time, granted by someone who did not have authority, disobeyed laws, outright fraud)
32. What happened to the Californios in the early years of the Gold Rush? (prospered)
33. What did the Californios do with their new-found wealth? (most spent on rich living)
34. What finally caused the end of the ranchos? (severe flood then drought)
35. What kinds of problems existed between the Indians and Californios after the missions were destroyed? (horse theft, violence, massacre)
36. How did the Indians benefit from contact with the American Christian culture? (standard of living increased, women escaped drudgery, heard about Jesus Christ)
37. What did John Bidwell do to help the California Indians? (built a village for them on his land, wife helped to train them)

Project Suggestions

1. Visit Gold Discovery State Historic Park in Coloma. Do a report on the discovery of gold. Perhaps make a model of Marshall's sawmill. Where is Coloma? Find out more about James Marshall.
2. Find out more about gold. How has it been used in history? What is a carat? Why is metal mixed with gold to make jewelry? How much is gold worth? How can you buy gold? What is Fort Knox? When did the United States go off the gold standard? What has happened to our money since?
3. How is gold mined? How is it processed? What is quartz mining? Hydraulic mining? Visit Colombia State Historic Park. Visit Empire Mine.
4. Try your hand at panning for gold. Expeditions are offered at Jamestown as well as at many other places. What kind of equipment is needed? What kinds of problems would miners encounter? (Hard to get supplies, have to stand in freezing water, and health problems, for example.)
5. Write a story about mining life. Describe how the miners lived, how they cooked their meals, what they did for entertainment, how they washed their clothes, what they did with their leisure time. Who was Bret Harte? (An early California author who wrote about California. Some of his stories are questionable.)
6. Make a map of the Mother Lode region showing the location of different mining towns.
7. Make a model of a gold mining scene.
8. Find out who Sarah Royce was. (See *A Frontier Lady* by Sarah Royce—she was one of the few women in the mining camps.) Do a report on the Royce family. Pretend you are Sarah Royce and write a letter to home. Describe your experiences and feelings.
9. Make models of various mining equipment such as a long tom, cradle, or sluice. Describe how they work.
10. Make a model of a millrace and a waterwheel. Describe how the waterwheel could be used to run machinery. Visit Bales Grist Mill at Bothe-Napa State Park. How is a grist mill similar to a sawmill?
11. Find out what the miners did in their leisure time. What was a miners' ball? Who was Lotta Crabtree?
12. Do a report on the ways that pioneers reached the gold fields. Show the sea routes around South America and across the Isthmus of Panama, as well as the various overland routes. Why would a person choose one route over another? Illustrate your report with maps and/or pictures. Pretend you are traveling one of the routes, and write a letter home describing your adventure.
13. Research the location of the state capitol before it settled in Sacramento. Visit the site of the capitol in Benicia. Take a tour of the capitol in Sacramento. Describe what goes on there.
14. Find several Bible verses that state that God controls the weather.

Source Documents

First Protestant Service in San Francisco

William Warren Ferrier, *Pioneer Church Beginnings and Educational Movements in California*, Berkeley, 1927.

An interesting account of that preaching service in the old adobe hotel building in San Francisco in April 1847 has been given by Mr. J. H. Brown, the proprietor, in a book of reminiscences written by him in 1886. "On board the ship (*The Whiton*) en route for Oregon, was a Methodist preacher by the name of Roberts, accompanied by his wife and daughter. While the vessel lay in the harbor he often came ashore. He informed me that if it was convenient and would be agreeable to the citizens to have him do so, he would like to hold services on Sunday. I told him he could have the use of the dining room, and that I knew he would have a good congregation. On Sunday morning I posted a notice that there would be preaching that day at the hotel. The room was filled, and the Reverend Mr. Roberts preached a good sermon; and it was the first Methodist sermon ever preached in San Francisco." Mr. Brown stated further: "The congregation was not very fashionable, but deeply attentive, and well pleased with the sermon. I can say that many who were at that meeting had not been to any place of worship for ten or fifteen years previous to that occasion. One old sailor who was greatly pleased with the sermon put a five dollar gold piece in his own hat and went around the room and collected over fifty dollars, which he gave to the minister, and with tears in his eyes he tapped the minister on the shoulder in a sailor-like way and exclaimed: 'That was a damned good sermon.' He further showed his appreciation by inviting the minister and his family to take dinner with him the next day at the hotel."

Describing the situation and the conditions, Mr. Brown stated in his story: "The dining room was in the center of the house; on one side was a billiard room and a saloon; on the other were two rooms used for card-playing." The story concludes with the observation: "I do not suppose another instance could be cited, where, under the same roof there was preaching, drinking, card-playing and billiards all going on at the same time and hour. Those who did not wish to attend the religious services had too much respect for the minister to make the least noise or disturbance."

Writing from memory so many years after the event, Mr. Brown stated the date of this service incorrectly, fixing it in June, whereas it was in April. pp. 33-34

Gold Rush Caused by God

William Taylor, *California Life Illustrated*, Carlton & Porter, New York, 1858.

Let any man weigh the facts we have in part indicated, and he will see that the gold magnet of California was pointed by an all-wise and merciful Providence, for the purpose of attracting and enriching the nations, not in gold, but godliness; and that when these "strangers and foreigners" shall have acquired our language, and some knowledge of the institutions of Christianity, a Pentecostal gust of glory may burst upon them, and they by thousands see and experience "the wonderful works of God," and return to their homes God's own embassadors, to carry the truce flag of redeeming mercy to their perishing brethren, and declare to them in their own vernacular tongue, the royal proclamation of peace and pardon through the blood of Jesus. Upon a careful review of the foregoing facts, taken together with the proximity of California to the heathen millions of Asia, and Japan, and Oceanica, etc., and her constant inter-communication with them, I come to the deliberate conclusion that California is to-day, in the openings of Providence, the most important missionary field under the sun. "The harvest truly is plenteous, but the laborers are few: pray ye therefore the Lord of the harvest, that he will send forth laborers into his harvest." p. 332

Californios' Extravagance

W. W. Robinson, *Los Angeles From the Days of the Pueblo*. California Historical Society, San Francisco, 1959.

With its new prosperity, El Puelbo went mad. Californians knew how to spend money. They bought fancy clothes, added second stories to their town houses on the Plaza, built bigger ranch homes, put on better horse races, and were heavy patrons of the gambling houses. They imported carriages, thousand-dollar shawls, and lace-curtained, four-poster bedsteads. Don Jose Spelveda and Don Vincente Lugo wore thousand-dollar suits, and their horses were equally resplendent. The money Californios spent did things to the shopkeepers, to the craftsmen in leather and silver, to the gamblers, to all the unsavory characters who came in for a share, and to the town itself. p. 54

Major Horace Bell, edited by Lanier Bartlett, *On the Old West Coast, Being Further Reminiscences of a Ranger*, William Morrow & Co., New York, 1930.

They were so rich, potentially, that they never suspected that they could, by any possibility, become poor. But they had one weakness common to all Spanish-Americans. When they wanted cash they wanted it immediately. The Californian couldn't wait, neither would he; and with his ample security he could bet all the money he wanted. But how he paid for it! He would pay interest as high as twelve and a half per cent. per day on each dollar borrowed, compounded daily! That was for small amounts. For large amounts he would pay the low (!) rate of five per cent. per month on the dollar, compounded monthly. p. 5

Decline of the Californios

Leonard Pitt, *The Decline of the Californios*, University of California Press, Berkeley, 1966.

When Benjamin Hayes reflected that the Lugo family of southern California had possessed $150,000 in 1852 but had practically no wealth by 1865, he concluded that "the finger of Providence seems to mark the decay of the old Californian families." Why God's wrath? "We must not judge," Hayes answered. "But the Indians have suffered great crimes and injustices from the later Mexican governors and people." In explaining the fall of the Californians, Hayes thus supplied the "unrequited toil" theory which Abraham Lincoln suggested in his second inaugural as an explanation of the Civil War. p. 277

In Hayes's time the Yankee still felt sufficiently free of guilt to regard the Californians' defeat as self-inflicted. The oldest and perhaps most highly respected Yankee pioneer in the state, Alfred Robinson, in a late postscript to his famous "Life in California," described the downfall as inevitable and regrettable, but as altogether the product of the Californios' passivity. His argument supposed a belief in the idea of progress:

The early Californians, having lived a life of indolence without any aspiration beyond the immediate requirement of the day, naturally fell behind their more energetic successors, and became impoverished and gradually dispossessed of their fortunes as they idly stood by, lookers-on upon the bustle and enterprise of the new world before them, with its go-aheadativeness and push-on keep-moving celebrity. p. 277

Problems With Indians

Robert F. Heizer, Ed, *The Destruction of the California Indians*, Peregrine, Smith, Inc., Santa Barbara, 1974, pp. 191-193

This letter, sent by California state legislators, to the governor, describes some of the problems encountered by the clash of two cultures.

Sacramento City, Cal.
April 6, 1852
To His Excellency
John Bigler, Governor of California

The undersigned Senators and Representatives from the Counties of Trinity, Klamath, Shasta and Siskiyou, most respectfully represent to your Excellency that the constant and continued depredations committed by the various tribes of Indians on the lives and property of our citizens demand your prompt, efficient, and constant resistance that the citizens of this district are no longer able to make, as a short review of the past history of this Section of our State and the present alarming situation of our citizens will demonstrate. Since the winter of 1848-50 the Pitt river Indians have been constantly hostile, and their incessant depredations and murders have been only occasionally checked by expeditions of the whites made into their country. All the other tribes, to wit: the Cottonwood, Trinity, Klamath and Shasta Indians, have, in turn, been hostile since the first settlement by the whites; but it has only been within the last few months that there appears to have been a general combination among them of hostility to the whites.

From our own personal knowledge, and from information obtained from reliable sources, we feel satisfied that the following statement of losses, both in life and property, that have occurred in our Section of the State from Indian depredations are considerably below the reality:

Shasta County:
No. of whites murdered 40
Amount of property destroyed and stolen $100,000

Trinity County:
No. of whites murdered 20
Amount of property destroyed and stolen $50,000

Klamath County:
No. of whites murdered 50
Amount of property destroyed and stolen $50,000

Siskiyou County:
No. of whites murdered 20
Amount of property destroyed and stolen $40,000

These enormous losses have all been sustained by the people of a small portion of this State, within a very few months. The evil is increasing every day as a more intimate knowledge of the whites makes the Indians more bold and reckless in their attacks. Already they enter our towns and villages at night and steal or set fire to property. The habitations of the industrious miners, while they are at their labors, are entered with impunity and robbed of their contents. The pack animals on which the miners must depend for their provisions, are either killed on the spot where found, or driven away to be roasted and eaten by the depredators. The people are compelled to travel from one portion of the country to another in companies, well armed to repel attacks.

It has been charged that the hostility of the Indians was superinduced by acts of injustice committed by the whites. As a general thing, we can state, from our own knowledge, that this has not been the case; and have no hesitation in saying that it emanates from the known character of the Indians—a mischievous disposition and desire for plunder. In but few instances have the first offences been committed by the whites.

[Illegible] . . . order out the militia for that purpose. Eighty or one hundred men, in addition to those proposed to be located at Cow Creek, properly distributed in bands of ten to twenty, along Trinity and Klamath rivers, and always in readiness for service, would probably be sufficient; for the Indians now generally act in small parties, although, there has not often been much difficulty in repelling them yet, it has been almost impossible to follow them to their haunts to chastise them. Instances have occurred where miners have attempted this, and return only to find their habitations despoiled of every thing valuable.

For these reasons we now ask of you protection for the people of that portion of the State that has never yet received any thing at the hands of the Government, confidently expecting your speedy attention to the same.

We remain very Respectfully
Your obt Servants

Signed Thomas H. Coats of Klamath County,

Samuel Fleming, E.D. Pierce of Shasta County,
Geo. O. McMullin of Trinity County,
J.W. Denver, Senator from Klamath & Trinity Counties,
R.J. Sprague, Senator from Shasta

Teacher's Supplement

American Units

Units 9 & 10

Teaching Aids—Unit 9 & 10

The American Units

Teacher's Overview

AFTER THE EXCITEMENT OF THE GOLD Rush had died down, California continued to grow and prosper. It found that it was a state in a mighty nation with thousands of miles separating it from its sister states. This worked for the good of California at first, since it had a very small part in the War Between the States. No fighting occurred on California's soil.

The Railroad

The railroad ended this isolation. It is hard for those of us living in modern times to appreciate the magnitude of this accomplishment. At that time rails had to be laid at a five percent or less grade for the locomotives to be able to travel. This is very slight. When we consider the massive Sierras that had to be scaled, we can admire the skill and determination possessed by the early Californians. At the completion of this incredible project, California was linked to the Union and able to share the wealth and resources of the East.

Southern California

Southern California especially benefited from the railroad. People from all over the United States, attracted by the beautiful climate, migrated in a very unusual fashion. First came the very wealthy, followed in turn by those in medium and middle circumstances, and finally the working class. This pattern is backwards from the experience of most states. Christianity thrived in Southern California.

Dominion

Californians began to take dominion over their land, changing the landscape into the form that we recognize today. The most important accomplishment was to bring reliable sources of water to the farms and cities. This resulted in the rise of agriculture, supporting industries, and prosperity.

California also benefited from the Industrial Revolution being experienced world-wide. Oil was discovered in Los Angeles and was used to fuel trains. Automobiles were invented which caused roads and highways to be built the length of the state. Houses soon had electric lights and central heating. California boasted of several fine universities, most of which were founded by Christians.

When we study this period, we are sometimes told by modern scholars that the early Californians destroyed the environment. This is the prospective of those who hold to an animistic worldview. (See the introduction to *His California Story*.) Most of these people would agree that any change at all to the environment is unacceptable. The Bible tells us that God made the world for man's use and God's glory. We are to take dominion over the land and make it fruitful.

This is exactly what the early Californians tried to do. Not all of their efforts were successful. Early forestry methods were quite primitive. Hydraulic mining was very destructive. However, Californians of the time learned from their mistakes. Forestry methods have greatly improved, and hydraulic mining was halted by law.

Even with the mistakes that the early Californians made, we must applaud their efforts. The irrigation systems they designed have provided water to millions of people in areas that were once deserts. Other projects have made life more enjoyable for all.

American Units

Units 9 and 10 are treated together in this section. Unit 9, The Americanization of California, discusses the events following the Gold Rush as California changed from a Mexican province into an American state, including the transcontinental railroad and the settlement of Southern California. Unit 10, Californians Take Dominion, discusses more specific accomplishments, such as irrigation projects, the rise of agriculture, and the rise of industry.

Stops Along the Grapevine

MORE THAN ONCE I'VE ENDURED THE TEDIUM OF Highway 5 from the San Francisco Bay area to Southern California but until recently, never by myself. Usually my husband drives and like many men, if I could be allowed a stereotypical remark, he drives to the destination. I needed to take frequent breaks, so I looked for interesting stops along the way and found a couple to share with you.

My most important discovery was a drive-thru Starbucks. I know this will interest some of you more than others, but I was pretty surprised to find it off Lavada Rd. just before the Grapevine. I don't think I've ever seen a busier Starbucks. Go figure.

Fort Tejon

The temperature dropped about fifteen degrees between Starbucks and my next stop, Fort Tejon. It had snowed the morning of my journey and "slush" as we called it in Minnesota blanketed the fort's ground. Located just north of Lebec, this small state historic park offers a great place for children to run off some energy, soak up some history and if you travel in the winter, throw snowballs. I had to duck as a couple of children aimed wet ones at their dad, who pitched them back. It looked like fun. Sort of.

Fort Tejon was operated by the U.S. Army for a brief ten years between 1854 and 1864. Founded to protect and control the Indians living at the nearby Sebastian Indian Reservation as well as the miners in the gold fields, deployment at Fort Tejon was considered dismal duty and frankly, in my opinion, still is. All that remains of the fort is a few buildings, some mediocre displays and posters, and a fenced-in oak tree with a carving from 1837 announcing that "Peter le Beck was killed by a x bear."

Civil War Re-enactment

The fort comes to life on several weekends when Civil War Re-enactors descend to re-live and re-fight the battles of that time. Although I've never attended a reenactment in the South, I've been to several in my area. One time when my college-age daughter was quite young, she fainted. Through the noise of a battle raging around us I heard, "Make way! Make way! Emergency!" as Civil War medics pressed though the crowd. Flustered, I tried to minister to my daughter and move out of the way until the medics landed at our feet. We were the emergency.

The soldiers offered her water out of a rusty tin cup—which I rubbed on her face and forearms rather than let her drink—then carried her to the hospital tent. As I looked around at the archaic medical instruments, I wondered what they had in mind. Then they took us to the back where the real first aid supplies were hidden. Whew! She was fine. She just locked her knees and after some rest, rose to carry on.

For more information on Fort Tejon, scheduled Civil War Reenactments, and information on Living History Programs for school children, look up their Web site at www.FortTejon.org.

State Water Project

My latte had cooled considerably by the time I reached my next stop, the Vista Del Lago Visitors Center at Pyramid Lake, which houses a display on the State Water Project, the controversial aqueduct that carries water from the wet to the dry portions of the state. What a fabulous find.

Filled with interactive displays, the visitors' center makes water more interesting than I ever thought it could be. One display shows common, household, and food items and explains how much water it takes to produce each. Another projects a movie onto a large map of California, highlighting the locations of various water projects, which is actually more interesting than it sounds. A timeline of the effort required to complete the project fills the wall along one room, an observation deck with telescopes allows viewing of the dam creating Pyramid Lake, and my favorite, a video called *Wings Over Water* presents a wordless panorama as an airplane (sometimes you can see its shadow) flies over the aqueduct from inception to termination. I think you will enjoy an hour or so here and more if you decide to picnic by the lake.

For more information visit their Web site (it's easiest to find if you just type "Vista Del Lago Visitors Center" into your favorite search engine). The center offers free publications to educators, which are reviewed on the Web site, along with tours for school groups.

Fort Tejon and Vista Del Lago provided an educational and enjoyable break from the road. By the time I reached Santa Clarita, I felt refreshed enough to tackle Southern California's traffic. I even found another Starbucks and indulged in a second latte. Why not? I figured a little extravagance now and then can't hurt!

History Makes a Difference

The Story of William Mulholland

Does it really matter if we record history accurately? History reports the deeds of dead people. Since they are gone, what difference does it make? Why go to all the trouble to unravel the past?

Let me tell a story to answer this question. It concerns William Mulholland who was either a great man who made it possible for the city of Los Angeles to survive, or a villain who caused 450 men, women, and children to perish. History needs to tell us which.

Meet Mr. Mulholland

We meet Mr. Mulholland in the early part of the 20th century. The native of Ireland and self-educated man who became Los Angeles' chief engineer had a problem. Los Angeles had no water. A growing population coupled with two years of drought had nearly exhausted the city's water supply. Searching for a solution, Mulholland located ample water at Owens Lake. The only problem—it was 253 miles from Los Angeles.

After studying the situation, Mulholland devised a plan. The city of Los Angeles would purchase the property along the Owens River, then build an open, gravity-powered aqueduct to bring the water to the Los Angeles basin, a project not without controversy. The fact that no aqueduct that long had ever been built did not faze Mulholland in the least. He set the price tag at $24 million and said it would take five years to complete.

Five years later, and within the set budget, 30,000 Los Angelenos gathered to watch the first flow of water cascading down the completed aqueduct.

The Hero

William Mulholland was a hero, his accomplishment noted all around the world. The University of California at Berkeley awarded him an honorary doctorate while newspaper editors urged him to run for mayor. His answer? "Gentlemen," he replied, "I would rather give birth to a porcupine backwards than be mayor of Los Angeles."

Several years passed and once again Los Angeles was running short of water. Mulholland proposed building several reservoirs to capture excess water during time of plenty for use during droughts. One of these was his twenty-second dam, the St. Francis. Construction, although arduous, was uneventful. Slowly, over the course of two years, the dam was filled. As it neared capacity, leakage occurred, but did not cause alarm.

Then, near midnight on March 11, 1928, the unexpected happened. Bursting abruptly, the massive concrete dam was ripped asunder. Lillian Curtis' husband, a dam employee, suddenly woke. Thrusting his three-year-old son into his wife's arms, he pushed her out the back window of their cottage while he went back for the couple's two older daughters. With water lapping at her armpits, Mrs. Curtis and her son reached safety. Her husband and other children did not. A 140-foot wall of water rushed down San Francisquito Canyon, brushing away sturdy bridges and annihilating everything in its path. In five and one half hours, 450 souls perished.

The Villain

William Mulholland was a villain whose negligence caused death and destruction. Threats were made and an armed guard had to protect his home. A coroner's inquest followed to investigate the failure, but gallant Mulholland said, "Don't blame anyone else, you just fasten it on me. If there was an error in human judgment, I was the human." He died seven years later, a broken man who never understood what had caused the dam to fail.

And there the matter would stand except for two people of our own time: an historian, Charles F. Outland, who asked the right questions, and a geological engineer, J. David Rogers, who found the right answers.

The St. Francis Dam collapsed due to factors which were completely unknown to William Mulholland, or anyone else at the time. The site abutted an ancient landslide, undetectable with equipment of that era. When the dam was filled to capacity, the ground beneath thrust upwards, the ancient slide moved, and the dam's left abutment broke. A severe tragedy, but an accident which could be attributed to no man.

History Matters

Does it matter if history is correct? Most definitely, say the descendants of William Mulholland who have lived to see the name of their grandfather cleared. Absolutely, say the friends and relatives of those who perished in the deluge who find it easier to forgive. Without a doubt, say the civil engineers and geologists who in their training have profited from a study of the St. Francis Dam.

William Mulholland, a giant of a man can once again take his rightful place in the pageant of California's heroes, a man of strong character and integrity. We all benefit from our acquaintance with this man and we find that yes, history does matter.

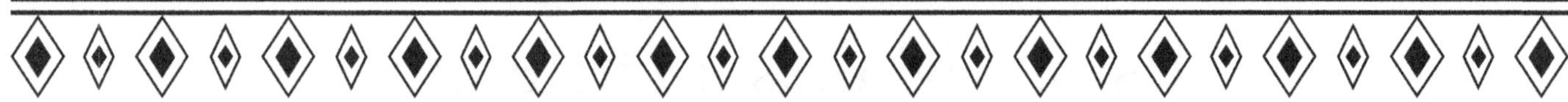

The Blessings of Progress

PROGRESS. IT SOUNDS LIKE AN UGLY WORD TO MODERN ears with its connotation of greenhouse gasses and smog-laden skyscrapers. But wait. What about the eradication of small pox, or the pleasures of central heat and air, or freedom from household drudgery? Shouldn't the word *progress* uplift and encourage us?

I remember my first experience with progress in terms of technology—a gift of a bulky transistor radio that picked up music from all of four radio stations, but only if the listener didn't mind a tinny whine filled with static. Today, a few short years later, an eye blink in the span of history, my students delight in showing off their latest gadgets—iPods, Razrs, and Vaios. They along with all of California have benefited from dramatic changes as progress has shaped society and brought freedom and prosperity to many.

In 1769, thousands of California Indians lived in the mountains and valleys of our state, never dreaming that another people lived far beyond the ocean. Spanish Catholic missionaries brought the two cultures together. They also brought the wonders of 18th century technology—improved farming methods, woven cotton clothes, beds, education, sturdy homes, and my personal favorite—chocolate.

From a materialistic perspective, the peoples' lives improved substantially. California Indian women were rescued from hours of painful toil as they learned to cook *pozoli* instead of acorns. Homes provided better protection from the elements. Certainly not without its problems (as I will discuss below), improved technology greatly enhanced the California Indians' daily comfort. It was a wonderful time to be alive.

One hundred years later, by 1869, hundreds of thousands of people from all parts of the globe called California home. Drawn by the riches of the mines and seduced to stay by the riches of the land, these men and women enjoyed the wonders of 19th century technology. Isolated from family beyond the deserts and mountains, they embarked upon an arduous plan to tie California to the rest of the Union—the transcontinental railroad.

Progress followed and soon an iron and steel skeleton connected markets and communities across the land. Separated families, who had bid tearful farewells just a few years earlier, were reunited for today's equivalent of $100. Goods from the East chugged over California's treacherous Sierra summits, including those from that new wonder, the Sears catalog. It was a great time to be alive.

In 1969, millions of people surged in California's coasts, valleys, and foothills. Henry Ford's Model T transformed into Lee Iacocca's Mustang. The gramophone developed into my beloved transistor radio. Miles of concrete highways, some paved over rusting railroad tracks, allowed people to stand on Sierra summits. On July 20' 1969, man accomplished one of the greatest technological feats of all time: He stood on another cosmic body, the moon, and bragged about the giant step for mankind. It was a wonderful time to be alive.

Closer to home, on October 29, 1969, a young man named Charley Kline, at UCLA, scored an even bigger victory for progress—he was the first to send a message over the ARPANET, the forerunner of the Internet. More than any other innovation, the Internet has shaped modern times. When I wrote my first book in 1995, the Internet was cumbersome and complex. Only techies could fathom its mysteries. Today our house sports five computers, all connected to each other and the Internet through a wireless network. When I want to send an e-mail to a friend, look up today's equivalency of 1885 dollars, or order that book I saw advertised on the pages of *Homeschooling Today*, I pull out my laptop and type away. It's a wonderful time to be alive.

Progress can be painful. The same padres who brought Spanish technology to the California Indians also brought diseases for which the Indians had no immunity. The same railroads that opened California's markets to the East also closed many local businesses bringing depression and despair. The same Internet that imports the delights of the world into my living room also imports filth and lies. I can use a cell phone to talk to my children. Terrorists can use cell phones to destroy two towers of progress. Most of all, progress requires one to keep up, to move forward, to adapt. Sometimes this means a career change as an entire industry undergoes massive modifications, something that strikes close to my home. Even so, I would not trade my grandparent's carpet cleaner and ice box for my vacuum and freezer any day.

Technology is wonderful, but it doesn't save. Only Christ can change a sinful heart, and only Christ can equip Christians to use technology to further His kingdom. As He blesses and empowers us to use the resources He provides to fulfill His Dominion Mandate, let us not forget that it's a wonderful time to be alive.

Out With the Old—In With the New

A WHILE BACK, MY SON TOOK A COLLEGE-LEVEL California history class and I couldn't wait to peruse his textbook. "Wait a minute," I thought to myself as I skimmed along the surface. "I've read this before!" and sure enough, I had. It was an update of a book that had been published in the 1970s. The new book added roughly 90 pages to bring it current to Pete Wilson's time. Thinking it might be fun to compare the two versions, I dug out my highlighter and jumped in.

Not surprised, I noticed a trend I've seen in many of the postmodern history books of our time, which can only be termed "revisionist." I want to share some specific examples from my son's college text and compare it to the original, but not because I want to disparage either author; in fact I'm just going refer to the two books as the old and the new. Rather, I want to illustrate some trends in postmodern history-writing.

Christianity Scrubbed

The first trend that these two books illustrate is the complete eradication of Christianity, especially Protestant Christianity. While neither book could be considered a friend of Christianity—far from it—the old contained minor passing references to the faith which have been completely scrubbed from the new. For example, the old text tells us that by 1870 federal Indian agents were appointed after consultation with Christian churches and that the reservations in California were run by the Methodists. That tidbit didn't make it into the new book.

Black and White History

The second trend is the extraction of color and detail. To many people history comes across very dry, even boring, and postmodern texts perpetuate this tendency. I realize some detail had to go to make room for the new material, but history in color is so much more interesting than history in black and white. Consider these sentences. In the new book the italicized words are omitted in the following accounts:

- Speaking of a rusty cannon used in a conflict between the Americans and Californios during the Mexican War: "Dug up and lashed to the running gear of a wagon, *fired with homemade powder and a cigarette, and moved rapidly about by skilled horsemen,* it proved a deadly weapon, and the Battle of the Old Woman's Gun was a brilliant *little* victory for the Californios."
- Speaking of the surrender of Andrés Pico at the end of the skirmishes: "…Andrés Pico chose to surrender the rebel forces to Frémont, who had reached the San Fernando Valley from the north. *Andrés Pico had heard of the clemency Frémont had recently shown to Jesús Pico, another of the officers who had broken parole by joining the rebellion, and whom Frémont had captured at San Luis Obispo. Military law would have permitted his execution by a firing squad, but the tearful pleas of the wife and the 14 children of Jesús Pico led Frémont to spare his life."*

Plain Revision

Then there's the revision. Many postmodern books reinterpret events using today's perspective and seek to "correct" the errors of the past by making subtle changes in language. I'll share two examples of how the new book does this.

In 1781 the Yuma Indians along the Colorado River, for reasons both real and imagined, massacred a Spanish expedition and destroyed two missions. All of the men were killed and the women later ransomed. Old history books, without exception, refer to this event as the Yuma Massacre. The new book calls it "an instance of violent resistance" and reduces the original 2-page description to a paragraph. Further the old book states that the Yuma Massacre was one of the worst disasters in the whole history of the Spanish frontier, while the new agrees it was a terrible disaster, but only if examined from the Spanish point of view. This leaves the postmodern impression that the concept of "disaster" is relative and while being massacred is a disaster, committing massacre may not be.

The second example is even more subtle and concerns word choice or what the English books call *connotation*. I'll just give one example. When speaking of the original five Indian reservations established in California the old book says, "The first, at Tejon in the Tehachapi foothills, attracted about twenty-five hundred Indians." The new book replaces the word *attracted* with *contained.* While the first word implies that the Indians came to the reservation by their own choice and enjoyed some benefits there, the second implies the exact opposite. Isn't the impact of one word amazing?

Postmodern books contain a changing "truth" based on the worldviews and values of groups or cultures. In a quest for *the* truth, we need to evaluate historical actions based on the absolute standard of the Bible and point our children back to history's source documents, that is, the ones written by the people who lived through the events. We need to exercise wise discernment as we examine today's texts. Only then can we combat the errors of postmodernism.

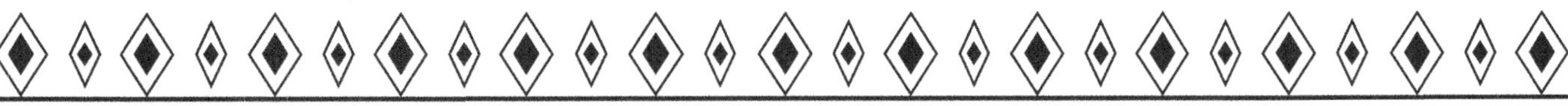

Teaching the American Units

Lesson Plans

Unit 9

1. Introduction ideas:
   - If you have not had time to visit a railroad museum, this might be the time to do it. The railroad had a phenomenal impact on California's development. The premier museum is in Sacramento, the California State Railroad Museum, but most towns have their own museums.
   - You might also look for model railway clubs by searching the Internet for "model railway club California." Men (and some women) who set up model trains for a hobby often construct elaborate settings. I've visited several of these clubs throughout the state, and I've always been warmly welcomed and informed.
   - If a field trip is not possible, you might find pictures of old Sears and Roebuck and Montgomery Wards catalogs, and discuss the catalogs' impact on the people of the time. Most students take the Internet for granted, but most teachers remember a time when we couldn't easily lookup and order a product from the other side of the world. The catalogs were an early, paper version of the Internet. (My great-grandparents ordered a Sears and Roebuck home for their North Dakota farm.) Try to impress upon students the enormous change the railroad brought to California. Just as the Internet has drawn our global community closer together, the railroad did the same for California and the rest of the nation.
2. Discuss the early transportation methods that connected California with other parts of the country (Ch. 27). Do Roundup questions.
3. If students enjoy the stories about the Pony Express riders, you might look for other tales of these intrepid men.
4. Teach the transcontinental railway verse (1869) of the "California Date Song."
5. Do a character sketch on Theodore Judah and if desired, one of the Big Four. You might also do a compare and contrast on Judah and the Big Four—a three column chart (Judah, both, Big Four) or a Venn diagram.
6. If available, watch at least the western portions of the video *The Iron Road.* Fascinating!
7. A choral reading of "What the Engines Said" by Bret Harte is fun. Select a narrator, then divide the class into sections to read be the train from the East and the train from the West. Practice to become familiar with the poem, and then read or recite it with expression.
8. Teach about Los Angeles and Southern California (Ch. 28). Do Roundup questions.
9. Discuss the concept of *competition* and how it benefits the economy. To give students some background on the topic, make connections to sports competitions and how tougher games make competitors train and try harder.
10. Test students on all geographical features learned so far, and then create the salt-dough maps.

Unit 10

1. Teach how the early Californians obtained water (Ch. 29 and 30). Do Roundup questions.
2. Find out how water is delivered to your community. Visit or obtain information about your water district.
3. Do character sketches on John Muir and

William Mulholland.
4. Teach about the rise of agriculture and industry (Ch. 31 and 32) and do Roundup questions.
5. Research the types of agriculture and industry near your area.
6. Research your local history and visit historical sites or host visitors or storytellers—check with your local library or historical society for possibilities.
7. Teach the last verse of "The California Date Song."

Objectives

Objectives for Unit 9

At the completion of this unit students should be able to:

1. Describe California's contributions to the War Between the States.
2. List some early methods of transportation in California.
3. Describe the hardships and obstacles that had to be overcome when building a railroad across the Sierra Nevada.
4. Understand the changes that the railroad brought to California.
5. List the four stages of migration to Southern California.
6. Describe what was so unusual about the settlement of Southern California.
7. Articulate the effects of Christianity upon the growth of Southern California.

Objectives for Unit 10

At the completion of this unit students should be able to:

1. Define the word *dominion.*
2. Describe the water problems in California and how they were solved.
3. Understand the difference between *preservation* and *conservation.*
4. Describe several changes Californians made as they took dominion over their land.
5. Articulate how agriculture helped California to grow and prosper.
6. Describe how California's agriculture differed from that of other states.
7. List and describe the advances in gold mining techniques.

Definition of Dominion

Definition of "Dominion" from Noah Webster's First Edition of the *American Dictionary of the English Language*, 1828.

1. Sovereign or supreme authority; the power of governing and controlling. The dominion of the Most High is an everlasting dominion. Dan. iv.
2. Power to direct, control, use and dispose of at pleasure; right of possession and use without being accountable; as the private dominion of individuals.

Character Sketches

(See Appendix A for further detail on character sketches)

Choose from the following:

- Charles Crocker
- Mark Hopkins
- Colis P. Huntington
- Leland Stanford
- Theodore Judah
- John Muir
- William Mulholland

California Date Song

(See Appendix B for entire song)

1869 - Completion of transcontinental railroad
Dominion and end of the unit

In eighteen hundred and sixty-nine,
Railroaders worked to build one line,
Two oceans joined and that was fine,
The transcontinental railroad.

We sing one part of God's great plan,
To bring the gospel to each man,
And take dominion of the land—
His California Story!

Geography

(See Appendix D for further discussion of geography.)

All of the geographical features of California should have been learned by this point. To reinforce learning, administer the geography test in Appendix D, and then begin the map described in the Class-Time Activities of this section.

Journal

1. Do character sketches on Hopkins, Crocker, Stanford, Huntington, and Judah.
2. Write a paragraph or two about the effect of Christianity on the settlement of Los Angeles.
3. Do a character sketch on John Muir and William Mulholland.
4. Record the definition of *dominion*. Write a paragraph or two discussing at least five ways Californians took dominion over their land.

Unit Roundup Answers

Unit 9 Introduction

1. How did religion motivate people to come and settle California? *See introduction to Unit 9.*
2. What part did California play in the War Between the States? *Very little. Supplied gold and contributed to the Sanitary Commission. The California Battalion fought with Massachusetts.*
3. Name some generals who lived in California before the war. *Sherman, Halleck, Hooker, Sheridan, Grant, Farragut, Johnston.*

Chapter 27

1. What early methods of transportation brought people and goods to California? What was the common problem with all of these methods? *Panama Railroad, Camel Corps, Stage coach, Pony Express, clipper ship. Too slow and expensive.*
2. Would you have liked to have been a rider on the Pony Express? Why or why not? *Opinion. Answers will vary.*
3. Why was Theodore Judah called "Crazy Judah"? Do you think he was crazy? *People thought it was a crazy idea to build a railroad over the Sierras.*
4. Write a short description of each of these men: Theodore Judah, Charles Crocker, Leland Stanford, Mark Hopkins, Colis P. Huntington. *Answers will vary, but should include details about the men's personalities.*
5. Describe some of the hardships in the

construction of the transcontinental railroad. *Tunneling through granite; crossing rivers, chasms, valleys, and streams; snow; avalanches.*

6. Did the railroad help California to prosper? Explain. *Yes, by opening up territory for settlement, bringing goods from the East, and providing a safer and less arduous method of transportation. No, caused economic hardship at first.*

Chapter 28

1. Describe the early days in Los Angeles. *Crime, murders, and wickedness.*
2. What event in 1885 brought many Mid-Westerners to California? How does this event illustrate the benefits of competition? *Rate war between Southern Pacific and Santa Fe caused rail prices to drop. Competition caused the rate war.*
3. What was unusual about the migration of Southern California? *The very wealthy came first, followed by those in medium and middle circumstances, and then the working class. Was backwards from other migrations. Also, neighboring territory was not settled first.*
4. What effect did Christianity have on the growth of Southern California? *Was responsible for the prosperity and law and order that the Southern Californians enjoyed.*

Chapter 29

1. How does California today differ from the land that the California Indians inhabited? *Many improvements have been made, especially to control flooding and provide water in the summer.*
2. What does it mean to "take dominion"? *To wisely rule over what God has created to make the world fruitful.*
3. Why are California's water laws based on Spanish law rather than English common law? *Because Spain has a dry climate similar to California. In England water is abundant.*
4. What problems did California's rivers cause and how were they tamed? *They flooded in the winter and were dry in the summer. Dams were built to control the flow of water.*
5. What is a *levee* and what problem did it solve? *A high bank of dirt or concrete built along rivers to prevent them from flooding the land.*
6. Give some examples of early Californians working together to solve their problems as communities. *They built levees, irrigation districts, and dams.*

Chapter 30

1. What is the difference between *preservation* and *conservation*? Conservation *means to conserve resources for the future.* Preservation *means to preserve them in their natural state.*
2. Why do you think John Muir worked so hard to preserve California's natural resources? *Because of his animistic worldview and ideas about preservation.*
3. What were the three water projects for Southern California? What did each accomplish? *The Los Angeles Aqueduct provided water to Los Angeles from the Owens Valley. The Imperial Canal provided water to the Imperial Valley. The Hoover Dam provided water to Southern California.*
4. What is hydroelectric power? *Electricity produced by water power.*

Chapter 31

1. How did the orange industry begin? *A missionary from Brazil shipped some naval orange trees to Luther Tibbetts.*
2. Describe the variety of agriculture that is raised in California. *More variety of crops raised in California than in any other part of the world.*
3. What advances were made in gold mining? Were they good or bad? *Hydraulic mining and dredging destroyed the landscape and were eventually outlawed. Others advances were good as new inventions made mining*

easier and safer.

4. What is "black gold" and how was it discovered in California? *Oil. Doheny and Canfield drilled a well in downtown Los Angeles.*
5. What was the Temperance Movement? *A move to make the sale, manufacture, and transportation of intoxicating liquor illegal.*
6. What changes did the automobile bring to California? *Power of the railroads decreased, more areas accessible, new necessities such as garages and shopping centers.*
7. Do you think the many changes the early Californians made to the land would be allowed today? Why or why not? *Opinion, answers will vary.*

Supplemental Activities

Literature Suggestions

The Pony Express by Samuel Hopkins Adams. Describes the formation of the Pony Express and the daring young riders. A Landmark book. Highly recommended.

The Building of the First Transcontinental Railroad by Quentin Reynolds. Helps give students an appreciation for the monumental effort involved in completing this project. A Landmark book. Highly recommended.

Men to Match My Mountains by Irving Stone. The sections of this book on the building of the transcontinental railroad are just wonderful (as is the rest of the book). For very strong readers or adults. Highly recommended.

Check with your local historical society regarding books suitable for students on your community's history.

Field Trips

Since you will now be nearing the end of your study of California, you will want to consider field trips that didn't quite fit into previous sections. Families might also consider taking vacation to visit more distant parts of the state.

Field trips specific to Units 9 and 10 include Fort Point in San Francisco, a fort built to protect the harbor during the War Between the States, which was never used, and which was obsolete even before it was completed.

The Wells Fargo History Rooms in San Francisco and Los Angeles describe early transportation methods in California along with many other interesting exhibits. The California State Railroad Museum in Sacramento is wonderful. Students can walk through many trains as they get an appreciation for this part of California's history. Other places to consider visiting are the Luther Burbank Gardens in Santa Rosa, and the Crocker Art Museum in Sacramento.

John Muir lived for several years on a ranch owned by his wife's parents in Martinez. Today his house has been preserved as the John Muir National Park. Many California wilderness areas bear his name, including Muir Woods and the John Muir Trail.

In addition to parks and museums, you will want to look for evidences of how water was provided to the people of California. Many dams offer tours. A visit to your own local water district can be especially rewarding. Many large commercial farms will offer tours to your group or family. One of the most interesting field trips we have ever taken was to a dairy.

Finally, this is a great time to investigate your own local history and find out about the people who today have streets, schools, creeks, and cities named after them. Your local historical society might be able to provide speakers and presentations on local history.

Class-Time Activities

Railroad Video

The video *The Iron Road* from the PBS series *The American Experience* is wonderful. It describes the obstacles that the railroad builders faced and how they were overcome. Running time is 58 minutes, but may be shortened by skipping the parts that deal with the Union Pacific. The video jacket describes this documentary as follows: "*The Iron Road* recounts the six years of harsh labor, searing heat, Indian attacks, and frontier lawlessness these railroad men endured to complete this visionary enterprise."

Salt, Water, and Flour Maps

Map Construction

1. Materials Needed
   Each student will need: plywood boards (precut and sanded, for map base—finished size 12 x 20 inches), two cups of flour and one cup of salt, two small bowls (one to mix the salt-dough mixture and the other to hold water), a small hand towel. (Note: a smaller version of this project can be made using thick, corrugated cardboard, 8 1/2 x 12 inches.)

   Additionally, you will need precut large maps of California so that students can trace the outline of the state on their board (see Appendix D), extra bowls and pitchers for water, overhead or map showing geographical features, and protective table coverings.

2. Advance Preparation
   Cut 1/4-inch plywood into 12 x 20 inch pieces. Sand rough edges. (Or, corrugated cardboard.)

3. Objective
   By now, students should be fairly familiar with the geographical features of California. This activity will allow them to build a scale model of the state, including all of the mountains, rivers, valleys, lakes, and other features, in a raised-relief format.

4. Procedure
   Instruct students to trace the outline of California on their plywood. Also direct them to write their names on it.

   Mixing the salt-dough: Supervise students as they add water to their salt and flour mixture, a little at a time, and mix with their hands until it is the consistency of bread dough. It is important that the mixture is not too wet, or it will take too long to dry. (If the mixture is sticky, it is too wet.) If the mixture is too dry, the maps will crack. (If the mixture is hard to knead, it is too dry.) Most students will need help with this step. When the right consistency is reached, it is important that the students wash their hands in their water bowls and dry them on their towels before they continue to work with their salt dough mixture, otherwise, the mixture will become too wet.

Begin to form the salt dough map by applying flour to the outline of California, being careful not to cover any of the bays. Continue by adding the Sierra Nevada, the Central Valley, and the other geographical features. Remind students to dry their hands on their towels.

Once the geographical features are in place, the flour mixture may have to be smoothed, especially around the base of the mountains. Direct students to dip their fingers in a little water and smooth the map. It should not have any large cracks in it

The maps should dry in the air over the next several days. If they are drying too slowly, the map can be placed in the oven with just the oven light on. If the temperature is too high, they will bake like cookie dough. Once the map is dry it can be painted in two steps.

Painting—Step One

1. Materials Needed
   Dried salt dough maps, paint brushes, and tempera paint (green, brown, and yellow), plastic covers for table, bowls for water, pitcher to fill water bowls, and small paper cups for paint.

2. Advance Preparation
   None

3. Objective
   To learn the geographical features of California. The first part of the painting will concentrate on mountains and valleys.

4. Procedure
   Direct students to paint their maps according to the following guidelines:
   - Yellow - valleys (Central, Salinas, Imperial, San Fernando, and Los Angeles Basin).
   - Green - coast and forested areas (coastline, Sierra Nevada)
   - Brown - desert areas (Mohave, Colorado)
   - Green/Brown - mixed areas (note: this week paint the dominant color, either green or brown. Next week, when the paint is dry, the remaining color can be "splotched" on top.)

Painting—Step Two

1. Materials Needed
   Dried salt dough maps, paint brushes, and tempera paint (green, brown, yellow, blue, red, and orange), plastic covers for table, bowls for water, pitcher to fill water bowls, and small paper cups for paint.

2. Advance Preparation
   None

3. Objective
   To continue to learn the geography of California, concentrating on the lakes, rivers, and bays.

4. Procedure
   Students can begin by "splotching" brown or green paint over the areas that are a combination of desert and forest.

   Direct students to draw the lakes and rivers on their maps in pencil before they paint.

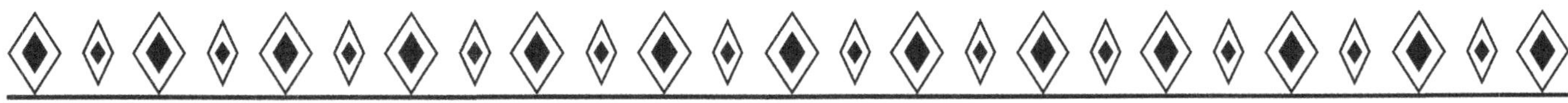

Make sure they use a fine paint brush to paint the rivers. If a fine paint brush is not available, a pencil or the opposite end of a paint brush dipped in blue paint works well. A permanent blue marker also works well. Students tend to forget the Colorado River which separates California and Arizona.

When all lakes and rivers are painted, students may paint the ocean, the states, and the country that borders California:

- Ocean - blue
- Oregon - yellow
- Nevada - orange
- Arizona - green
- Mexico - red

Oral Review Questions

Use these questions for review, to close a lesson, or for a review game like Around the World or Jeopardy.

1. How did the admission of California as the thirty-first state lead to the War Between the States? (The balance of power was upset in the Senate.)
2. Why weren't Californians required to fight in the War Between the States? (The cost of transporting them to the East was too high.)
3. What was the "California Battalion"? (men from California who fought with the men from Massachusetts)
4. Besides sending soldiers, what else did California do to support the North? (supplied gold and contributed to the Sanitary Commission)
5. Before the railroad, what methods of transportation were used to link California to the rest of the states? (Camel Corps, stagecoach, Pony Express)
6. Tell one interesting detail about the Pony Express. (Answers will vary. See p. 175 in *His California Story*.)
7. Who was the man with the dream of building a transcontinental railroad? (Theodore Judah)
8. Why was Theodore Judah called "Crazy Judah"? (People thought he was crazy to believe that a railroad could be built through the Sierra Nevada.)
9. How did Charles Crocker find men to work on the railroad? (He employed thousands of Chinese.)
10. What were some of the difficulties encountered in building the railroad through the Sierras? (They had to tunnel through granite; build trestles over chasms; build bridges; and cross valleys and streams. Dangers from snow and avalanches.)
11. What amazing feat did the Chinese workers of the Central Pacific accomplish in just one day? (laid 10 miles of track)
12. Where did the rails from the west join with the rails from the east? (Promontory Point, Utah)
13. The Central Pacific changed its name to what? (Southern Pacific)
14. Why was the Southern Pacific considered a mixed blessing to California? (Linked California to the Union, but exercised undue control over the people)
15. Name two of the Big Four. (Crocker, Hopkins, Stanford, Huntington)
16. Describe the pueblo of Los Angeles in the years before and just after the Gold Rush. (wickedness unequaled in entire state. Crime flourished.)
17. How did people immigrate to Southern California? (on emigrant trains)
18. What event brought many people from the mid-west to Southern California? (rate war between Southern Pacific and Santa Fe)
19. What was unusual about the migration to Southern California? (Wealthy came first be-

fore middle or working class. Was not settled by spill-over from neighboring territories)

20. Describe the spiritual condition of Southern California after the railroad. (mostly Christian)
21. What does "to take dominion" mean? (To make the world fruitful and to wisely rule over what God has created.)
22. What natural resource did California require to grow? (water)
23. What was the Wright Act of 1887? (A law which made irrigation districts possible.)
24. How did early farmers protect their land from flooding? (by building levees)
25. What is a causeway? (A bridge built over vacant land. During the winter excess water from the river is released into this land by weirs.)
26. How did farmers solve the problem of storing water for California's dry summers? (by building dams to save winter run-off)
27. Where does the water supply for San Francisco originate? (Hetch Hetchy)
28. What is *preservation*? (The position of a person who believes that the earth's natural resources should be preserved in their natural state.)
29. What is *conservation*? (The position of a person who believes that the earth's natural resources should be used, but also conserved for the future.)
30. Describe John Muir's religious views. (animistic)
31. What talent did God give to John Muir which he later rejected? (mechanical inventions)
32. Which president went camping with John Muir in Yosemite Valley? (Theodore Roosevelt)
33. Who was the engineer in charge of bringing water to Los Angeles? (William Mulholland)
34. Where does Los Angeles' water originate? (Owens Valley primarily, but also Colorado River)
35. How was the Salton Sea created? (by a break in the bank of the Colorado River which flowed into the Imperial Valley for two years)
36. What was California's first agricultural crop? (wheat)
37. What was its first fruit crop? (oranges)
38. What is hydraulic mining? (a highly destructive method in which entire hillsides were washed away to acquire gold)
39. What is black gold and where was it discovered? (Oil. Los Angeles and other parts of Southern California)
40. What group of people started most of the early colleges? (Christians)
41. What is the Temperance Movement? (a move to outlaw the sale, manufacture, and transportation of intoxicating liquor)
42. Who uprooted all of his grapes and stopped producing wine on his farm? (John Bidwell)

Project Suggestions

(See Appendix B for a description of the Class Project)

1. Draw a map of California showing historical details. Prepare a report on some of the places shown, such as the state and national parks.
2. Prepare a map/report of places that would be fun to visit for field trips (state historic parks, museums, and the like). Describe any you might have been to.
3. Find out how dams are constructed. Try to visit one. What kinds of engineering problems do they face? How are they solved?
4. Research your own local history. Identify landmarks (schools, streets, and creeks for example) that were named after early settlers and pioneers. You local historical society and library should be able to help you with this project.

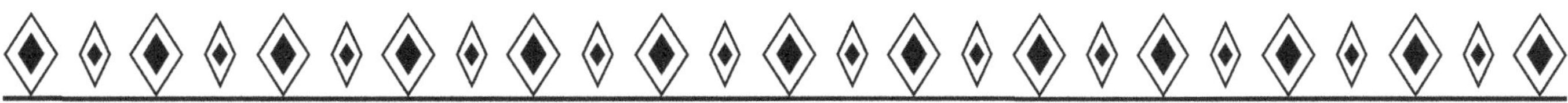

5. If your grandparents grew up in California, interview them. Pay particular attention to the changes that they have seen in their lifetime. Find out how and under what circumstances they came to California.
6. Research the churches in your community. Try to find out which are the oldest and the circumstances under which they began. Again, your local historical society should be able to help you.
7. Pretend you are one of the first people to ride the transcontinental railroad from New York to San Francisco. Write a letter describing your experiences. Or, pretend that you came to California originally by wagon, and have just returned to the East on the railroad. Write a letter describing the differences.
8. Dress in a costume similar to what Theodore Judah would have worn and tell the story of his life and his dream to build the transcontinental railroad.
9. Besides the Camel Corps, stagecoach, and Pony Express, people came to California on clipper ships before the railroad connected it to the other states. Research these fascinating and fast ships.

Source Documents

Christianity in Southern California

Carey McWilliams, *Southern California Country, An Island on the Land,* Duell, Sloan & Pearce, New York, 1946.

After 1900 the tide of immigrants to Southern California was increasingly made up of people of moderate means who came west to retire, to take it easy rather than to have a good time. As the type of immigrant changed, the character of the region itself began to change. From 1850 to 1870 Los Angeles was "the toughest town in the nation," but it became the most priggish community in America after 1900. A glacial dullness engulfed the region. Every consideration was subordinated to the paramount concern of attracting church-going Middle Westerners to Southern California. In 1896 the gambling houses were closed in Los Angeles and, a few years later, the saloons were required to close on Sundays. By 1906 the number of saloons was restricted to two hundred, and Los Angeles began to boast that it had more churches than any city of comparable size in America. In 1922 San Francisco voted against a prohibition measure by 91,000 "no" votes to 32,000 "yes" votes, but Los Angeles, the home of the vineyard industry, cast 143,000 "yes" votes and 84,000 "no" votes. Over the years, the mores of Los Angeles have undergone similarly swift changes reflecting the changing character of the immigrants to the region. p. 157

Imperial Valley Developed with Private Funds

Carey McWilliams, *California: The Great Exception*, Current Books, Inc., A.A. Wyn, Publisher, New York, 1949.

Basic to an understanding of Imperial Valley is the fact that its development, the first large-scale development on the Colorado, was undertaken under private auspices. In one sense, Imperial Valley was the first large-scale development project in the west, for its development dates from 1896, and the Reclamation Act was not passed until 1902. The development of the valley was a most heroic undertaking, and the story of this development is fascinating and dramatic. p. 301

Shasta Dam Improves Fish Habitat

Raymond F. Dasmann, *The Destruction of California*, The Macmillan Co., N.Y., 1965.

The construction of Shasta Dam seemed to threaten the highly valuable salmon run of the Sacramento River. There was no hope of bringing adult fish, migrating from the ocean, upstream to spawn above the high dam. Consequently the dam would deny the vast area of spawning ground on the upper Sacramento and its tributaries to the salmon, and it was expected that the salmon-fishing industry would suffer a severe decline. However, the Bureau of Reclamation, as part of its construction plan, included a major fish hatchery, built below the dam, to produce salmon to take the place of those lost through denial of access to the head water streams. It was hoped that this would at least cut the loss to the fishery. When the dam was completed, however, and the hatchery in operation, it was found that salmon production in the Sacramento had actually increased. The steady flow of cool, silt-free water from the dam improved the quality of the lower Sacramento for salmon. Survival of wild fish produced on the lower tributaries, as well as of hatchery fish, was enhanced, and there was a net gain to the fishery. Something had been lost. A hatchery fish is not a wild fish, but in this instance such an aesthetic consideration could be ignored. p. 165

Improvements in Forestry

Jonathan Adler, Policy Review, Spring 1993, quoted in Summit Journal, June 1993.

At the turn of the century, leaders in the emerging conservation movement warned that the United States would soon run out of trees. Both President Theodore Roosevelt and Gifford Pinchot, the father of the U.S. Forest Service, foretold severe timber shortages, a prediction based on the high rate of deforestation at the time.

At one point, farmers were clearing forests at the astounding clip of 8,600 trees a day, a rate that continued for nearly 50 years.

But something remarkable happened, though it may come as some surprise to those taken in by the idea that America's environment is being destroyed at breakneck speed: In the past 70 years, American forests have been reborn...

There are three major reasons for the improvement of America's forests:

- The development of better forest management techniques such as wildfire control...
- Rapid technological advancement that has reduced timber demand by enabling more efficient use of forest resources. The development of wood preservatives, for example, has lengthened the life span of timber products. The rise of the automobile saved millions of acres of forest, as rural communities no longer had to depend on wood-intensive rail transportation. The spectacular advances in farm productivity—resulting from chemical fertilizers and pesticides, hybrid seed varieties and farm machinery—also limited the need for cropland acreage, even as America's population continued to rise.
- Timber mills also have become vastly more efficient in using wood, and the introduction of fiberboard and other wood products has turned what were once wood scraps into marketable products...

Were Theodore Roosevelt and Gifford Pinchot still alive, they would be in for a shock. The "timber famine" they believed was imminent has been forestalled indefinitely, and America's forests are healthier than at any other time in this century.

With continuing technological improvements, there is every reason to believe that this trend of robust forest growth—led by private individuals motivated by market incentives—will continue. p. 5

Variety of Agriculture

California State Grange Cookbook, "California Gold (Grange Recipes Are Naturally Good Eating)," quoted in *The Californians*, Volume 11, Number 4.

More than 250 different crops and livestock commodities are grown within California, with no one single crop dominating the state's farm economy. California ranked the #1 agricultural producing state since 1947, in 1990 generated cash farm receipts of more than $18.3 billion, plus more than $70 billion in related economic activities. Though our 30 million acres of farmlands are less than 4% of the U.S. total, we produce more than 50% of the nation's fruits, vegetables, and nuts. p. 50

Teacher's Supplement

Appendices

A to F

Appendix A

Character Sketches

Webster's Definition of *Character*

Webster, Noah. "character." *American Dictionary of the English Language, 1828.* 01 Mar. 2008. <http://1828.mshaffer.com/d/search/word,character.>

1. The peculiar qualities, impressed by nature or habit on a person, which distinguish him from others; these constitute real character, and the qualities which he is supposed to possess, constitute his estimated character, or reputation. Hence we say, a character is not formed, when the person has not acquired stable and distinctive qualities.

7. By way of eminence, distinguished or good qualities; those which are esteemed and respected; and those which are ascribed to a person in common estimation. We enquire whether a stranger is a man of character.

Online Definition of *Character*

"character." *Dictionary.com Unabridged (v 1.1).* Random House, Inc. 01 Mar. 2008. <http://dictionary.reference.com/browe/character>.

1. the aggregate of features and traits that form the individual nature of some person or thing.
2. one such feature or trait; characteristic.
3. moral or ethical quality: *a man of fine, honorable character.*
4. qualities of honesty, courage, or the like; integrity: *It takes character to face up to a bully.*
5. reputation: *a stain on one's character.*
6. good repute.
7. an account of the qualities or peculiarities of a person or thing.

Synonyms of *Character*

"character." *Dictionary.com Unabridged (v 1.1).* Random House, Inc. 01 Mar. 2008. <http://dictionary.reference.com/browse/character>.

1. CHARACTER, INDIVIDUALITY, PERSONALITY refer to the sum of the characteristics possessed by a person. CHARACTER refers esp. to moral qualities, ethical standards, principles, and the like: *a man of sterling character.* INDIVIDUALITY refers to the distinctive qualities that make one recognizable as a person differentiated from others: *a woman of strong individuality.* PERSONALITY refers particularly to the combination of outer and inner characteristics that determine the impression that a person makes upon others: *a child of vivid or pleasing personality.* **5.** name, repute. See REPUTATION. **14.** sign.

Character Sketches

When we study the men and women who lived in California in the past, it is very important to study their character. What motivated them? Were they Christians living their lives in a way that pleased God? Were their accomplishments a result of their Christian character? Were they non-Christians living their lives in a way that pleased themselves? Did God use them anyway?

Many modern textbooks do not address these questions, and so we have students admiring men who were rebellious (Ps. 34:16). A good example of this is John Sutter. However, even rebellious men were used for good by God in California's history. A good example of this is, again, John Sutter.

To help students study the character of people who lived in California, the form latter in this section may be used. Do not expect students to answer every question with every person. Sometimes the information is not available. However, even then encourage students to make good guesses and offer opinions (and defend them).

Question-Answer Relationship

The skill of looking at clues in the book, looking at what the book says about a person—and then making good guesses is called *inference*, and it is very difficult for upper elementary students. Even so, it is not to early to begin teaching this skill as it becomes the basis of all analysis in later grades, as well as a necessary skill in exercising Christian discernment.

Begin by teaching students that there are four different ways to answer questions and to think about a person's character.

Based on Question-Answer Relationship or QAR (Raphael, 1982; 1986). There is a wonderful graphic that describes these four relationships at http://www.greece.k12.ny.us/instruction/ela/6-12/Tools/Qar.pdf

1. Right There

Some elementary students think that all questions can be answered by finding the sentence(s) in the book that answer the question, and sometimes they are correct—the answer is right there. These are called literal questions. Look at the description of William Taylor on pages 155-156 in *His California Story*. What is "right there" in the description? Students might answer:

- William Taylor was twenty-seven when he went to California.
- His wife was Anne.
- He read his Bible on the ship.
- He started a ministry for sailors called Bethel.

All of these answers come directly from the book, and some like #4 even use the book's exact words. They are basic facts about Taylor that address the *who*, *what*, and *where* of the man.

2. Think and Search

Sometimes students need to combine information from two or more parts of the book to answer questions. They need to think about how ideas from one part of the book relate to ideas in another part.

For example, to answer the question How did Taylor feel about the gamblers? students might find information from page 156:

- spoke courageously against gambling evils
- became a friend to gamblers
- performed funeral services for them
- warned them
- earned their admiration and confidence

They might find more information on page 154:

- the gamblers did not interfere when Taylor spoke
- they were orderly and attentive
- he asked them what they would profit if they lost their souls

They might combine the information from both pages and answer the question by saying, Taylor tried to befriend the gamblers and warn them.

Another type of "Think and Search" question might require students to compare or contrast (or both) one person, object, or event discussed in one section of the book to a different person, object, or event discussed in another.

3. Author and You

The "Author and You" question requires students to make an inference; that is, to come to a conclusion using what they already know combined with information in the book. They take their own

background knowledge, add clues from the book, make a good guess, and arrive at an inference. Expressed mathematically, it looks like this:

Book + BK + GG = Inference

When asked about William Taylor's devotion to God, students might make an inference as follows:

- Book: William Taylor read his Bible and prayed on the ship to California. He did not stop even when everyone else rushed off to see the shark. He said it would be disrespectful to stop a conversation with God.
- Background Knowledge (BK): People who are devoted to God read their Bible and pray, but most people would put their Bible aside for a moment and go see the shark. I think I would go see the shark.
- Good Guess (GG): Since Taylor continued reading and praying, he must have been sincerely devoted to God, more than most men.
- Inference: William Taylor showed steadfast devotion to God. He put serving God first in his life and would not let any activity distract him from his prayers.

Many students will do the above thinking automatically, never realizing they have made an inference. However, others need to be expressly taught. Sometimes these students think it is "cheating" to take information that is not in the book to answer a question and need specific permission to do so and instruction on how to do it.

4. On Your Own

The final category of question in Question-Answer Relationship occurs when students use their own background knowledge to answer a question. The background knowledge might include what they have just learned and might ask them combine this new information learned from the book with what they already know to draw a conclusion.

There are several of these questions in the Unit Roundups, but you might form others. For example, at the end of Unit 5, you might ask students to think about life on a rancho, and then talk about whether they would like to live on one or not and why.

To answer this question, students would need to activate their background knowledge, perhaps like this:

1. People who lived on ranchos got to ride horses, and I like horses.
2. They had to dance, and I don't like dancing.
3. They got to spend lots of time outdoors, and I like that except when it is very cold or raining.
4. Children did not have to go to school. I like my school, but sometimes it is hard.
5. Fleas were everywhere. I got bit by a flea once and it itched a lot.

After thinking about rancho life, students form their own conclusions, aside from the author. The question called for an opinion, and the students' opinions may be similar or very different from the author's.

Questions that fall into the "On Your Own" category of the Question-Answer Relationship can call for discernment on the part of students. They might ask students to determine if something was right or wrong or if something agrees or disagrees with the Bible. They might also ask students to form opinions on the author and the author's worldview. As students grow in knowledge and understanding, they will be able to tackle challenging "On Your Own" questions.

Making Inferences about Character

To make character sketches, students will need to make inferences. Explain to students what an inference is and then model it for them. Think out loud and share with your students how you infer.

For example, you might say something along the lines of the following:

1. I think William Taylor was courageous.
2. On page 153 I read that William Taylor planned to preach on Portsmouth Square, but

a friend was afraid he would be shot." (Read the passage aloud and allow students to highlight it in their books.) Wouldn't a man have to be courageous to face death?

3. Then on page 155 I read that Taylor did not stop reading his Bible to see the shark. This seems very courageous because he did not do what other people did. He went against the actions of the crowd. It takes courage to act differently from everyone else.
4. I know that *courage* means acting bravely, even if one is afraid. It also means holding on to convictions and beliefs, even when others do not.
5. Combining my knowledge of the meaning of *courage* with William Taylor's actions, I find him a very courageous man.

Do not be concerned if you have to do a lot of modeling before students understand how to make inferences about a person's character. Some students will catch on quickly and others will need more time. Give them the time.

Samples of Students' Character Sketches

To make a character sketch, begin with the questions on the form at the end of this section. Ask students to answer them by getting information from one or more places in the book and by making inferences. Students should not copy words from the text; instead, they should put the information and thoughts into their own words.

If you are teaching more than one student, after students complete their sketches, you might put them into groups and ask them to share their ideas. Students should expand their sketches by incorporating other students' ideas. After a short time, choose one person from the group to share the group's thoughts with the class. (Let the students choose a spokesman or you can choose deliberately or randomly—the person whose birthday is closest to today for example). The objective of this sharing activity is to let students hear others' thoughts and get ideas not only about what to look for next time, but how others think.

The following character sketches were created by some of my fourth and fifth graders. I made no attempt to correct grammar, punctuation, or spelling. Some of the answers are surprisingly insightful.

Name of person: **John Sutter**
1. Lived in what time period: Mexican
2. Is the person a Christian? No. He was atheisst. He didn't beleve that man have to bleve god's law.
3. What is this person remembered for? For helpping people.
4. What admirable character traits did he possess? Generous
5. What character weaknesses did he possess? self-centered
6. What else can you say about this person? Rich, but spent more then he had.

Name of person: **John Marsh**
1. Lived in what time period: Mexican period
2. Is person a Christian? No.
3. What is this person remembered for? Helping the Bidwell party.
4. What admirable character traits did he possess? helpfullness
5. What character weaknesses did he possess? Selfishness
6. What else can you say about this person? He studied chemicals. [I think that's supposed to be medicine.]

Name of person: **John Frémont**
1. Lived in what time period: Mexican & American
2. Is person a Christian? Maybe. Not sure. He was a good man.
3. What is this person remembered for? Industrious and remarkable explorer
4. What admirable character traits did he possess? spending time whith his family And

close freinds.

5. What character weaknesses did he possess? rash. impulsive. Did not know how to choose men to work with him.
6. What else can you say about this person? Helped the Bear Flag. Let Jesus "Tito" Pico go free. was a generall and running for presedent.

Name of person: **James Marshall**

1. Lived in what time period: Gold Rush
2. Is person a Christian? Probably not.
3. What is this person remembered for? He is rememberd for being the first to find gold on Sutters property.
4. What admirable character traits did he possess? He was willing to work. He was a good worker.
5. What character weaknesses did he possess? greediness
6. What else can you say about this person? He Just bumped into the gold

Name of person: **Lewis Manly**

1. Lived in what time period: Gold Rush
2. Is this person a Christian? Don't know, but Mrs. Bennett, as they (the men) left said "God bless you & help you to bring food to my starving children."
3. What is this person remembered for? Getting water & supplies for the wagon train. Crossed the desert without food or water in order to save the people.
4. What admirable character traits did he possess? A young courageous man. Adventursome. Strong Caring, unselfish.
5. What character weaknesses did he possess? Can't see any. Bad judgment? Didn't go back and find the trail.
6. What else can you say about this person? He was very brave to walk back all that way to save those peeple.

Presenting Character Sketches

You may complete your character sketch activity after students fill in the organizer and perhaps discuss it. On the other hand, if you do more with the information, if you emphasize it in some way, it will become more memorable. Ideas to present character sketches follow.

Create a Booklet

Ask students to use the information on their organizers and their own information plus other ideas (from discussion) to write a paragraph about the character. Ask them to write on a page that looks like this:

In the box, students may draw a picture of the person or of something associated with the person. For example, students might draw a picture of Sutter's Fort to go with John Sutter.

Something that requires some higher thinking skills is to ask students to associate an object with the character. For example, students almost always choose a shark for William Taylor, and he is forever known as "the shark guy." Even today some of my former students, who have children of their own, still remember "the shark guy." Other objects for William Taylor might be a cross because he was a minister, rotten eggs because he didn't let the fear of being covered with them stop him from preaching, or a hospital because he ministered to sick men in San Francisco's decrepit hospitals. It doesn't matter what object students choose as long as it makes sense and helps them make an association between the object and the person. It needs to stimulate memory.

Here is an example of an entry for William Taylor with spelling corrected:

> William Taylor came to San Francisco in 1848. It was during the Gold Rush. He was a minister. He told people about Jesus Christ. William Taylor was very faithful to the Lord. He did not stop reading his Bible and praying when others saw a shark. William Taylor was also very brave. He sang to the people and then talked to them. Even though some people wanted to throw eggs at him. William Taylor lived in San Francisco for seven years.

Ask students to create a cover for their booklet. They might decorate the cover of a three-pronged folder or choose sturdy paper to decorate, and then fasten the booklet together with yarn or staples. If you use yarn or staples, you will need to collect the character sketches in a folder until you are ready to conclude the project.

Create Folding Characters

To create folding character displays, you will need sturdy paper (construction paper or card stock), markers or colored pencils, scissors, glue, and finished paragraphs written on paper that will fit inside the folds.

Fold and cut the paper like the examples provided. The section that extends above the middle fold could either be a face or an object or a title. It might be a circle, a rectangle, or some other shape. Students should paste their paragraphs in the center section, as show.

To interject even more creativity to this project, you might ask students to decorate the outside of their character. This might be abstract, it might be a drawing of the object students associate with the character, or it might be clothes—a brown robe with a belt for Father Serra, a checkered shirt with patched jeans and boots for a gold miner, or a suit and tie for a businessman like William Coleman.

These folding characters may be any size you choose, limited only by the materials you have on hand. They make excellent displays that provide a visual reminder of the people in the pageant of California's history.

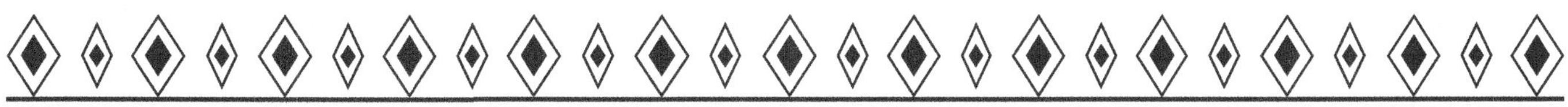

Writing Instruction

One more idea for character sketch presentation is to take the opportunity it provides for writing instruction. The above sample paragraph describing William Taylor is a perfectly good paragraph in terms of content and basic structure. It is typical of what I receive from upper elementary students. Incorporating ideas from the character sketch organizer, it begins with a topic sentence that tells what the paragraph is about and ends with a concluding or clincher sentence that brings the paragraph's thoughts to a close.

Once students are comfortable with the idea of developing character sketches by making inferences (and not before—be careful not to introduce too many new concepts at a time), you might look at some ways to improve on the style of the paragraph, beginning with sentence structure.

I am a huge advocate of the writing methods taught by the Institute for Excellence in Writing and promote their method and products whenever I can. (Disclaimer: I wrote two of the resources for high school students. However, I incorporated IEW's ideas into my teaching methods for many years previous.) For more information go to www.excellenceinwriting.com.

One of the first style techniques IEW teaches is a variety of sentences openers and introduces them to students one at a time. These are the sentence openers:

1. Subject
2. Preposition
3. Adverb (or "ly" word until students become comfortable with the unfamiliar *adverb*)
4. ing,
5. Clausal
6. VSS

The student above, and most students, does not need to be taught the subject opener, although he or she does need to learn to recognize it. All of the sentences begin with a subject: *William Taylor*, *it*, and *he*. (The sentence that begins with *even* is a fragment.)

In the IEW method, students put a number in the margin of their paper identifying the type of opener the sentence uses, like this:

1 William Taylor came to San Fran-
1 cisco in 1848. It was during the Gold
1,1 Rush. He was a minister. He told people
1 about Jesus Christ. William Taylor was
1 very faithful to the Lord. He did not stop
reading his Bible and praying when oth-
1 ers saw a shark. William Taylor was also
1 very brave. He sang to the people and
? then talked to them. Even though some
1 people wanted to throw eggs at him. William Taylor lived in San Francisco for 7
years.

Next, teach the first sentence opener, the preposition, and ask students to rewrite one of their sentences so that it begins with a preposition:

- In 1848, William Taylor made the long voyage to California.
- At the beginning of the Gold Rush in 1848, William Taylor sailed to California.

Whenever they open a sentence with a preposition, students put a 2 in the margin of their paper. Over the course of several weeks, teach all of the openers and encourage students to use all of them in their paragraphs. Shortly, they should be able to produce paragraphs that look like this:

2 At the beginning of the Gold Rush,
5 William Taylor sailed to California. Since
he was a minister, he wanted to tell the
4 people about Jesus Christ. Showing his
faithfulness, Taylor did not stop reading
his Bible and praying when others saw a
6, 2 shark. He was also brave. Courageously,
1 he sang to the people, even though some
1 wanted to throw eggs at him. William
Taylor lived in San Francisco for seven
years, and then he moved to Africa.

While students are learning the sentence openers, make paragraph construction a game with its object to include all six constructions in each paragraph. After students have internalized the sentence openers, they may use them as needed. Even so, you may have to review from time to time and ask students to go back to using all six.

When students are comfortable with the sentence openers, the IEW method teaches more sophisticated sentence structures, calling them *dress-ups* and *decorations*. Not only do students learn to make their writing more interesting and stylish, they also learn some grammar (parts of speech) and mechanics (comma placement) in context. I can't say enough about this program and the results it produces in the youngest of students. Be sure to check it out.

Character Sketch
California History

Name ________________________________

Date ________________________________

Name of Person ____

Lived in what time period?____

Do you think this person a Christian? Give reasons for your answer.

____

____

What is this person remembered for?

____

____

What admirable character traits did he possess?

____

____

What character weaknesses did he possess?

____

____

What else can you say about this person?

____

____

Class Project
California History

Name ___________________________________

Date ______________________________________

Project selection (briefly describe your project):

What information do you think your report will contain?

What do you think your display will look like? What are your ideas?

What will you talk about in your oral report? (This might be the same as your report.)

List at least two books or resources you will use to complete this project.

Do you need any help? If so, please tell me what kind.

Appendix B

Class Project

ONE OF THE MOST EXCITING AND challenging parts of a study of California's history is the completion of a class project. At the end of each unit earlier in this *Teacher's Supplement*, I've listed numerous project suggestions, although students may think of others. (If they do, make sure they check with you before proceeding so that you can give them direction. Sometimes I've helped students rethink their ideas because I knew they would not be able to find many resources.) Students' first challenge will be to narrow their selection to one project.

When considering a topic, have students ask themselves questions such as: Is this topic interesting to me? Can I find enough material to complete my project? If much research is required, do I have the time to pursue it? In my California history classes, many good ideas had to be changed because of lack of time or resources. Additionally, if you are teaching a class or leading a co-op, you will want to have each student choose a separate topic so that the students will learn as much as they can when the other students present their projects. To reserve their topic, ask students to turn in the project selection form (found on the previous page).

The Report

The first part of the California history project is a report of between 500 and 700 words in length (one and a half to two pages if it was typed and double-spaced.) For many students this will be the first time they have tackled a report of this size. If your language arts materials include a section on writing a report, you might consider combining that section with the California history report. If your language arts program does not contain a report writing section, follow the directions below or look for help online.

There are several steps involved in writing a report. One system breaks the process into smaller steps as follows: Read and gather, think and plan, write and rewrite, and check and polish. Another uses the acronym TOWER to organize the steps: Think, Organize, Write, Evaluate, and Rewrite.

Think (and Research)

"Think" involves choosing a topic, reading about it, and taking notes. Generally note-taking is a new adventure for students. Since only a few resources will be used for this report, this step will become more important in future projects. Introduce the art of note-taking, but don't expect mastery.

Students will be able to find resources for their report from many places. The student who wrote the following report on Carmel Mission was privileged to visit it, take pictures, and receive a great deal of first-hand information. In addition to the references listed in the other parts of this manual, check with the children's librarian at your local library. Sometimes copies of popular books are located in the reference section of the library so that they are available for patrons' use in the library. Generally these cannot be checked out, but portions can be copied. Additionally, librarians sometimes maintain a pamphlet file stocked with copies of booklets, or portions of books, on the more popular California history topics.

There are also many resources available online—so many that it's hard to keep track of them. Years ago, when one of my students wanted to learn about life on a rancho, her best resources were *Josefina's Craft Book* and *Welcome to Josefina's World*, both from Pleasant Company Publications, part of the *American Girl* series. Today, I did a quick search on the Internet (California rancho tours) and found six wonderful resources in less than a minute. Most include pictures on their websites and many include videos. Students should have no difficulty finding resources for their reports.

In my classes, I restrict Internet sources. For every Internet source students use, they also have to use one non-Internet source. I have several reasons for this restriction. First, unless students print out the Internet sources, it is difficult to work with them to take notes and create an outline. Second, working with print sources is easier on the eyes and wrists. I realize that I am fighting a losing battle and that the Internet is becoming the preferred research tool, but I have worked with computers my entire life and as a result struggle with radial tunnel syndrome. If children use the Internet, they need to have a station that works for them ergonomically, and grows as they do. Third, print sources often contain wonderful pictures and diagrams that aid understanding. These are not always available on the Internet—especially the artwork. Fourth, as students get older, they tend to use fewer and fewer non-Internet sources. When I require my high school students to go to the library to check out a book, many are appalled, don't have a library card, and don't even know where the library is. That is very sad. Finally, a wide variety of older sources that support a Christian worldview exist, which is not always the case with the Internet. On the other hand, more and more of those resources are disappearing, making their way to library sales. Of course, it's your choice as to what materials your students use for their California history reports, but I encourage the use of some non-Internet sources.

Think and Research Checkpoints:

- ☐ Bring books and notes to class for teacher's OK.
- ☐ Create notes or note cards
- ☐ Prepare bibliography in correct format

<u>Organize</u>

The next step is to organize the notes using an outline. Generally, at this point the student's topic is too broad. An outline can help to narrow it to reasonable bounds. For example, students often choose a mission for their project. Reams have been written about each individual mission and the student's first decision will be to decide the scope of his or her topic. Will he include how the mission was founded? Mission activities? Biographies of the padres? Important incidents such as an earthquake or Indian attacks? Architecture? The mission today? An outline serves to define the boundaries of the report, organize it, and break it down into more workable sections. Students will require a great deal of help at this point. If they are struggling, give them as much help as they need to complete their outline. See the following examples of outlines.

Organize Checkpoints:

- ☐ Outline—Roman numeral or graphic organizer

<u>Write</u>

The third step in writing a report is to actually write. If you have helped your students to prepare an outline, this step will be markedly easier as they can write their reports in sections over a period of days. In the example that follows, the student could write section one, "History of the Missions," the first day, followed by "Beginning of Missions" another. Writing the report in sections will relieve tedium and allow students to do their best on smaller units. Instruct students to double space their reports and use their own words. It is very important to check to be sure that they are not copying directly out of the reference books. The result of this step will be the

student's rough draft.

Once the rough draft is complete, students (and teachers) should evaluate what they have written. The report should be checked for grammatical, punctuation, and spelling errors, but it should also be checked for style. One of the most common problems with reports at this age is abrupt beginnings, missing transitions, and rushed endings. The report needs an opening paragraph to introduce the subject to the reader (introduction) and a closing paragraph to wrap it up (conclusion). Additionally, sometimes a transition sentence is needed between paragraphs.

For example, if a student is writing a biography and writes about the subject's early life in one paragraph and later life in the next, he will need some sort of transition sentence to fill in the missing years such as, "Father Serra continued to work diligently at his studies until he was chosen to be a missionary to the New World." While evaluating the rough draft you might decide that additional topics could be included or that the report is unwieldy and has to be cut. Mark all changes on the student's rough draft.

Write Checkpoints:

- ☐ Evaluate individual paragraphs or rough draft

Re-write

The final step is to rewrite the rough draft. At this age it is best to require one rewrite so that the student will not be discouraged from further writing. Make sure that you have edited the rough draft carefully. The final report should be copied on wide or college-ruled notebook paper. Most of my fourth graders do not type very well, and since I would like them to practice handwriting (rapidly becoming a lost art), I ask for handwritten reports. You, of course, may differ.

Design an attractive cover (see Class-Time Activities for the Mexican period) and include a bibliography. Finally, congratulate yourself! You have survived one of the major challenges of California history!

Rewrite Checkpoints:

- ☐ Write report final draft
- ☐ Create final bibliography

The Display

The second part of the California history project is the display. The student who prepared the report on Carmel Mission built a model of it. Many of my students have chosen missions as their projects. Some build models out of sugar cubes, Styrofoam, or salt, water, and flour. Other projects have ranged in size from a small replica of Patty Reed's doll to a full-sized model of a Gold Rush sluice. We have had costumed visits from Theodore Judah and Pasquala and have heard the story of their lives. We have seen models of ships, forts, ranchos, and gold mines. We have sampled tortillas. We have seen student-authored and -illustrated books on sea otters and grizzly bears. We have also seen large maps of grizzly habitat and routes of various mountain men.

Have your students look over the various project suggestions. (All of the project suggestions from each section of this manual are reproduced on the following list so that you may copy it and give it to your students.) They can also obtain help from their local librarian. If students will be presenting their displays at a history fair or at a co-op presentation day, they will want to consider some kind of backdrop. Pictures, captions and information glued to reinforced poster board will help to introduce their project. For more information on display design, look for books in the science project section of the library.

The Oral Presentation

The climax of the California history project is the oral presentation. Students make a five-minute presentation about their project before a group. This could be before the family, before their class, at a presentation night, or at a history fair. For some students, this will be the most challenging part of the class. Students can use index cards for notes, but they may not read their reports. (One year one of my students came with a huge stack of index cards on which he had copied his entire report. He proceeded to read them, one by one!) The objective here is a gentle introduction to public speaking. Encourage students to practice their speeches before they actually give them on the presentation day. This will greatly increase their confidence.

Roman Numeral Outline Example

San Carlos Borremeo del Río Carmelo

1. Introduction
    - A. Oldest mission
    - B. Founded Monterey August 1771
    - C. Fray Junípero Serra
    - D. Mudejar star

II. Founding
- A. Portolá, Serra, Crespi
- B. Worked together

III. Buildings
- A. Kitchen
- B. Adobe construction

IV. Contents
- A. Mudjar star
    - i. Stained glass window
    - ii. Also San Rafael
- B. Graves—Serra, Crespi, Lasuen
- C. Statues
    - i. Jesus
    - ii. Virgin Mary, baby Jesus
    - iii. Crowns donated sailor
- D. Belltower
    - i. 8 original
    - ii. View—pond
- E. Other
    - i. Indian workshops
    - ii. First library

V. Use of mission
- A. 2,000 books
- B. Sir Harry Downie restore
- C. Mass today
- D. Fray Junípero School

VI. Conclusion
- A. Astounding founders, historical beginnings
- B. Tourist attraction
- C. First library in CA

Graphic Organizers

Some students, especially those who are visually-oriented, do better with a graphic organizer rather than a Roman numeral outline. Many options exist. Just search for "Graphic Organizers" on the Internet, and you will be overwhelmed with choices. Two simple organizers follow, one that works best with information organized topically, like life on a mission, rancho, or the report about gold. The other works best with information organized chronologically, like a biography or narrative.

Body Web

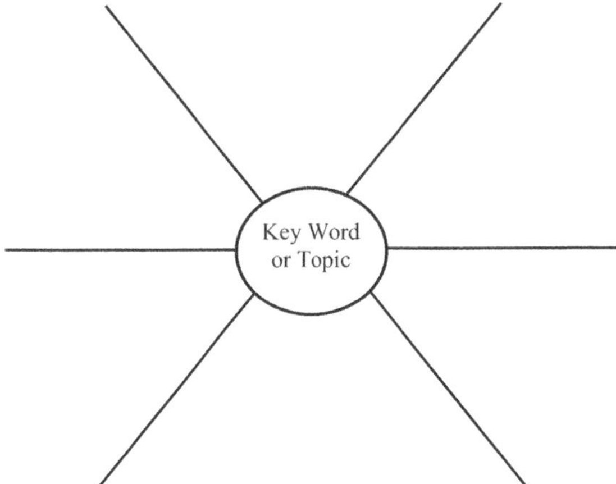

Write the subject, idea, concept, person, or topic in the center. Surround with important details or pertinent information.

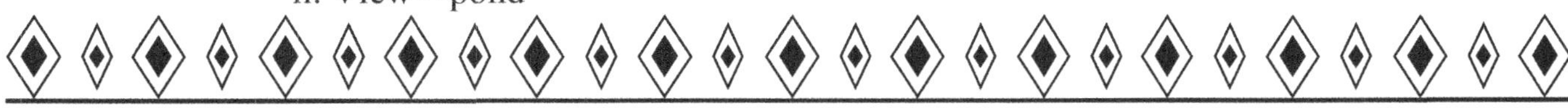

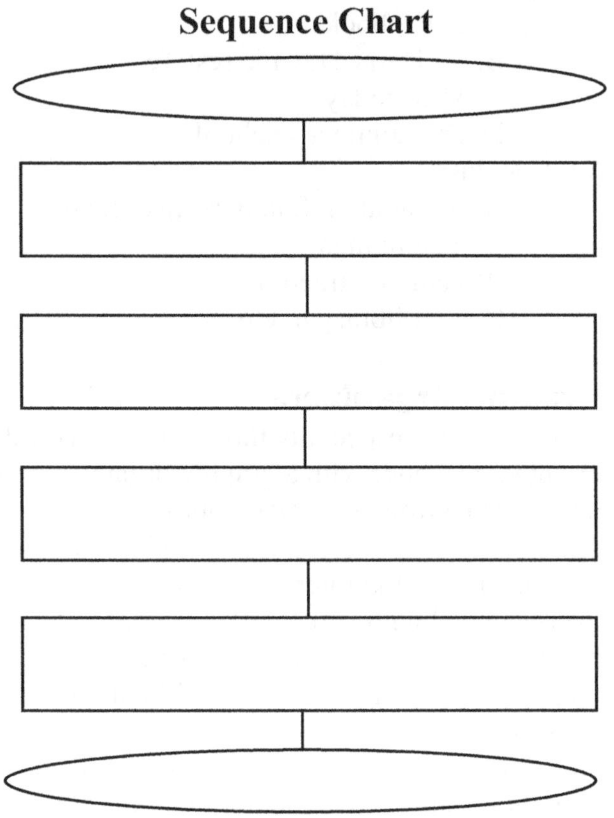

Sequence Chart

To use the sequence chart, identify the topic in the top oval, then list the facts and details in order beneath it.

Graphic Organizer Outline Example

The technical term for the organizer illustrated at the bottom of this page is *body web*, but my students all call it the spider. I have included two levels of detail on this web, but students could expand it by writing key word outlines under the horizontal lines

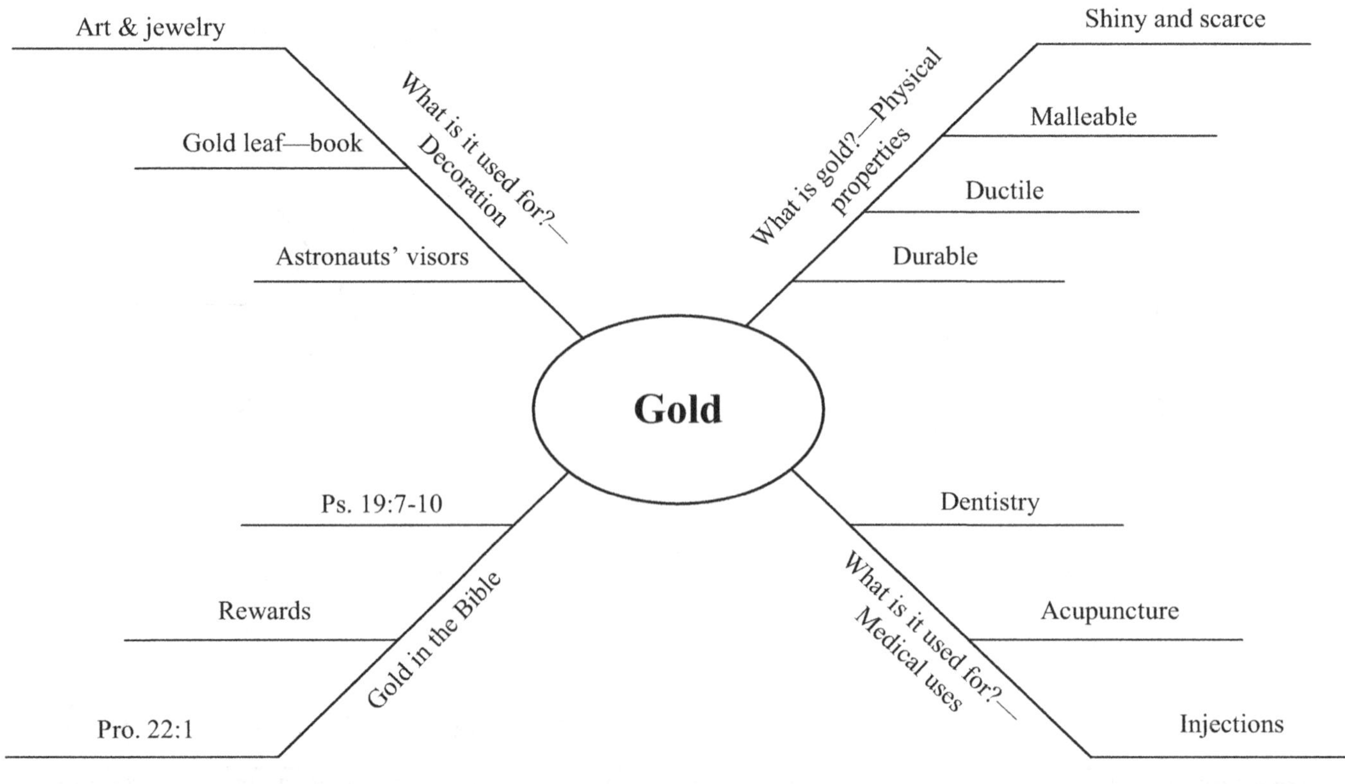

Report Examples

These are all final drafts of California history reports by students in my classes, reproduced exactly as I received them.

San Carlos Borremeo del Rio Carmelo
By Daniel Roberts

Mission San Carlos Borremeo del Río Carmelo remains the oldest continuously used mission today. In 1770 the construction began in Monterey. The mission was dedicated in August 1771, having been founded by Fray Junípero Serra. One of the mission's most fascinating features is the Mudejar star. This mission remains a historical landmark to this day.

Captain Don Gaspár de Portolá, who served in the military, helped Fray Serra with the beginnings of mission San Carlos Borremeo del Río Carmelo. Juan Crespi willingly served as one of the friars at the mission as well. Because these founders all worked together they made this mission a reality.

The mission church had its own kitchen. Before the beginnings of this mission, Serra blessed it in the Carmel valley. In August of 1771, he dedicated it. Some structures which were constructed out of adobe, were skillfully made. These beginnings are important because they play a notable part in the history of Mission San Carlos Borremeo del Río Carmelo.

The Mudejar star is a stained glass window, which is embedded in a rock wall. Although this star is at Carmel mission, it is also at Mission San Rafael Arcangel. Because Serra, Crespi, and Lasuén were influential people, they were honored by having their graves in the church. There is a statue of Jesus in the church. In the Chapel there is an altar of the Virgin Mary and Baby Jesus which are the originals. Their crowns were donated by a sailor. Most of the eight bells in the belltower are the originals. From there is a view of a pond. The south side of the quadrangle originally housed Indian workshops. The first library in California was at this mission. These features are fascinating sites to see.

By 1820, 2,000 books occupied the mission's library. Sir Harry Downie willingly restored the church's altar because it was the main attraction of the church. Mass is still held there today. There is a Fray Junípero Serra school, which is Catholic. These changes are a significant part of the history of mission San Carlos Borremeo del Río Carmelo because they reflect the past and present of this mission.

Mission San Carlos Borremeo del Río Carmelo has some astounding founders and some historical beginnings. The features are fascinating and they remain a tourist attraction. The most significant part of this mission is that it occupied the first library in California.

Bibliography

Ambrosio, Katie. Mission San Carlos Borromeo. Carmel, 2000. pp. 2, 4, 5, 18-19.

Edgar, Kathleen J. The Missions of California: Mission San Carlos Borremeo del Rio Carmelo. New York: The Rosen Publishing Group, Inc. pp. 4, 17-19, 24, 26, 30, 38, 50, 52-57.

Kuskoi, George. Live Again Our Mission Past. Larkspur: Arts' Publications. 1983. pp. 76-77.

Roberts, Daniel. Mission Tour Notes

Gold
By Shannon Gerhard

What is gold? What makes gold so valuable and what is it used for? Is there anything more valuable than gold? What does the Bible say? I will answer these questions in my report.

Gold is a heavy metal and it is very shiny. Throughout history it has been treasured in every country of the world. Glistening bright yellow in color, it captures people's attention. Gold is very scarce and it has many qualities that make it

special. It is very malleable which means gold is pliable and can be pounded and bent into shapes without being broken. Its also very ductile so it can be hammerd very thin and stretched and extended out into a long wire. In fact, a chunk of gold the size of a pea, can be stretched into a wire two miles long without breaking. A little larger piece, the size of a plum, can be beaten into a thin sheet of gold leaf that can cover a tennis court. Gold is very durable which means it can last a very long time and is not worn out easily. It doesn't react to air, water, and most chemicals. Gold keeps its luster even when acids are put in contact with it. Heat and electricity flow through gold easily. All of these qualities make gold very useful.

Gold is used for more than just jewelry and coins. It is used for medical care. Because gold doesn't react to acids in people's mouths, dentists use it for gold fillings in teeth. Acupuncturists use goldplated needles because gold is safe to use in people's bodies. Did you know injections of solutions containing some gold, are helpful to treat tuberculosis, rheumatoid arthritis, and some types of cancer? Researchers are still looking for more ways that gold can be used in medicine.

Because of gold's surpassing beauty, it is used for jewelry and art. Gold leaf is used sometimes on the cover of a book to engrave a name. Did you know that a very thin layer of gold is used on astronauts' visors? This is done to protect astronauts from harmful sun rays while in space. This reflective value of gold has been useful on many different spacecrafts, such as satellites, space shuttles, and the Pathfinder Probe. I think it is interesting that strands of gold are used in astronauts' tethers. Gold is used because it will not corrode and break causing the astronaut to drift off into space. According to these outstanding facts about gold, it is magnificent.

The Bible describes something more valuable than gold. Do you know what it is? In Ps. 19:7-10 the following things are more desirable than gold: God's law, testimony, precepts, commandments, judgments, and the fear of God. By keeping or obeying God's Word, we can get a great reward. Seeking wisdom and understanding is better than the profit of gold. Another thing that is more valuable than gold is to have a good name or reputation. (Pro. 22:1).

Wouldn't it be cool if there was a Bible rush, just like the 1849 Gold Rush?

Bibliography

Adkins, Jan, "Gold." Muse Magazine. April 1998, pp. 32-34

Angliss, Sarah. The Elements of Gold. New York: Benchmark Books, 2000. pp. 1-30.

Coombs, Charles, Gold and Other Precious Metals. New York: Morrow. pp 16, 94-107.

McMorrow, Catherine, Gold Fever! New York: Random House, 1996, p. 8.

The World Book Encyclopedia, "Gold."

The Transcontinental Railroad

By Ryan Harral

"May God continue the unity of our country, as this railroad unites the two great Oceans of the world." These words are found on the Golden Spike, which was the last Spike driven at Promontory Point, Utah, when the Transcontinental Railroad was completed. Theodore Judah and the Big Four started the Central Pacific and although there were many hardships, the railroad helped California in many ways.

Theodore Judah, who was often called crazy Judah, thought up the first plan for the Transcontinental Railroad. He came to California in 1854 and later went to Washington, D.C. to ask if it was OK to build the Transcontinental Railroad. When he was surveying some land, he saw Donner Pass. That gave him an idea. He could build the tracks through the Sierra Nevada.

Now he needed money to build it so he went to the Big Four who were Charles Crocker, Leland Stanford, Mark Hopkins, and Colis P. Huntington. When they agreed to finance it, they formed the Central Pacific.

There were a lot of problems when building the Transcontinental Railroad. There were not enough workers so Crocker hired Chinese men because they were hard workers. Even though they only got paid two dollars a day, they never went on strike. Another challenge was to make a tunnel through the mountains because the tunnel had to be fifteen miles long. But the hardest problem was digging through Cape Horn because it was made of the hardest granite. Also, Cape Horn was very wide and tall. The workers used gun powder to blast their way through the rock. In the end more than twenty thousand men had hammerd down 1,175 miles of track in a little more than three years.

The Transcontinental Railroad made it safer and easier to travel to California. Traveling by wagon or ship was very slow and difficult. The Railroad helped settlers want to come to California because they could still stay in touch with their family by sending letters or visiting them. Also California could get food, clothes, tools, toys, supplies, and other goods from the East which was brought by train.

The Central Pacific was formed by Theodore Judah and the Big Four who had a vision for a railroad to connect the Atlantic and the Pacific Oceans. Although building the railroad was challenging, California benefited from it in many ways.

Bibliography

Blumberg, Rhoda, Full Steam Ahead: the race to build the Transcontinental Railroad, Washington D.C., 1996

Everds, John, The Spectacular Trains, North Brook, Illinois, Hubbard press, 1973

McCready, Albert L. Railroads, in the days of steam, N.Y., American Heritage, 1960

Myers, Lesha, His California Story, Concord CA, Cameron Academy, 1995

Stein, Conrad, The Story of the Golden Spike, Chicago, Childrens Press, 1978

Bears in California

By David Wilcox

Bears are one of the most ferocious creatures of the forest. There were a whole lot of them in California back in the 1800's. There aren't many bears living in California now and no grizzlies. They were hunted and so many were killed that they couldn't reproduce. The people that came to settle in California were afraid of the bears and treated them badly. They also thought they were strong and a good symbol to put on the California flag.

In California there are the American black bears, brown bears and there used to be grizzly bears. All these types of bears pretty much live the same way. Bears are omnivores which like to eat leaves, roots, berries, insects, grubs, small rodents, salmon, honey, dead animal flesh and hooved animals. They also will eat humans if they have to protect themselves of if they are very, very hungry.,

Bears will have their cubs and hibernate in the dens and caves of the cool mountain forests during the winter. In the spring, the mother bears will go out into the meadows first to protect the cubs from all other bears who will eat them; then the cubs will come out to help her search for food. All the bears come to the river to try to catch the salmon as they spawn. The cubs will stay with their mothers for about three years. Bears can live up to 25 years; but when there's a lot of them being hunted, the average age of a bear would be only about fifteen years old.

During the Mexican Period of California's history, the bears were used for entertainment by being tied together with a bull and having to fight each other. Even though fur traders didn't use the furs of the bears to make a lot of money, the bear hunt at La Cañada de Los Osos ("Bear Valley")

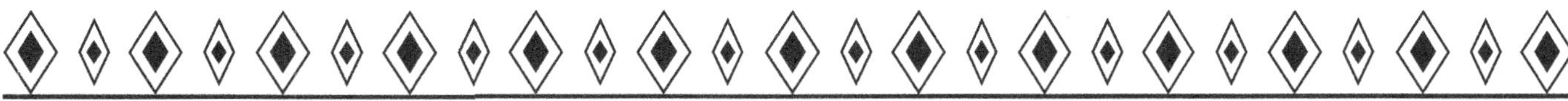

in 1769 killed enough grizzlies to make 9,000 pounds of bear jerky to feed starving missionaries. There were thousands of grizzly bears in the 1800s in California' and today, the only grizzly bear I have seen is a stuffed one in the Lindsey Museum. It was the beginning of the end for the California grizzlies.

The American settlers of California didn't like that the Mexicans were trying to rule California. In 1846, the Americans captured the pueblo of Sonoma. It was known as the "Bear Flag Revolt" because they used the bear flag until they later replaced it with the American flag. The bear flag was made by William Todd. It has a red stripe with a picture of a grizzly bear next to a star, copied from the lone star of Texas, with the words "California Republic" under the bear. The grizzly bear was used as the symbol because there were so many living in California at the time.

Bears look cute and cuddly and can seem friendly at times, but they are still one of the most ferocious creatures of the forest. Jedediah Smith, the mountain man and fur trapper, met up with a grizzly bear in the forest which slashed the side of his head and broke three ribs. We need to be cautious around bears, but they don't usually kill people unless they get surprised and think you will hurt them. I'm sad that there aren't any grizzly bears in California now, but we do have black bears. Bears need to live where we can be protected from them, and where they can be protected and live and grow their families.

Bibliography

Berger, Ralph. "The Bear Flag Revolt." CCNet. 1996. <http://www.ccnet.com/~laplaza/calhist4.htm>.

"The California State Flag." Netstate. 2001. <http://www.netstate.com/states/symb/flags/ca_flag.html>.

"The Long History of La Cañada De Los Osos." Los Osos—Baywood Park Chamber of Commerce. 2001. <http://www.losososbaywoodpark.org/chamber/history/index.html>.

Myers, Lesha. His California Story. California" Cameron Academy, 1995.

Pringle, Laurence. Bearman. New York, N.Y.: Scribners, 1989.

Swinburne, Stephen. Moon in Bear's Eyes. Brookfield, CT: Millbrook Press, 1998

Common Grammatical and Punctuation Errors

1. Forgetting to capitalize proper nouns (for example the mission at San Juan Capistrano vs. San Juan Capistrano Mission)

2. Using abbreviations instead of spelling out the entire word (for example Ca. for California).

3. Forgetting to write out numbers under 100 (12 instead of twelve).

4. Starting a sentence with "and," or "but."

5. Having a paragraph of just one sentence or omitting paragraph breaks altogether.

6. Improper use of there and their.

7. Capitalizing a word in the middle of a sentence.

8. Using incomplete sentences and run-ons.

Suggestions for Class Projects

Indian Period

1. Make a model of an Indian village. Include the sweathouse, dwellings, roundhouse, and perhaps some utensils (baskets, acorn-pounding rocks). You could use plaster of paris to make the setting, aluminum foil for water, weeds for marshlands, and grass and twigs for structures.
2. Learn how to weave an Indian basket, or make a soaproot brush or other Indian tool. Some Indian museums offer instruction.
3. Research the different ways California Indians made their homes. Build models of plank houses, tule huts, desert shelters, and earth mounds (see *California Indian Days*, by Helen Bauer). Discuss how the climate influenced the kind of house the Indians made.
4. Make a model of a tule boat using hard-stemmed grass or weeds. Make a model of a boat like the Chumash used. Use thin pieces of wood or egg shell cartons, and "sew" together with thread. Use "tar" or "asphalt" (or plain glue) to seal the seams. Paint. See if your boats float. Discuss merits of each.
5. Make up some Indian legends. For example, why are there earthquakes in California, why do birds fly, why is the moon not always round? Read some actual legends (have your parents or teacher help you make your selection) so you can make yours sound authentic.
6. Visit an Indian museum and prepare a report. Take pictures if you can.
7. After reading Unit One: The California Indians, make a list of similarities and differences to compare and contrast the Indians' culture and a Christian culture.

Explorer Period

1. Prepare a report on Juan Rodríguez Cabrillo. Include a map of his voyage. Write a story about his encounter with the Indians of San Diego or San Miguel Island—what did they do, look like, and say?
2. Find out all you can about galleons and other Spanish ships. Draw some pictures or diagrams.
3. Prepare a report on Sir Francis Drake. Include a description of Indians he met. Perhaps visit Drake's Bay near Pt. Reyes.
4. Learn how to navigate with a compass. Set up a route for your friends or classmates. Make it your goal to have them begin and end in the same place. Are they able to do it?
5. Research the art of knot-tying. Learn to tie a square knot, bowline, and half-hitch.
6. Research and write a report on scurvy or rickets. Why were sailors prone to these diseases? What were their symptoms? How were they cured? Why are these diseases no longer a problem?
7. Learn how ships communicated with each other using flags. Write a message in "flag code" (semaphore).
8. Find out all you can about anchors. How are they made, what are they used for, how can they be used to move a ship, and how are they raised? Make a report illustrated with pictures.

Spanish Period

1. Draw an "event map" (words or pictures illustrating what happened along the way) of Portola's march to San Diego and Monterey. Record what happened at each place along the

way. Pretend you are Portolá and write a letter to place under the cross at Monterey. Record the most important things that have happened in your journey. Discuss the reason you are returning to San Diego.

2. Do a study of the La Brea tar pits from a creationist point of view. Find out how the Indians used the tar. What else was found in the pits? What does this tell you about California's past?
3. Compare San Francisco Bay as it was when originally discovered to the area today. What parts were filled in and why? What is there now? (Downtown San Francisco!)
4. Draw an "event map" of the Anza Expedition. Research Juan Bautista de Anza.
5. Research and report on the California sea otter. What was its habitat? Why and how was it hunted? What was its fur used for? Now that it's a protected species, how is it doing? What would it be like if sea otters were as abundant as they were originally? Would their voracious appetites affect abalone and other seafood along the coast?
6. Research and report on the grizzly bear. Find out more about the bear hunt at El Cañon de los Osos (near San Luis Obispo). Describe a bull and bear fight. Do you think this was cruel? Are you glad grizzlies do not live in California anymore? Describe their temperament and habits. Write a fictional account of a person meeting a grizzly. Find out more about Jedediah Smith's meeting with a grizzly.
7. Report on Doña Concepción and Count Rezanov (several authors have written fictional accounts of this romance. See Gertrude Athernon in the adult section of the library). How did their different religions cause problems for them?
8. Make some adobes. Make a model of an adobe home. Describe how the Spaniards made their adobe homes. Why did they coat them with limestone? Why did the San José Mission, and other missions, add tar to the adobes when they reconstructed them? (So they wouldn't "melt" in the rain.)
9. Learn how to do some of the things Mission Indians would have done such as carding and spinning wool or weaving cloth.
10. Do a report on the Russian colony at Sitka, Alaska. What was their religion? Who were the Aleuts? What did the Russians do at Sitka?
11. Do a report on any of the missions. Build a model using sugar cubes and egg white icing or glue. You could also build a model from Styrofoam. What took place at the mission? Perhaps paint or draw pictures of some of these activities.
12. Make a map showing the location of all twenty-one missions. Perhaps draw pictures or make models of some of these. Visit as many as you can, take pictures, and build a display.
13. Dress up as Pasquala and tell the exciting story of your kidnap, escape, and dangerous journey to save Mission Santa Ines.

Mexican Period

1. Find out all you can about the hide and tallow trade. Draw a map to mark the routes the Boston ships followed to California, and Hawaii. What routes did the English ships follow? How were hides prepared for the trip? How were they loaded on board ship? What kinds of things did the Mexican-Californians trade their hides for? (*Two Years Before the Mast* by Richard Henry Dana has a good description of this trade.)
2. Research the old California rodeos. What kinds of activities took place? How were cattle roped? What kinds of social activities took place? What were bull and bear fights? What kinds of horses were used? How were the horses ornamented? Illustrate with pictures or build a model of a rodeo. What is a vaquero?

3. Find out how tortillas were made in Mexican-California. Try to make one. Grind the corn by hand on a metate or similar surface. Learn how to make bread as the early Californians did. What other kinds of food can you think of to make? Perhaps make a display and offer samples.
4. Make a model of a pueblo. Perhaps choose the Los Angeles pueblo, a reconstruction of the original pueblo in downtown Los Angeles. Write for information on Los Angeles Pueblo State Park or look it up on the Internet. Or prepare a report on the San José pueblo. Visit Kelley Park in San Jose. You could illustrate your report with pictures of activities that took place in a pueblo. What was the plaza used for?
5. Find out more about frontier men such as Jedediah Smith. Draw maps of their expeditions. What procedures did they use to trap? What did they trap? What kinds of experiences did they have with Indians?
6. Research beavers. Where do they live? What are their habits? Why were they trapped? How was their fur used? Would it be good to have a quantity of beaver near civilization today? (The forest service usually relocates beavers to remote areas because their dams create problems with water supplies.) Could you find a beaver dam?
7. How were covered wagons made? How were wagon trains assembled? How were captains selected? What happened at night? What trails were used to get to California? What difficulties were faced? Research specific wagon-train parties such as the Stevens-Murphy party (*First Wagons to California*, by Michael Chester) or the Donner Party. What kinds of landmarks did the pioneers look for? (Courthouse Rock, Chimney Rock, Independence Rock.) Where are they located?
8. Make a model of Sutter's Fort. Prepare a report on John Sutter. Where was he from? How did he build his fort? What activities took place there? Perhaps visit the reconstructed Sutter's Fort in Sacramento.
9. Research whales. How was the whaling trade important to California? Where did the whalers go? (The Sandwich Islands, as Hawaii was called). Research William Richardson who lived in what is now Sausalito. How did he help the whalers? (through trade). How was whale oil obtained? What was it used for? Illustrate with pictures and maps. Find out what whaling ships looked like.
10. Draw pictures of some of the costumes worn by rancheros during Mexican California. Make costumes for dolls, clothespin people, or yourself. Where did the clothes come from? Learn how to embroider or do needlework like the California women did.
11. Find out which Mexican ranchos existed in your area. Find out all you can about some of the founding families. Draw a map of the ranchos. Are there any adobes that you can visit in your area?
12. Make Patty Reed's doll from a clothespin and pipecleaners. Dress it as Patty would have. Find out how Patty and her family were rescued by their father when the Donner party became trapped in the winter of 1845-46.

Gold Rush

1. Visit Marshall State Historic Park in Coloma. Do a report on the discovery of gold. Perhaps make a model of Marshall's sawmill. Where is Coloma? Find out more about James Marshall.
2. Find out more about gold. How has it been used in history? What is a carat? Why is metal mixed with gold to make jewelry? How much is gold worth? How can you buy gold? What is Fort Knox? When did the United States go off the gold standard? What has happened to our money since?
3. How is gold mined? How is it processed? What is quartz mining? Hydraulic mining? Visit Colombia State Historic Park. Visit

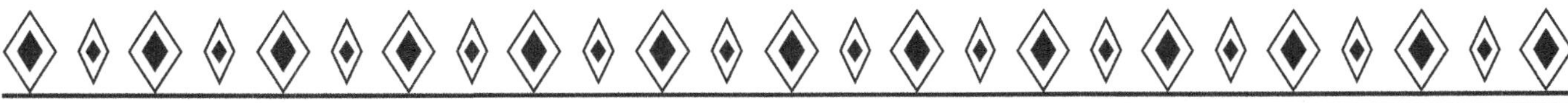

Empire Mine.

4. Try your hand at panning for gold. Expeditions are offered at Jamestown, as well as at many other places. What kind of equipment is needed? What kinds of problems would miners encounter? (Hard to get supplies, have to stand in freezing water, and health problems, for example)
5. Write a story about mining life. Describe how the miners lived, how they cooked their meals, what they did for entertainment, how they washed their clothes, what they did with their leisure time. Who was Bret Harte? (An early California author who wrote about California. Some of his stories are questionable.)
6. Make a map of the Mother Lode region showing the location of different mining towns.
7. Make a model of a gold mining scene.
8. Find out who Sarah Royce was (see *A Frontier Lady*, by Sarah Royce -- she was one of the few women in the mining camps.) Do a report on the Royce family. Pretend you are Sarah Royce and write a letter to home. Describe your experiences and feelings.
9. Make models of various mining equipment such as a long tom, cradle, or sluice. Describe how they work.
10. Make a model of a millrace and a waterwheel. Describe how the waterwheel could be used to run machinery. Visit Bales Grist Mill at Bothe-Napa State Park. How is a grist mill similar to a sawmill?
11. Find out what the miners did in their leisure time. What was a miners' ball? Who was Lotta Crabtree?
12. Do a report on the ways that pioneers reached the gold fields. Show the sea routes around South America, and across the Isthmus of Panama, as well as the various overland routes. Why would a person choose one route over another? Illustrate your report with maps and/or pictures. Pretend you are traveling one of the routes and write a letter home describing your adventure.
13. Research the location of the state capitol before it settled in Sacramento. Visit the site of the capitol in Benicia. Take a tour of the capitol in Sacramento. Describe what goes on there.
14. Find several Bible verses that discuss the relationship between God and the weather.

American Period

1. Draw a map of California showing geographical details. Prepare a report on some of the places shown, such as the state and national parks.
2. Prepare a map or report of places that would be fun to visit for field trips (State Historic Parks, museums, and the like). Describe any you might have been to.
3. Find out how dams are constructed. Try to visit one. What kinds of engineering problems do they face? How are they solved?
4. Learn how water is provided to your home. Find out what irrigation project you are a part of. Visit your local water district.
5. Research your own local history. Identify landmarks (schools, streets, and creeks for example) that were named after early settlers and pioneers. Your local historical society and library should be able to help you with this project.
6. If your grandparents grew up in California, interview them. Pay particular attention to the changes that they have seen in their lifetime. Find out how and under what circumstances they came to California.
7. Research the churches in your community. Try to find out which are the oldest and the circumstances under which they began. Again, your local historical society should be able to help you.
8. Pretend you are one of the first people to ride the transcontinental railroad from New York to San Francisco. Write a letter describing

your experiences. Or, pretend that you came to California originally by wagon, and have just returned to the East on the railroad. Write a letter describing the differences.

9. Dress in a costume similar to what Theodore Judah would have worn and tell the story of his life and his dream to build the transcontinental railroad.

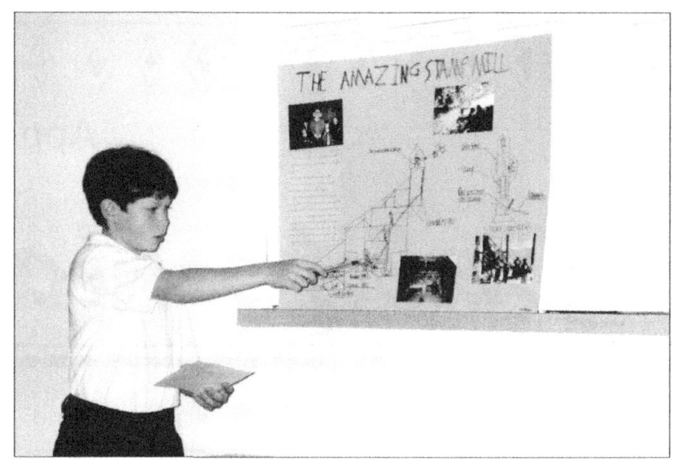

My students' projects, clockwise from top right: Clay Bedinger and stamp mills, Shannon Gerhard and gold, Janae Werner and Mexican food, and Daniel Roberts and Mission San Carlos Borremeo del Río Carmelo.

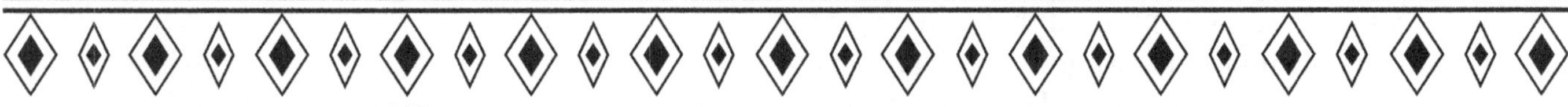

Appendix C

California Date Song

The "California Date Song" was written by one of my California history students, who was nine at the time, to help her memorize the dates I assigned. She meant it to be sung to the tune of "Paddy Works on the Railway," but students have written to me with other tunes that also work such as "Yankee Doodle." I'll give the dates and leave the tune to you.

Dates

Sometime after the flood—
the Indians came to California
1542—Cabrillo (Discovery of California)
1579—Drake (English visit to California)
1602—Vizcaíno (Last major Spanish explorer)
1769—Beginning of Spanish period
1781—Yuma Massacre
1811—Russians build Fort Ross
1821—Beginning of Mexican period
1826—Jedediah Smith visits California
1839—John Sutter immigrates to California
1841—First overland wagon trip (Bidwell)
1848—Gold discovery
1850—Statehood
1856—Vigilance Committee
1862-63—Great Drought
1869—Completion of transcontinental railroad

California Date Song Verses

Some unknown years after the flood,
When all the land was dried from mud,
Maybe after our Savior shed His blood,
Came the California Indians.

In fifteen hundred and forty-two,
Cabrillo sailed the ocean blue.
Searching for a short cut through,
He discovered California.

In fifteen hundred and seventy-nine
Sir Francis sailed the *Golden Hind*,
The Strait of Anían to find,
But he only found Drake's Bay.

In sixteen hundred and only two,
Vizcaíno sailed the ocean blue,
Of Monterey Bay he wrote and drew,
The last of the explorers.

In seventeen hundred and sixty-nine,
Portolá crossed the Baja line,
San Francisco Bay he'd finally find,
With the Sacred Expedition.

In seventeen hundred and eighty-one,
Captain Rivera's men were stunned,
By what the Yuma Massacre had done.
The Anza trail was closed.

In eighteen hundred and eleven,
Long after Serra went to heaven,
Fort Ross was built by Russian men,
Who came to trap the otter.

In eighteen hundred and twenty-one,
Mexican independence was won,
For California it was no fun,
The poor, neglected province.

In eighteen hundred and twenty-six,
A man blazed trails west through the sticks,
Of beaver pelts he took his picks,
Bible-totin' Jed Smith.

In eighteen hundred and thirty-nine,
John Sutter left his debts behind,
To settlers he was always kind,
And he built a fort in the valley.

In eighteen hundred and forty-one,
The first wagons rolled toward the setting sun,
They met John Marsh when the trip was done,
John Bidwell's seven-month journey.

In eighteen hundred and forty-eight,
James Marshall found a shining bait,
Soon men would flood the Golden Gate,
In the California Gold Rush.

In eighteen hundred and fifty years,
Congress overcame its fears,
And a thirty-first star appeared -
California joined the Union.

In eighteen hundred and fifty-six,
San Francisco's Coleman was called to fix,
Its crimes and murders and corrupt politics,
With the Vigilance Committee.

In eighteen sixty-two and three,
First flood, then drought, oh mercy me!
Dead cattle led to bankruptcy,
And the end of the old ranchos.

In eighteen hundred and sixty-nine,
Railroaders worked to build one line,
Two oceans joined and that was fine,
The transcontinental railroad.

We sing one part of God's great plan,
To bring the gospel to each man,
And take dominion of the land—
His California Story!

California Date Song

Appendix D

Geography

The objective of the geography portion of each unit is to introduce the physical features of California to the student, a few at a time. Once all features are learned, the salt, water, and flour map, described in the American Units section of this manual, can be completed.

Make one copy of the large outline map which follows for each student. Each week, the student should draw the new geographical features on his or her map. The map should be placed in the student's notebook and used for review and as a guide for the salt, water, and flour map.

Indian Unit

Bays:
Humboldt
San Francisco
Monterey
Santa Barbara
San Pedro
San Diego

Mountain Ranges:
Sierra Nevada
Tehachapi*
Coast Range
Klamath
Santa Ana
San Gabriel

*Pronounced Te-HATCH-a-pee

Explorers Unit

Capes and Points:
Cape Mendocino
Point Conception

Islands:
Santa Catalina
San Clemente
Santa Rosa
Santa Cruz
San Miguel

Spanish Units

Rivers:
Colorado
Sacramento
San Joaquin
Feather
American
Mokelumne
Stanislaus
Tuolumne
Merced

Valleys:
Sacramento
San Joaquin
Imperial
San Fernando
Salinas

Mexican Units

Lakes:
Goose
Shasta
Lake Almanor
Tahoe
Clear Lake
Mono Lake
Salton Sea

Deserts:
Mohave
Death Valley

Gold Rush Units

Mountains:
Mt. Shasta
Mt. Lassen
Lava Beds
Mt. Whitney
San Gorgonio
San Jacinto

American Units

Review all features learned, administer the accompanying quiz to test retention, and then make salt, water, and flour maps.

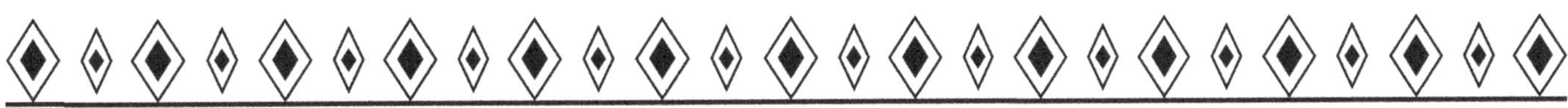

His California Story
Geography Quiz

Name ________________________________
Date ________________________________

Directions: On the map which follows, draw and label as many of the following features as you can:

Bays:
Humboldt
San Francisco
Monterey
Santa Barbara
San Pedro
San Diego

Mountain Ranges:
Sierra Nevada
Tehachapi
Coast Range
Klamath
Santa Ana
San Gabriel

Capes and Points:
Cape Mendocino
Point Conception

Islands:
Santa Catalina
San Clemente
Santa Rosa
Santa Cruz
San Miguel

Rivers:
Colorado
Sacramento
San Joaquin
Feather
American
Mokelumne
Stanislaus
Tuolumne
Merced

Valleys:
Sacramento
San Joaquin
Imperial
San Fernando
Salinas

Lakes:
Goose
Shasta
Lake Almanor
Tahoe
Clear Lake
Mono Lake
Salton Sea

Mountains:
Mt. Shasta
Mr. Lassen
Lava Beds
Mt. Whitney
San Gorgonio
San Jacinto

Deserts:
Mohave
Death Valley

Name ______________________________

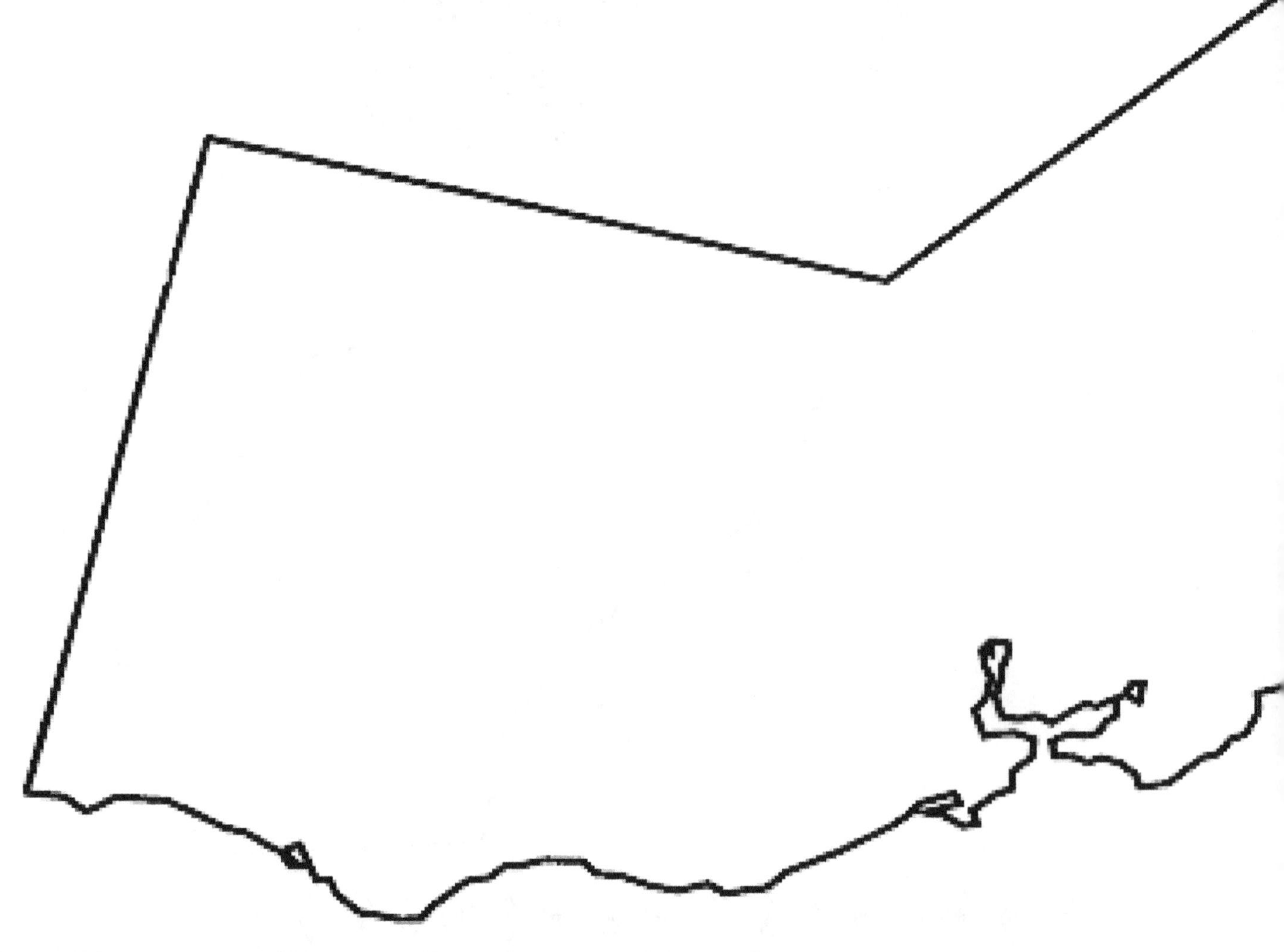

Klamath Mountains
Goose Lake
CAPE MENDOCINO
Mt. Shasta
Lava Beds
Shasta Lake
Mt. Lassen
Sacramento
Coast Range
Feather
Lake Almanor
Clear Lake
Sacramento Valley
American
Lake Tahoe
Drake's Bay
San Francisco Bay
Mokelumne
Stanislaus
Tuolumne
Sierra Nevada
Mono Lake
Monterey Bay
Merced
Salinas Valley
Coast Range
San Joaquin
Mt. Whitney
San Joaquin Valley
Tehachapi Mountains
Death Valley
POINT CONCEPTION
San Fernando Valley
Santa Barbara
San Gabriel Mtns.
Mojave Desert
San Miguel
Santa Rosa
Santa Cruz
San Gorgonio
San Jacinto
San Pedro
Catalina
Santa Ana
Imperial Valley
Colorado River
Salton Sea
San Clemente
San Diego Bay

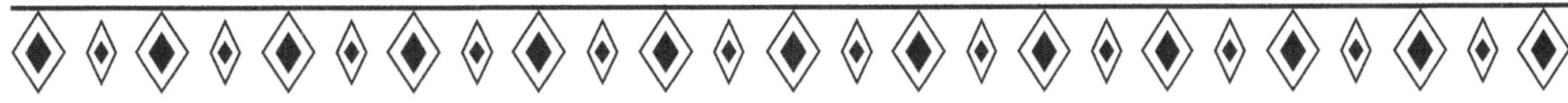

Appendix E

Organizing Co-ops

If you have read the previous sections of this manual, you might be overwhelmed with the great variety of projects and supplemental activities that accompany a study of California's history. This might be a good place to remind you that the supplemental activities are *supplemental*, and are designed to enhance a study of California's history. If they overwhelm instead of enhance, drop them.

Another way to include several of these activities while lessening the burden of preparation is to organize a co-op class. While cooperative classes have many advantages, they also can have some problems. Make sure that everyone is aware of and agrees to the rules of participation before the class begins.

Co-op Organization

Co-op classes can be designed in one of two ways. First, the course can be taught by a group of parents. If the group contains five parents, each could teach two units of *His California Story*. The first parent could teach the California Indians and the Explorers (Units 1 and 2), the second could teach Spanish Colonization and Spanish Days (Units 3 and 4), and so on. Each parent would be responsible to digest the material in her unit, prepare discussions and teach four classes, obtain all materials for the activities involved, and set up field trips.

The second way to design a co-op class requires a main teacher and several parent-helpers. The main teacher sets the overall schedule, selects field trip dates, arranges for speakers, and teaches the discussion portion of the class. Each parent-helper gathers the materials for the activities and conducts the activity part of the class.

Mandatory Meeting

During the seven years that I taught California history cooperatively, I always had a mandatory meeting about two weeks before the class started. At this meeting I explained my philosophy of education (Christ-centered), discussed my classroom rules, and gave an overview of the course. I passed out all materials, including field trip directions. We discussed the class project and shared books that I had collected over the years, ones I made available for loan. Finally, I had a sign-up sheet of activities I needed help with. Parents selected the activities with which they were willing to assist. Each parent was required to select one or more activities (depending on the number of parents). Some tasks required classroom participation while others, such as hemming the bear flags, could be done at home.

Organizing the Course

When you are organizing your course, submit the matter to the Lord in prayer. Ask Him to guide and direct you to the proper people and places that He desires. I have been constantly amazed at the resources the Lord has brought our way, things that greatly enhanced our study of California. Inquire about teaching resources in your area. Look for story-tellers. Your children's librarian may be able to recommend several. If one of your

students has grandparents who were raised in California, they might be willing to come and share their experiences with your group. Contact your local museums. Oftentimes, they make teaching kits available to teachers for loan or for a small rental fee. We have discovered a kit filled with Indian artifacts, one with exploration equipment, and another with nineteenth-century school supplies.

Next, you will need to decide how long you will take to teach the course—three quarters, leaving one quarter for local history, or a full year. When I taught, I began in September, took almost all of December off, and continued through March. That left us April to prepare for and participate in a delightful environmental living program offered through one of our local historical sites.

A suggested lesson plan appears at the beginning of each unit in this manual. Use it to plan your own class.

A Typical Class

Our co-op class was conducted one afternoon a week for two hours. Prior to the class, students did the required reading and homework (which included date-memorization and looking up geographical features). This way, they came to class ready to discuss what they had read.

We began with prayer, and then spent the first fifteen minutes of the class reviewing geography. I drew a large outline of California on my portable white board and invited students to fill in the geographical features learned to-date. We also sang the "California Date Song."

The next forty-five minutes were devoted to a discussion of the material learned over the past week, focusing specifically on one or two topics.

To provide for a bit of a break, the next thirty to forty-five minutes of the class were devoted to an activity—a writing assignment, a project, or something from the class-time activity section of this supplement. Parent-helpers made sure all of the materials were set up and ready to go.

Finally, we spent the remaining time on whatever was needed: more discussion, reinforcement, or explaining homework. Sometimes I had the students write a reflection on the activity they had just completed. I wanted it to be more than fun and games, I wanted students to learn something from it, as outlined in the objectives sections of the activity directions. Not only did this allow students to think about the reason we did something, it connected the objective to the hands-on activity so that students were more likely to remember what I hoped they would learn.

We had a fabulous time and I miss it.

Contact Me

When I first wrote *His California Story* in 1995, I invited parents and teachers to contact me and share their experiences teaching California history. I'm always interested in what creative people are doing so that I can improve my own teaching methods. It's been thirteen years and exactly three people have contacted me. It makes me feel very lonely.

With this new edition of the *Teacher's Supplement* to *His California Story*, I would like to make the offer again. Please give me feedback on these lessons and how you have adapted them to teach your children and classes.

You may get in touch with me through www.Cameron-Publishing.com. Look for the Contact Us link. You will be joining a very elite group!

Appendix F

More Articles

There are a few more articles that I must share with you. You might use these as a basis to tell more California history stories to your students and/or share them with older students.

The Angel of Chinatown

The Story of Donaldina Cameron

Part 1 of 3

MANY YEARS AGO, WHEN I COULD MANAGE A NEEDLE and thread and when my mother-in-law hosted Christmas dinner in her home, I made her a beautiful apron and potholder set. I envisioned her using these creations as she bustled about the kitchen, working magic with her culinary skills. She was properly enthusiastic when she opened my gift and then exclaimed, "These are just too good to use! I might spill something and ruin them." They've sat in a box surrounded by mothballs ever since.

A Gem Discovered

During the course of my studies of California history, I've discovered a gem, a strong woman of faith who lived out her convictions in constant ministry for almost forty years. She is my heroine. I admire this lady so much, I named my independent study program for her. So why have you never read about her in this column? I think, like my mother-in-law, I was afraid I would ruin her. I was concerned my writing skills would not bring her the honor and respect she richly deserves. But I've come to my senses. How can you admire someone you've never heard of? It's time to share the story of San Francisco Chinatown's angel.

To set the stage, we need to understand the California of the late 1800s and the Chinese immigration occurring at the time. Beginning with the Gold Rush and accelerating with the building of the transcontinental railroad, thousands of Chinese came to California and made positive contributions to the building of our state. They conquered the mighty Sierra Nevada summit by chisling a tunnel through some of the hardest granite in the world, all by hand, eighteen painstaking inches a day. Industriously, they set up shops in cities and towns, especially in parts of Los Angelos and San Francisco that became known as "China Town."

Looking for Riches

Originally, the Chinese (and everyone else) did not come to California to settle. They came to get rich. Most were men who left wives and children in China or who dreamed of returning to their homeland, marrying well, and living in luxury. Consequently, Chinese women and children were so rare in California, they attracted attention on the streets. The abundance of men, lack of family support, and feelings of despair that resulted when men found that riches eluded them resulted in an opportunity for some. A very small portion of Chinese brought a very great evil to California: chattel slavery.

If we were to walk through San Francisco's Chinatown before 1900, we would feel like outsiders in a foreign land. Strange sights and smells would assault our senses: bright lanterns, flaring dragons, ill-smelling fish markets, odorifious herb stores, cellar shops, bazaars, gambling dens, and joss houses. We might walk by a cellar shop and notice a sweet smell. It's an opium den. Historians estimate opium addiction held as much as forty percent of the Chinatown's population captive, as well as many Americans.

Up ahead we might see a group of men wearing black shirts and loose-fitting trousers, their hair neatly plated in a long braid called a queue, and their placid faces showing no expression at all. They are tong members, benevolent societies that evolved into bands of criminals

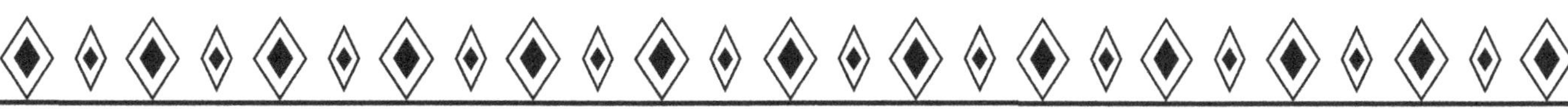

similar to gangs. Their violence often errupted into tong wars, which terrorized the law-abiding Chinese in Chinatown.

Sad-Faced Girl

Finally, we would see a child, a sad-faced girl chopping wood in the cellar of a Chinese shop. She is a slave. Already at the age of seven, she has been sold time and again. She spends her days washing, cooking, and cleaning with her owner's baby tied to her back. When the day's work is done, she sews until midnight. If she happens to fall asleep from sheer exhaustion, she is roused by a hot iron. Scars cover her body, betraying years of abuse.

As evening approached, we would see other girls behind tiny, grated windows calling out to passersby and trying to entice them into their dens of iniquity. These girls have been tricked into a life of the lowest degree. Some were daughters of wealthy merchants in China, kidnapped and sent to America. Others were lured by offers of marriage to prominent merchants in America, then cheated at the last minute by irreputable men. Still others were sold by their families. Who can save these poor women? Who can rescue them from their life of futility? Donaldina Cameron, that's who.

Donaldina Cameron came to San Francisco determined to fight this very great evil. For the next forty years, she rescued 3,000 Chinese girls. The stories of these rescues are very exciting as Miss Cameron and her police escort braved every imaginable obstacle in their determination to save the helpless girls. More about that next time.

I'm anxious to share some stories about Donaldina Cameron in my next column. However, if you can't wait, look for two books at a used book store or Web site: *Chinatown Quest* written by Carol Green Wilson in 1931 before the slave trade ended, and *Chinatown's Angry Angel* with its wonderful pictures, written by Mildred Crowl Martin in 1977.

Part 2 of 3

A FEW YEARS AGO, MY DAUGHTER AND I traveled to Washington, D.C. to participate in HSLDA's "Freedom Works" rally. Arriving a few days early, we visited the Smithsonian history museum and saw another family with five well-behaved children. "Homeschoolers," we thought, and sure enough, we were right. It's not unusual to know a homeschooling family with many children. Those of us with smaller families admire them and secretly wonder how they do it. If God blessed us with large families, we silently think, would we be able to serve?

Today I'd like to introduce you to the mother of 3,000 children and continue a subject I began last time in this space. I want to share some stories about a little-known servant of the Lord, who ministered in San Francisco's Chinatown in the early 1900s, Donaldina Cameron. Every school child should know about this great lady.

Rescue and Restore

Many Christians shared the gospel with the Chinese community in California through mission work and churches. Miss Cameron ministered to Chinatown's slave girls. Touched by the plight of these helpless young women, Miss Cameron came to San Francisco determined to rescue and restore. She served in a house on the outskirts of Chinatown that would eventually be re-named in her honor. The slave trade ended long ago, but the Cameron House still stands and aids the people of San Francisco's Chinatown.

Miss Cameron took part in thousands of rescues between 1895 and 1938. Although she downplayed these rescues, concentrating instead on the work that followed, they contain so much romance and drama I can't resist sharing one.

One day a terrified Chinese gentleman appeared at "920" as the Cameron House was then called, with an urgent plea. He had met a slave girl who reported she must pay for all of her food and clothing plus clear $300 a month. Her life was miserable. They fell in love and the young man promised to take care of her should she choose to run away. She did, but her owners traced her to a rival tong that held her hostage. The young man appealed to "920" for help.

Donaldina Cameron lost no time. Quickly she rounded up an interpreter and a police escort and raced off to rescue the girl. The trio hurried past the doorkeeper of the house and scurried down the hallway only to have huge solid oak doors slammed in her faces. The policeman scrambled for help while Donaldina fretted for twenty minutes outside the impenetrable door, powerless to help.

There Was Hope

Finally, three more policemen arrived and battered down the door. Inside all was calm and quiet as thirteen men sat around a long table, smoking their water pipes. A careful search revealed nothing. Discouraged, the policemen got ready to leave thinking Miss Cameron was wrong this time.

Donaldina stepped out onto the balcony to get a breath of fresh air and heard a muffled cry. A painter called to her, "They took her up through the skylight, across the roof next door." There was hope!

Quietly, Miss Cameron and one of the policemen slipped unseen from the room and dashed to the house next door. Although the owner protested, Miss Cameron brushed him aside. She noticed that the skylight was open and a long ladder lay nearby. After another long, futile search, the police were ready to give up when Miss Cameron noticed a dresser out of line with the wall. Investigating, she found the girl! Hearing that her rescuers came from the mission house, she gladly allowed herself to be carried away. Law-abiding Chinese cheered, and another soul was saved.

Real Work Begins

Then the real work began. To prevent unscrupulous owners from regaining possession of the rescued girls, Donaldina became their legal guardian. Over 2,000 at one time or another lived at the Cameron House. Here they learned about their unseen Father and His Son Jesus Christ, who died for their sins and who would restore those years the locust had eaten. Many became His children. In addition to prayer, days were filled with chores, lessons, and recreation. Girls learned to sew, cook, and support themselves.

Matchmaking became a pleasant task, but first the young man had to pass Miss Cameron's granite inspection. Always concerned that her girls could be recaptured, Miss Cameron carefully investigated each suitor and made sure he loved the Lord and could support a family. She required a courtship period to see if friendship would bloom. If the girls did not express love, Miss Cameron shooed the suitors away.

Over her long life, ninety-eight years, Miss Donaldina Cameron lived to serve others. Through setbacks, discouragements, and trials, she kept her eyes fixed on her Lord, relying on Him for strength. I want to devote one more column to my heroine and share my favorite rescue. Until then, I'll leave you with Miss Cameron's favorite verse: "Yet will I rejoice" (Habakkuk 3:18).

Part 3 of 3

THE BIBLE COMMANDS US TO LOVE OUR ENEMIES. THAT is, we must show compassion, concern, and forgiveness to those who seek our harm. An impossible task you think? Absolutely, if one operates in his own strength and power. Donaldina Cameron rarely operated in her own strength. Through love, this mighty servant of the Lord helped bring one particular enemy to Christ.

The time was the early 1930s, the place San Francisco's Chinatown, and the enemy a stunningly beautiful courtesan named Ah Peen Amy, sometimes called "Opium Amy."

Like many of the young Chinese girls Donaldina Cameron devoted her life to, Amy was tricked into marriage, brought to America, and sold into slavery. She embraced a life of debauchery. By selling opium, she managed to buy her freedom, and then purchased her own slave girls, forcing them into the trade. Ah Peen Amy despised Donaldina Cameron and with her strong intellect matched wits over the fate of her slaves. She railed at Miss Cameron's successful rescues and gloated over those thwarted.

Come Quickly!

One day, Miss Cameron received an urgent typewritten note desperately summoning her to Amy's home. Quickly responding, Miss Cameron hoped to rescue a young girl despicably treated and forced to wait on her mistress. But Amy was alone. Silent and sullen, Amy offered no protest while Miss Cameron's group searched her home. Then the truth dawned. Opium Amy sent the request. She wanted to be rescued.

Crying and clutching at Miss Cameron's skirt, she poured out her story. Her previous owner had turned on her and sold her to a rival. Amy, the opium dealer who had purchased her freedom and ruled over a house of ill repute, would be returned to slavery. Her only hope was the charity of Miss Cameron.

Miss Cameron reeled. Take this ravishing wolf, this scheming predator into the sanctuary built for her wounded lambs? Never! "Please!" begged Amy. "I want to change!" Miss Cameron made a phone call, then an offer. Would Amy submit to a short stay in prison while Miss Cameron worked out other arrangements? "I'll go anywhere you say I'm safe" Amy replied.

Trading her expensive finery for drab garb, Amy submitted to prison life for a time while Miss Cameron discussed Amy's plight with her board. Finally, they agreed to let her move to the unused schoolroom, but kept her locked away from the other girls. In the Lord's timing, Amy Law, a long-time missionary to China just "happened" to be visiting San Francisco. The two Amy's met daily for two weeks, discussing the claims of Christ. Amy Law returned to China, but Opium Amy repented of her sins and began a new life in Christ.

A New Life

Slowly, Ah Peen Amy entered the routine of the Cameron House, serving the very girls who were once her slaves. One day an abandoned baby arrived on the mission doorstep. Amy embraced the chance to raise this young boy and give him the love her own child, who had died at birth, never received. She eventually married a Christian man who met Miss Cameron's approval, and moved to the valley.

Several years after Amy's rescue in 1938, Chinatown's illegal slave trade ended. Two rescued girls found the courage to testify against their former owners, breaking up a formidable ring. By that time, Miss Cameron's children circled the globe living steadfast lives of service to the Lord Jesus Christ and bearing witness to His great power.

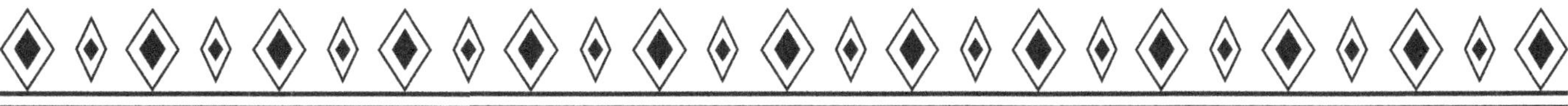

The End of Slavery

For more than forty years, Donaldina Cameron battled the frustrations of the work God had called her to. Rescues that failed weighed heavy, especially when the girls became examples to those who would hope for deliverance. Others loved finery and ease and returned to their sinful ways. She battled Christians who advised her to concentrate on saving the girls' souls rather than working to reform laws that could end mistreatment of the Chinese. Church and state should be separate, she heard, and Christians should not involve themselves in politics. Finally, she battled corrupt officials willing to take bribes rather than fight injustice. For more than forty years, Donaldina Cameron walked the path her Lord directed, and she prevailed.

I think of Donaldina Cameron on the days I grow tired of my ministry, when I think I have my hands full teaching my one remaining child. I am encouraged by her example because I serve the same Lord as she did, and I can call upon the same strength as she did. May we teach our children as diligently as she taught hers. May we be as faithful to our calling as she was to hers.

Beacons of Hope

ONE FOGGY, WINDY AUTUMN DAY, MANY years back, my husband and I found ourselves venturing down 308 steps to visit the picturesque Pt. Reyes lighthouse, all the while fully aware that the same 308 steps would be waiting for us on our return, uphill climb.

In due time we arrived at the imposing alabaster tower only to find it securely locked. Huffing and panting around the platform, we tried to gather our strength for the return trip when to our great relief a ranger arrived, took pity on us, and showed us around.

She explained how the myriad prisms of the Fresnel (pronounced fray-NEL) lens focused the rays of a small kerosene lamp into a mighty beam that would reach twenty or more miles out to sea. My heart was won that day and ever since, our family has sought every opportunity to visit the dozens of lighthouses still in existence on California's coast.

After the Gold Rush, ship traffic along with the inevitable shipwrecks, greatly increased along California's rugged coastline. Public indignation over these disasters, along with great safety concerns, prompted the federal government to embark on an aggressive building program to aid navigation.

Usually situated on points of land that jutted far out into the sea, lighthouse construction was an engineering marvel. Just transporting supplies to the foreboding sites proved challenging. Dedicated crews blasted level platforms, anchored foundations, and constructed sturdy towers on some of the most forlorn, rocky areas of the coast. Slowly, lonely sentinels began to line the coast, flashing their alerts to ships awash on angry seas, warning them away from the treacherous shoals.

Separated From Civilization

Although the lighthouses, with their marvelous Fresnel lenses, are beautiful, what is truly inspiring is the story of the families who carved these fortresses into homes. Many keepers had families who were accommodated near the lighthouses. Sometimes a family of five had to share a small one-room dwelling with no indoor plumbing.

Although the lighthouse keepers could often see a thriving metropolis, getting to it was another story. Miles of rugged coastal trails, roads if he were lucky, or choppy waters could separate the keeper from civilization.

Grocery shopping took ingenuity. If the lighthouse wasn't accessible by land, supplies could be imported by boat. The absence of a boat landing proved more challenging. In that case a supply ship was attached to cables and the goods were hoisted up to the keeper. Groceries arrived every three to four months. Keeper's wives learned to plan ahead.

Raising Children

Raising children on these lonely outposts offered its own set of unique difficulties. Keepers at Point Bonita Lighthouse were appalled when a family with young children was assigned to live in a house built on the edge of a cliff. Although the children could not be cooped up in the house, neither could they be left unattended in the frightfully small fenced enclosure. Mr. Martin, the keeper, fashioned harnesses and ropes to secure his wee ones from the rocky abyss.

One day, in the midst of hanging laundry, Mrs. Martin heard a muffled cry and saw a taut rope leading over the edge of the cliff. Hauling the dangling child up quickly but carefully, Mrs. Martin smothered him with kisses while her heart struggled to resume a normal rate.

Schooling offered challenges as well. When the lighthouses were located near a town, children learned to make the daily trek. If this wasn't possible, they were educated at home, often with a tutor who visited several times each year.

Thankfully for today's school children, the lighthouses are being lovingly restored. Many are accessible for field trips. Some are national monuments, such as popular Point Loma which marks the spot where Cabrillo first landed in California in 1542.

Others are on military installations and are closed to the public. Some Fresnel lenses are still in service, although powered by electricity. Although the lens is missing from Point Sur's Lighthouse (it's in the Monterey Maritime Museum), interpretive tours are offered for school groups and must be scheduled months in advance.

The Socialite Keeper

In one of my favorites, Point Piños, the light tower rises through the center of a Cape Cod home. Emily Fisk, known as the "Socialite Keeper," tended the light with her Chinese servant, Que. Furnishing the house with books, paintings, and silver, and planting the outside with trees and vegetables, Mrs. Fisk often entertained writers, artists, and naval officers. Fastidiously, she kept a feather duster near the door so that children could clean their shoes before entering.

Lodging in the old keepers quarters is available at some lighthouses, notably Pigeon Point and Montara (run by the American Youth Hostel), Pt. Arena (U.S. Coastguard), and East Brothers (a fancy Bed and Breakfast Inn on an island in San Francisco Bay). Lighthouses now serve as a surfer's museum (Santa Cruz), a restaurant (Oakland), and a yacht showroom (Vallejo).

Californians are fortunate to have such a rich sea heritage so close at hand. When you have the chance, be sure to visit one of these imposing sentinels who faithfully flashed their beacons of hope to reassure and warn lonely ships at sea.

World War II Comes to California

ALONG THE SHORE IN THE GOLDEN GATE NATIONAL Park stretch the skeletons of long neglected batteries and weapons fortifications. They are almost the only reminders of years past when California and the rest of the nation geared up to fight for our freedom in the early 1940s. We've heard of the patriotism of our young men who enlisted in the services, the dedication of the "Rosie the Riveters" who worked in factories building supply ships, and the sacrifices of all during World War II, but we almost never hear about events on our own California soil.

What Might Have Been

One in the category of "what might have been" was a deadly assault planned for Christmas Eve, just after the attack on Pearl Harbor. The Japanese had a fleet of I-class submarines, which were long range, aircraft-carrying vessels. Quietly and stealthily, nine of these submarines fanned out in the Pacific looking for American carriers and attacking merchantmen and tankers. At least five ships were attacked and another three sunk. Taking positions along the coast these submarines awaited orders to shell the coastal cities, or actually the lighthouses. Beacons from Cape Flattery in Seattle to Point Cabrillo in San Diego would be destroyed, plunging the coast into darkness and creating a hazard for ships attempting to reach safe harbor, not to mention breaking the morale of thousands of Americans celebrating the birth of their Savior.

Thankfully, the order never came and on December 20th the Japanese submarines were ordered away because of the anti-submarine measures taken by the United States. These measures consisted of small boats, many privately owned, and military planes, which vigorously patrolled the coast. The lighthouses continued to shine and not only acted as sentinels for ships, but as havens for coastal watchers who scanned the skies and seas for enemy craft.

The following February, Goleta, California became the first place on American soil to be shelled since the War of 1812. One of the I-class submarines, *I-17*, had returned. Residents, celebrating George Washington's birthday, had just tuned their radios to listen to one of President Roosevelt's fireside chats. No sooner had he begun than the shocked residents of Goleta saw an enemy sub shooting at them!

Half an hour later it was all over with *I-17* rapidly retreating. The damage was limited to about $500; however, while defusing a dud, an officer named Captain Hagen was wounded. He became the only U.S. serviceman to receive the Purple Heart as a result of enemy action within the United States during World War II.

The following April, in 1942, American forces bombed Tokyo, Yokosuka, Kobe, and Nagoya in the Doolittle Raid. Japanese citizens were stunned and jittery. Face-saving, a component of the Japanese culture, demanded that the United States homeland be attacked in return. Since submarine attacks had met with little success, another ingenious plan was formed.

Jet Stream Discovered

Unknown to the Americans, the Japanese had discovered the jet stream, the currents of high altitude air which flow in a path from Japan to the Pacific Northwest. After much experimentation, they devised a unique way to attack American shores from the safety of Japan.

Thousands of helium-filled airborne balloons, windship weapons, were launched into the jet stream. Carrying bombs filled with incendiary materials, these airships descended upon the northwest United States and Canada. While deadly within a 150-foot radius, their main purpose was to ignite forest fires. Fortunately, the jet stream is less powerful in the summer months when forests were tinder dry, so those launched in winter fell on snow or well-watered woods. These fires either fizzled or were easily controlled.

Although it is estimated that thousands of balloons were sent into the jet stream, only a few hundred were eventually discovered (including twenty-five in California), and only one caused any fatality. A minister's wife and five children out on a Sunday School outing discovered the odd object while looking for a fishing hole in Oregon's forest. The wife, Mrs. Mitchell, called to her husband who was parking the car, "Look what I found, dear." Seconds later he heard a horrible explosion as six people went to be with their Lord.

We don't hear much about action on America's soil in WWII. One reason was that the skirmishes were minor compared to those in other countries, but the other was a strategy of silence. Not only was it important for Americans to feel safe, especially since California and the Pacific Coast was a major manufacturing and supply station, but the silence made Japan feel their efforts were ineffective. Silence caused the balloon project to be scrubbed.

Now, with more than sixty years separating us from this difficult era, it's time to learn about the heroic efforts of our military and how the Lord protected our land.

The Spanish Influenza

MEANDERING HOME FROM A CRUISE TO CELEBRATE our twenty-fifth anniversary, my husband and I took the opportunity to visit one of California's historic delights. We visited Hearst Castle in San Simeon. While we waited for the bus that would whisk us up the hill to *La Cuesta Encantada*, we strolled through an exhibit on the Hearst family. There I discovered Phoebe Apperton Hearst, Mr. Hearst's mother, died of influenza in 1919.

Influenza? Could that have been The Influenza, the greatest pandemic of all time? The one that killed more people than WWI and perhaps 100 million people worldwide? And, the one that history books, astonishingly, say almost nothing about?

In the spring of 1918, World War I was drawing to a close when influenza, originating in Spain, swept through the European troops on both sides of the conflict. Quickly, it spread to Europe, Asia, and America, infecting many who sickened but did not die. In California, thousands called in sick to work in March and 500 of the 1,900 prisoners in San Quentin became ill in April. When summer arrived, good health returned, but scientists think this benign flu mutated into the nasty strain that caused the world so much grief.

End of WWI

By the fall, the Germans had signed the Treaty of Versailles, officially ending WWI. Thousands of soldiers who were exposed to the benign influenza were released from their war duties and thankfully returned to their homes. Little did they know that a killer had hitched a ride in their bloodstream.

The deadly influenza first camped on America's shore in August, arriving with a group of sailors in Boston. With amazing stealth, it spread to all corners of the country. Beginning with a headache, it rapidly developed into pneumonia followed by mahogany spots on cheekbones that quickly spread to the rest of the body. Fever and deliriousness and bone-aching pain assaulted people as they languished for several hours until gasping for breath, they drowned in their own blood. In total, about twenty-five percent of all Americans became ill, and of these, about 2.5 percent died.

Desperate for a cure, doctors approached a group of condemned sailors at the Naval Training Station on Yerba Buena Island and proposed a Faustian bargain. In exchange for a full pardon, would they volunteer to become deliberately infected with the flu so that doctors could learn how it operated and spread? Such a proposal would be illegal today, but in 1918 the doctors justified their offer with the hope that the study could save the lives of thousands.

Quarantine Station

Taking these fifty sailors to the quarantine station, which had been erected on Angel Island in San Francisco Bay, doctors tried various methods to expose them to the flu including inoculating them with mucus and blood from the sick and asking sick men to breath and cough on them. Surprisingly, all of the sailors remained healthy. Not even one contracted the flu. The doctors were dumbfounded. How, despite their best efforts, did the sailors remain healthy? Meanwhile, the virus spread through the world like gossip from an old fishwife.

People tried to cope. All across California officials canceled events that would attract crowds, even those celebrating the end of WWI. Places where the public gathered, such as bowling alleys, theatres, and lodges were shut down. Even churches ceased their services. In Richmond, the county health officers closed all of the public schools in October and did not reopen them until the following January. Cities and counties across the state did likewise.

Since the flu virus was thought to be airborne, volunteers at the Red Cross made masks consisting of several thickness of gauze for people to wear for protection. Pictures from the time show people working in offices, riding trams, and even playing baseball while wearing their gauze masks. Health officials tore down the roller towels popular in public bathrooms, inspected health practices at restaurants, and worked with a cooperative public. All the while, the killer continued to stalk.

Then, with the arrival of warm weather, the flu completely vanished. It had felled 550,000 people in the United States, but its reign of terror was over. It never returned. People put it out of their minds and moved on with their lives. Curiously, although almost every extended family lost a loved one, like Phoebe Hearst, no one spoke about the trauma. They refused to write about it, too. Newspapers, magazines, and history books contain very little on the subject. Even doctors who were involved in efforts to stop the pandemic don't discuss it in their memoirs. In my twenty-volume Grolier's Encyclopedia, I found exactly one sentence that referenced the Spanish Influenza of 1918.

Today with the advances in DNA research, interest in the influenza pandemic has revived. Remarkably, scientists have recovered tissue samples from an Eskimo flu victim who was buried in permafrost, which served to preserve the virus. Perhaps it will solve the mystery of the virulent virus that killed by conservative estimates 20-40 million people worldwide, although many virologists feel 100 million is a better estimate. It doesn't explain why history books loath to discuss this pandemic, but it does spur scientists in their studies to do everything possible to prevent another pandemic like the Spanish Influenza of 1918.

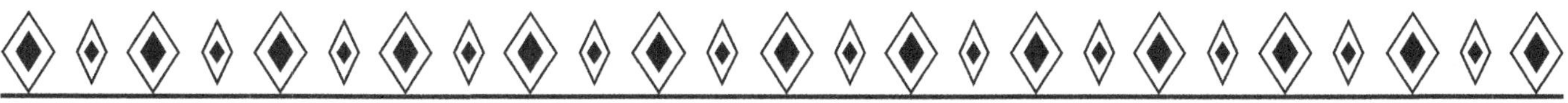

Made in the USA
Las Vegas, NV
07 November 2024

11244252R00109